Hattusili, the Hittite Prince Who Stole an Empire

Also available from Bloomsbury

A Short History of the Phoenicians by Mark Woolmer
Babylon by Michael Seymour
Imagining Xerxes by Emma Bridges
Warriors of Anatolia by Trevor Bryce

Hattusili, the Hittite Prince Who Stole an Empire

Partner and Rival of Ramesses the Great

Trevor Bryce

BLOOMSBURY ACADEMIC
LONDON • NEW YORK • OXFORD • NEW DELHI • SYDNEY

BLOOMSBURY ACADEMIC
Bloomsbury Publishing Plc
50 Bedford Square, London, WC1B 3DP, UK
1385 Broadway, New York, NY 10018, USA
29 Earlsfort Terrace, Dublin 2, Ireland

BLOOMSBURY, BLOOMSBURY ACADEMIC and the Diana logo are trademarks of Bloomsbury Publishing Plc

First published in Great Britain 2025

Copyright © Trevor Bryce, 2025

Trevor Bryce has asserted his right under the Copyright, Designs and Patents Act, 1988, to be identified as Author of this work.

Cover image: Hattusili III, on the right of the relief sculpture, making libation before the Storm God, the figure on the left. Chris Hellier / Alamy Stock Photo

All rights reserved. No part of this publication may be reproduced or transmitted in any form or by any means, electronic or mechanical, including photocopying, recording, or any information storage or retrieval system, without prior permission in writing from the publishers.

Bloomsbury Publishing Plc does not have any control over, or responsibility for, any third-party websites referred to or in this book. All internet addresses given in this book were correct at the time of going to press. The author and publisher regret any inconvenience caused if addresses have changed or sites have ceased to exist, but can accept no responsibility for any such changes.

A catalogue record for this book is available from the British Library.

Library of Congress Cataloging-in-Publication Data
Names: Bryce, Trevor, 1940– author.
Title: Hattusili, the Hittite prince who stole an empire : partner and rival of Ramesses the Great / Trevor Bryce.
Other titles: Partner and rival of Ramesses the Great
Description: London ; New York : Bloomsbury Academic, 2025. | Includes bibliographical references and index.
Identifiers: LCCN 2024011972 (print) | LCCN 2024011973 (ebook) | ISBN 9781350341821 (pb) | ISBN 9781350341838 (hb) | ISBN 9781350341845 (epdf) | ISBN 9781350341852 (ebook)
Subjects: LCSH: Hattusilis III, King of the Hittites, active 1275 B.C.–1250 B.C. | Ramses II, King of Egypt. | Hittites—History. | Middle East—History—To 622.
Classification: LCC DS66 .B726 2025 (print) | LCC DS66 (ebook) | DDC 939/.2092 [B]—dc23/eng/20240405
LC record available at https://lccn.loc.gov/2024011972
LC ebook record available at https://lccn.loc.gov/2024011973

ISBN: HB: 978-1-3503-4183-8
PB: 978-1-3503-4182-1
ePDF: 978-1-3503-4184-5
eBook: 978-1-3503-4185-2

Typeset by RefineCatch Limited, Bungay, Suffolk
Printed and bound in Great Britain

To find out more about our authors and books visit www.bloomsbury.com and sign up for our newsletters.

*This book is dedicated to
Diana McVeagh,
a distinguished musicologist and dear friend.
Her 1,000-page edition of the letters of the English composer, Gerald Finzi,
a meticulous work of scholarship published at the age of ninety-five,
has inspired me, many years her junior,
to begin writing once again.*

Contents

List of Illustrations		viii
Abbreviations		ix
Introduction		1
1	'He Will Not Live Long'	5
2	Our Sources	21
3	Benefactors of a Young Prince	31
4	The Prince Goes to Court	39
5	Unseating the Rightful King	47
6	'And She Gave Us the Love of Husband and Wife'	65
7	'Uneasy Lies the Head …'	81
8	The Eternal Treaty	95
9	The Royal Mail	111
10	Managing an Empire	127
11	'Beware of Greeks Bearing Gifts'	151
12	'Bleating in Cuneiform Across the Wine-Dark Sea'	163
13	A Poisoned Chalice	179
14	Hattusili's Reign in Review	193
Appendix 1 Chronicle of Events		211
Appendix 2 The Economy		213
Notes		227
Bibliography		247
Index		255

Illustrations

Maps

1.1	Plan of Hattusa. Adaptation by author	8
1.2	The Hittite homeland. Courtesy Hannah Bryce	10
1.3	The Anatolian peninsula. NASA satellite photo by Jeff Schmalz. MODIS Rapid Response Team, NASA/GSFC	11
1.4	The Hittite world. Author map	12
11.1	Bronze Age Greece and western Anatolia. Author map	154

Figures

1.1	Outline sketch of palace, Hattusa. Adapted from model at Hattusa. Courtesy Hannah Bryce	6
1.2	Acropolis, Hattusa. Author photo	7
3.1	Inscribing a clay tablet. Courtesy Tolga Örnek, Ekip Film*	33
3.2	Suppiluliuma I. Courtesy Tolga Örnek, Ekip Film*	36
6.1	Fraktin monument. Puduhepa and Hepat. Courtesy Hannah Bryce	68
8.1	Battle of Qadesh. Courtesy Tolga Örnek, Ekip Film*	95
9.1	Ramesses II, Abu Simbel. Author photo	123
11.1	Sign at entrance to Troy. Author photo	152
13.1	Tudhaliya and Sharrumma. Author photo	192
14.1	Hattusili. Courtesy Tolga Örnek, Ekip Film*	206
A2.1	Sword swallower and acrobats, Alaca Höyük. Author photo	226

* from the documentary, *The Hittites* (2003), [TV Programme] Dir. Tolga Örnek, Turkey: Ekip Film.

Abbreviations

AA	*Archäologischer Anzeiger.*
AfO	*Archiv für Orientforschung.*
AhT	*The Ahhiyawa Texts.* Gary M. Beckman, Trevor R. Bryce and Eric H. Cline. Atlanta, GA: Society of Biblical Literature, 2011.
ÄHK	*Die ägyptisch-hethitische Korrespondenz aus Boghazköi.* Edited by Elmar Edel. 2 vols. Opladen: Westdeutscher Verlag, 1994.
ANE	*The Ancient Near East.* Edited by Mark W. Chavalas. Oxford: Blackwell, 2006.
ANET	*Ancient Near Eastern Texts Relating to the Old Testament.* Edited by James B. Pritchard 3rd edn. Princeton, NJ: Princeton University Press, 1969.
AoF	*Altorientalische Forschungen.*
Apol.	*Apology of Hattusili III.*
AS	*Anatolian Studies.*
CANE	*Civilizations of the Ancient Near East.* Edited by Jack M. Sasson. 4 vols. New York, NY: Charles Scribner's Sons, 1995.
CoS	*The Context of Scripture: Canonical Compositions from the Biblical World.* Edited by William W. Hallo and K. Lawson Younger Jr. 3 vols. Leiden and Boston: Brill, 2003.
Fs Hoffner	*Hittite Studies in Honor of Harry A. Hoffner Jr. on the Occasion of His 65th Birthday.* Edited by Gary M. Beckman, Richard Beal and Gregory McMahon. Winona Lake, IN: Eisenbrauns, 2003.
HDT	*Hittite Diplomatic Texts.* Gary M. Beckman. 2nd edn. Atlanta, GA: Society of Biblical Literature, 1999.
HHE	*Handbook Hittite Empire.* Edited by Stefano de Martino. Berlin and Boston: de Gruyter, 2022.
JCS	*Journal of Cuneiform Studies.*
JEA	*Journal of Egyptian Archaeology.*
JNES	*Journal of Near Eastern Studies.*
OHAA	*The Oxford Handbook of Ancient Anatolia.* Edited by Sharon R. Steadman and Gary McMahon. Oxford: Oxford University Press, 2011.

OLZ	*Orientalistische Literaturzeitung.*
SMEA	*Studi Micenei ed Egeo-Anatolici.*
Taw	*Der >Tawagalawa-Brief<. Beschwerden über Piyamaradu: Eine Neuedition.* Edited by Susanne Heinhold-Krahmer and Elisabeth Rieken. Berlin: de Gruyter, 2020.
transl.	translated by.

Introduction

In 1970, the Turkish Minister for Foreign Affairs presented U Thant, Secretary-General of the United Nations, with a replica of a peace treaty between the two most powerful rulers of the Bronze Age as it entered its final decades. One of them is called Ramesses. This is Ramesses 'the Great', pharaoh of Egypt, famous throughout history as the builder of mighty monuments and statues honouring himself; infamous as the biblical pharaoh who under divine pressure permitted the enslaved children of Israel to return to their homeland, only to try to re-enslave them once their journey had begun. Terrible was the punishment a wrathful God inflicted upon him. So goes the biblical tradition.[1]

Ramesses' treaty partner you may never have heard of, if you haven't read any books about the Bronze Age Near East, or even if you have. He is called Hattusili, sometimes written Khattushilish, a much less evocative name than Ramesses, and sounding rather like a sneeze. He was the ruler of the Hittite empire, whose heartland lay in Anatolia, modern Turkey. Some devotees of Turkish history consider this empire to be a lineal ancestor of the Selcuk and Ottoman empires and the modern Turkish republic. The treaty is set up outside an entrance to the Security Council Chamber of the United Nations, New York City. It provides one of the focal points in this remarkable story of the life and career of Hattusili, 'Great King, King of the Land of Hatti', who rose from a sickly childhood and life-threatening illnesses to become one of the most important monarchs of his era. As such, he deserves special recognition in this stage of Turkey's long and often violent history.

Before you read any further, I should warn you that this is not a conventional history book. You will find in it three main strands. The first is a fairly straightforward historical one, telling you what we know about Hattusili from the surviving clay tablets of his reign. Indeed, the quantity of these tablets and the range of their contents – including the king's correspondence with his royal peers and vassal rulers, his treaties with his vassals, his famous treaty with Ramesses, and a document unique in Hittite literature commonly known as the

Apology or the *Autobiography* – tell us more about this king than do the tablets that record the careers of almost every one of his predecessors and successors on the Hittite throne.[2]

All fields of scientific enquiry, and history is one of them (at least in part), have an important basic requirement. Any conclusions that researchers in these fields reach should have firm evidence to back them up. Hence good professional historians show well-merited caution in advancing new theories, without fresh, supporting evidence, or earlier evidence that has been overlooked or misinterpreted. But I sometimes think that evidence can become a kind of sheltered, walled enclosure with us inside, fearful of straying beyond it to travel a world of unexplored possibilities – a world 'whose margin fades forever and forever when I move'.[3] My second strand takes us outside the limits of what has been or can be proved, into the realms of new ideas and theories which *could* one day be shown to be true. This calls to mind Professor Theo van den Hout's comment: 'Daring to be wrong is what often makes scholarship progress more than just daring to be right.'[4]

My third strand consists of a number of imagined scenarios. These are set apart from the main text by the different font I have used for them. Each has as its core a piece or pieces of solid evidence. But my elaborations go considerably further, with imagined dialogue, imagined settings and the imagined thoughts, emotions and reactions of the characters in each scenario. I have, however, tried to ensure that every one of my scenarios is historically feasible, even if never likely to be provable.

All three strands, which are often intertwined, are readily distinguishable from one another. After a lifetime of cautious scholarship, I hope I shall be forgiven any liberties I may take in the pages that follow. In any case, now that I am in the middle years of my ninth decade, I trust my critics will not be too severe. If they are, I'm afraid that by then I may no longer be in a position to address their concerns.

For me at least, writing a book can be a lonely experience. Mainly because my words are addressed to an audience totally unseen. I cannot hear even a cough or a sneeze to assure me that there really is someone out there. I miss that surge of adrenalin when I speak to a live audience. I can sense and adapt to what their body language tells me. I can anticipate what particularly stirs their interest and what is likely to lose it. I can communicate directly with them through eye contact and my own body language, as well as my words. I may not know any of my audience personally, but I quickly get a sense of what sort of people they are, even if they are a random gathering, including both retirees and persons of younger generations, wanting to learn more about the world, past and present, beyond their normal callings in life.

From delivering and listening to thousands of lectures for general audiences and, after writing some twenty books and reading thousands more, I've learnt that these books and lectures all have an important starting-point: as a speaker, you have five minutes to capture your audience's attention; as an author for a general public, three paragraphs to engage their interest. Fail to meet this requirement and your listeners' or readers' attention quickly wanes. It's not long before smartphone screens begin to light up and heads nod off. In my mind's eye, I am sitting in a comfortable armchair sipping a glass of red; my written words are really spoken ones which I address to a gathering of intelligent, well-educated people, many of whom know little if anything about the Hittites, but are interested to learn who they were. In keeping with the informality of my presentations, and I see each chapter as one of these presentations, I occasionally make a personal appearance in the tale that follows, sometimes with an anecdote which may begin or end one of my presentations, sometimes by relating my experience of places I have visited that are relevant to our tale.

One final comment. Though I began my career as a Classicist, I have since drifted eastwards in my research travels and back in time, some centuries earlier than the Classical era. But I have never abandoned my Classical origins. In fact, my grounding in the Classics has often enhanced my appreciation of the many traditions that link the Classical and Near Eastern worlds. Sometimes the links I make are direct and straightforward. Sometimes they require a long leap of the imagination. Let me give you an example of the latter. Chapter 11 begins with the Roman tradition of a Trojan prince Aeneas, shipwrecked on the coast of Africa in his flight from the ruins of Troy, and from there moves back in time via the eighth-century, epic poet Homer to the Bronze Age kingdoms of Greece and Anatolia. Our story is about a Hittite prince who stole an empire, an old empire whose foundations were already beginning to crumble. Never far from my mind as I tell this story is the legend of the refugee Trojan prince who laid the foundations of a new kingdom in Italy, the Land of the Evening Star. Two princes: one a genuine figure of history, the other a literary product of a long-evolving Classical tradition. Both are linked, though one just marginally, with the story of Troy.

IMPORTANT NOTE

The Turkish people now call their country 'Türkiye', on the grounds that it best represents the culture, civilisation, and values of the Turkish nation in the best way'.' (from a Türkiye website).

A word of thanks

May I express my sincere thanks to Lily McMahon, my editor, who answered all my initial queries so promptly and efficiently, and in such a cheerful, friendly manner, to Zoe Osman for her great cover design and editorial guidance, and to the members of the production team, Sophie Beardsworth (general oversight of the production process), Merv Honeywood (production management co-ordinator), Dorothy Luckhurst (copy editor), and Kevin Eaton (proof reader). It has been a pleasure to work with all of them. My warmest thanks also to my granddaughter Hannah, for the three sketches and technical assistance she so ably provided.

1

'He Will Not Live Long'

Already as a young lad he is becoming skilled in the arts of warfare. Indeed, he has been assigned for training to the army's most elite branch – the chariot corps. Already in his earliest years, his career in the chariotry had been foreshadowed when the honorary title 'man-of-the reins' was bestowed upon him.[1] A future as a great warrior – and perhaps much else – lies ahead.

But his career is threatened by recurring bouts of illness. Some of them so severe as to raise grave fears for his life. The best doctors in the land have been summoned to his bedside. But all their potions and salves, indeed all their attempted remedies, are of no avail. The city's Chief Scribe has searched the state's ritual tablets for a possible cure. Incantation priests mutter prayers for the restoration of the lad's health. In the courtyard outside, 'Wise Women' have gathered with all their ritualistic equipment, including a sheep and a piglet. The animals are of the finest quality. They are for sacrifice. 'Let the evil which afflicts this child be transferred to the bodies of these animals', the women chant, as the victims' throats are slit and their bodies cut into pieces, burnt and cast into a pit. Soil is heaped upon the pit. Maybe the child's illness will now depart his body and lie buried within the dismembered corpses of the sacrificial beasts – forever. That is the faith.[2] And indeed the rituals and incantations and, perhaps, too, the medicinal salves and potions, seem to be working. For a time.

This is something to be celebrated. For the child is of no common breed. He is a prince, son of the Great King Mursili, Supreme Ruler of the Kingdom of the Hittites. Yet, in truth, he is of limited importance in the royal pecking order, for he has two older brothers, Halpasulupi and Muwattalli. Only if both of these and their sons die before him will he likely have a chance of ascending his kingdom's throne. That seems a remote prospect. But who can tell? In any case, his recovery proves but a temporary reprieve. The oracles are consulted. What has he done to offend the gods? Has someone else offended them? How are they to be appeased? Despite repeated requests, oracular consultation proves fruitless. Then one night the child's father, King Mursili has a vivid dream – one that will change the course of history. In his dream, his son Muwattalli appears before him with a message from the goddess Ishtar. She is one of the most important deities in the Hittite pantheon.[3] His brother's life is destined to be short. But she has the power to change that. If the young prince is made a priest in her service, he will live and he will prosper.[4]

Divine communications conveyed by dreams are to be taken seriously. By royal command, the prince is hastily consigned to the goddess's service. Ishtar becomes his lifelong patron and protector and, with her guidance, he will become ruler of one of the ancient world's greatest empires. Well, maybe Ishtar will help pave the way for this. But his prowess as a military commander, his political skills and, above all, his ruthless ambition will play no small part in his rise to supreme power. Along the way, he will encounter many enemies, both at home and abroad, many plots and conspiracies to overthrow and destroy him – and so will his successors. Supreme power will not be easily attained, nor easily maintained.

This will be his story.

Place

Within the palace

The child's quarters lie in the innermost recesses of the large, heavily fortified building complex serving as the chief palace of the Hittite Great King. This is the residence he uses when he is at home,[5] which is probably not all that often. Here, too, in what is now called Büyükkale (Turkish for 'Big Castle') reside a number of

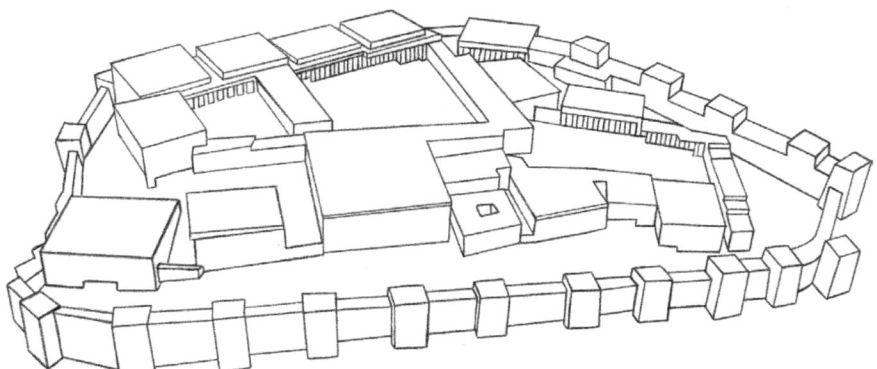

Figure 1.1 Outline sketch of palace, Hattusa. Adapted from model at Hattusa. Courtesy Hannah Bryce.

the king's relatives – and he has lots of them, some very problematic. Elsewhere within the palace are living quarters for important royal officials, including perhaps the Chief Scribe, and the king's special bodyguard, the 'Golden-Spear Men'.[6] Maybe there are also quarters for visiting VIPs. Envoys from foreign states no doubt figure prominently amongst them. When granted admittance to the palace, diplomats from abroad, vassal rulers and other high-ranking subjects of His Majesty will pass through a series of courtyards, connected by gateways and surrounded by colonnades, which lead to various parts of the palace. Including the great Audience Hall.

Located probably on a second storey, it is here that the Great King holds court, listening to letters from his Brother-Kings in Egypt, Babylon and Assyria (translated from Akkadian, the *lingua franca* of the age), accepting his vassal rulers' reaffirmations of their loyalty and their adherence to the terms of the treaties he has imposed upon them, giving final judgement on lawsuits referred to him as Chief Justice of the land, and dealing with a host of other matters too important to be entrusted to the kingdom's host of minor officials.

Within the capital

Let's zoom out a little. The palace lies on an elevated, sloping plateau at the southeastern end of the oldest part of Hattusa. This part is walled off from the

Figure 1.2 Acropolis, Hattusa. Author photo.

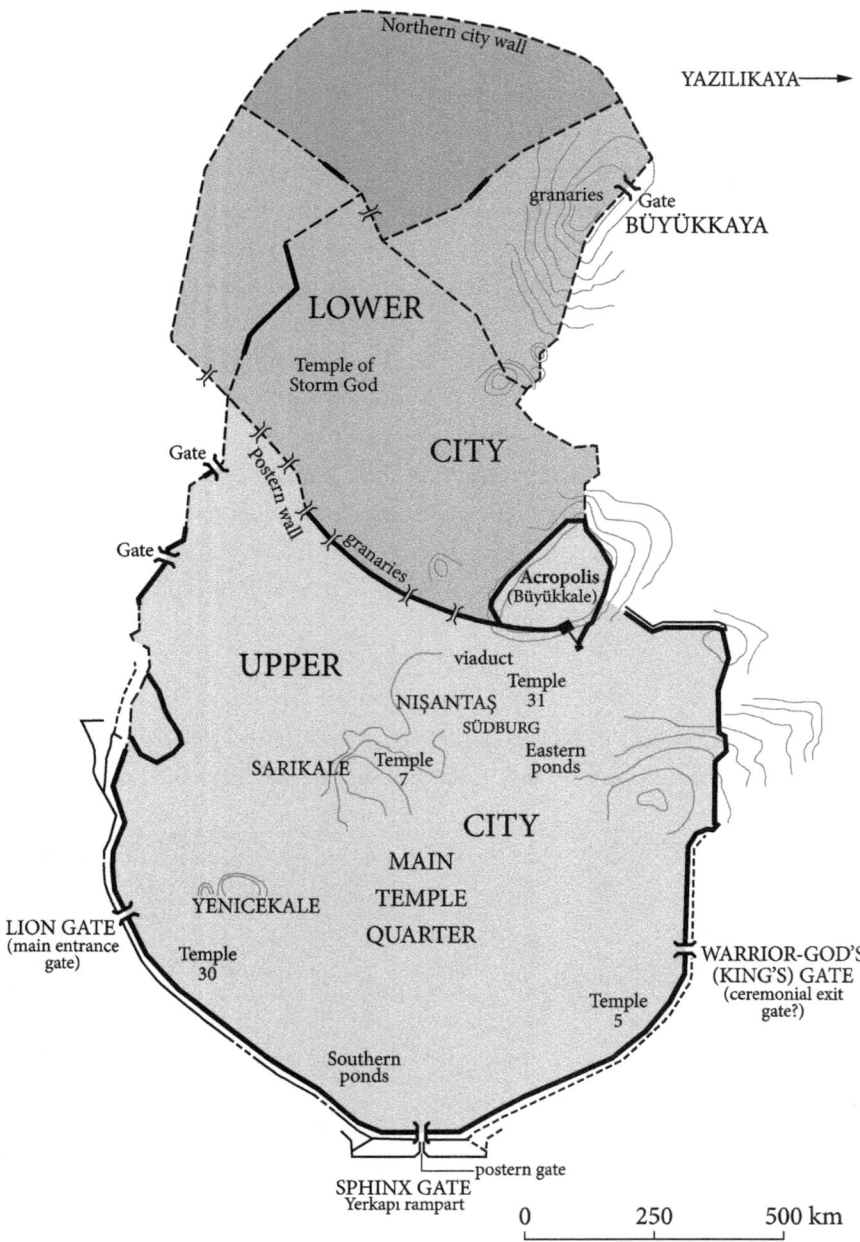

Map 1.1 Plan of Hattusa. Adaptation by author.

rest of the city, just as the palace is walled off from it. We refer to it today as the Lower City. At one time in its history, it contained what appears to have been an elite residential area, with houses probably occupied by some of the city's most important inhabitants – high-ranking bureaucrats or military officers and perhaps, too, heads of priestly establishments. Also in the Old or Lower City there is a huge, sprawling complex believed to be the Temple of the Storm (or Weather) God, the kingdom's most important deity. In contrast to almost all other temples, this one contains not one but two shrines, probably dedicated to the Storm God and his wife, the Sun Goddess of Arinna. Each deity has their own shrine, housing their own monumental statue.

When we zoom out a little further, the entire city comes into view.[7] By ancient standards, it's huge. Some 181 hectares in area, it is surrounded by massive walls, made of mudbrick on stone foundations, and rising 8.3 metres above ground level. Every twenty to twenty-five metres, the walls are punctuated by crenellated towers some 12.8 metres in height. Snaking across rocky, uneven terrain and spanning a large ravine, the walls, 6.6 kilometres long, enclose the entire city. Even at ground level this architectural and engineering achievement cannot fail to impress all who visit Hattusa. We see that access to the city is via a number of gates. The chief one is today called the Lion Gate, because it is flanked by the sculptured foreparts of two lions roaring their defiance at those who dare cross their threshold. All who do so find themselves in the Upper City. Completely walled off from the Lower City, it contains at its peak at least thirty temples.

On the rugged, downward-sloping terrain of this part of the city, several large rocky outcrops stand out. Some have become parts of building complexes, perhaps cult sanctuaries, perhaps residences for a few privileged members of the city's elite. Of particular note is a large cliff face, also part of a building complex today called Nişantepe. This is the Turkish word for 'marked hilltop', so called because it bears a long inscription, which has now almost entirely weathered away. It may have been inscribed by the very last ruler of the Hittite empire.[8] While we're looking down upon Hattusa, our attention might be caught by a number of other features of the Upper City, including seven ponds, five of which serve as reservoirs; the other two have special sacred purposes.

It's time to zoom out further. But wait. We should pause a moment. There is something odd about this city – something quite extraordinary. We need to talk about this since it's an important part of our story. But there'll be a later, more appropriate time for us to do so.

Within the kingdom

Let's continue our zoom outwards. Much further out this time. Hattusa is now little more than a speck in the landscape below us, the landscape that is its homeland. This homeland, so called by Hittite scholars, lies in the north-central part of the large plateau that extends across the Anatolian peninsula and rises about a thousand metres above sea level. From our lofty bird's-eye view, we see the dull brown shimmer of a river that circumscribes the homeland and defines for us the core part of the kingdom. Within it lie the capital Hattusa and, fairly short distances from it, a number of its regional centres. The Hittites called the river the Marassantiya, known in Classical sources as the Halys ('Salt River'). Today the Turks call it the Kızıl Irmak ('Red River'). The river isn't of much use to the Hittites. It's too shallow to be navigable and it provides no barrier worth speaking of to invading enemy forces. Incidentally, 'Anatolia' is an ancient word for Turkey, still sometimes used today by the Turks in the form 'Anadolu'. The word is Greek in origin. It literally means 'towards the rising (of the sun)'; that is, 'towards the east', which Turkey *is* from a Greek perspective.

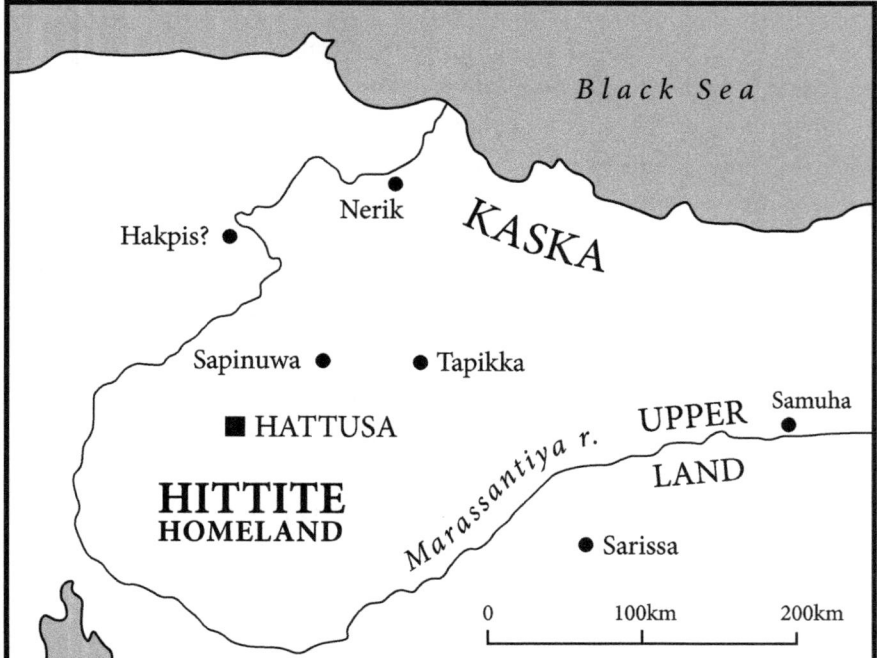

Map 1.2 The Hittite homeland. Courtesy Hannah Bryce.

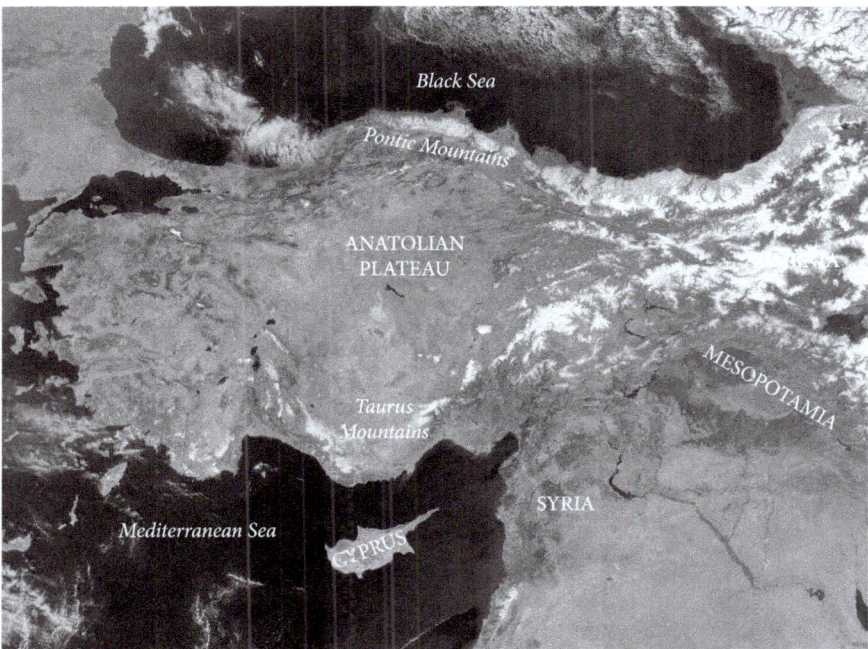

Map 1.3 The Anatolian peninsula. NASA satellite photo by Jeff Schmalz. MODIS Rapid Response Team, NASA/GSFC.

Zooming out further, we see that the Anatolian plateau is bounded by mountain ranges on both its northern and its southern sides. The northern ranges, which separate it from the Black Sea, are known as the Pontic mountains; the ranges on the south, which divide the plateau from the Mediterranean, are called the Taurus mountains. In the east, the plateau merges into the Armenian mountains. In the west, it slopes down more gently to the Aegean coast. The peninsula in between is commonly referred to as a land-bridge between the Near Eastern and western worlds, for through it pass important routes of communications conveying population groups, trade goods, cultures and armies from east to west, and west to east.

Why on earth did Hattusa become the capital?

Our final zoom brings into view the entire empire, in a period that encompasses the lifetime and career of our Hittite prince, the man destined to become 'Great King of Hatti'. We're looking down upon a vast conglomerate of core territories and subject states, stretching from the Aegean Sea in the west across the Anatolian

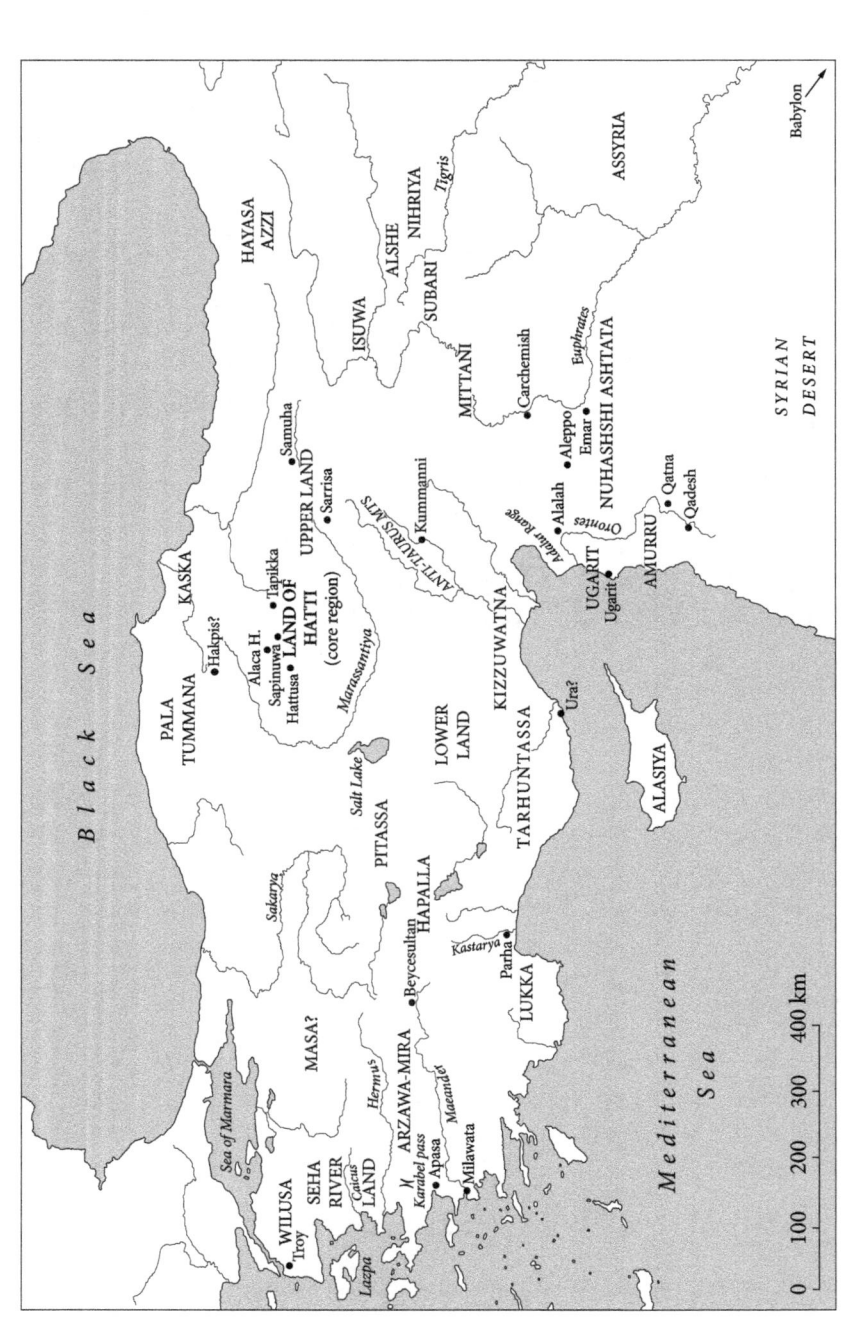

Map 1.4 The Hittite world. Author map.

peninsula to the Euphrates river in the east, and extending southwards deep into Syria as far as the region of Damascus. That's where Egyptian territory begins. What may strike you as particularly odd is the location of the empire's capital near the northern periphery of its own territory, far from its westernmost, southernmost and easternmost dependencies. This makes very costly, and sometimes very risky, the Hittites' long-distance campaigns against their enemies and rebel states, in terms of the human resources that have to be diverted for long periods from other activities, like the defence of home territory. Nor does its remoteness protect it against invasions by powerful groups of Hurrians from the east and southeast, and the highly aggressive, and highly elusive, Kaskan tribes from the Pontic mountains in the north. What's more, the Hittite core region is landlocked, so it has no seaports like Egypt and thus no navy or commercial fleets.

The kingdom's economy is primarily, indeed almost exclusively, an agricultural and pastoral one. In good seasons, the homeland's large cattle herds and flocks of sheep have plenty of fodder to sustain them, and grain crops fill to capacity, for redistribution to its populace, the large storage silos located in the capital and its regional centres. Skilful husbandry also ensures a bountiful supply of fruit and vegetables. That's all very well in good seasons. But the region suffers from harsh, hot summers, with periods of drought, and from even harsher cold winters when the capital is often snowbound, completely isolated from the rest of its kingdom. There is another danger that constantly threatens the land. Even in good seasons, flourishing crops and orchards can suddenly be flattened when an offended Storm God unleashes his fury. And it needs much more than emissions reductions or carbon-capture schemes to appease a wrathful Storm God – of whom there are a multitude.

So why on earth was the Hittite capital built where it is? One of the early Hittite kings chose it as the site for a capital. In its favour, it has an abundant all-year-round water supply, provided by a number of springs, and the large outcrop of rock now called Büyükkale provides an excellent location for a citadel. But I can think of little else to recommend it. Not even tradition. Indeed, a forerunner of the Hittite dynasty wiped out its predecessor, at that time an enemy capital called Hattus, sowed its site with weeds and declared it accursed. It was never to be resettled.[9] To be fair to the Hittite king who ignored the curse and probably rebuilt the city – calling it Hattusa and naming himself Hattusili after it[10] – he could have had little idea of its increasing strategic disadvantages as the kingdom grew and expanded. And his successors stubbornly maintained its status as the Hittites' chief city until our prince's elder brother, King Muwattalli shifted the royal seat to a new capital in the land of Tarhuntassa, south-central Anatolia.[11] Muwattalli's patron deity was the Storm God of Lightning. The very name of the new capital – Tarhuntassa, which means 'Storm God City' – exemplifies the king's homage to his deity.

All this leaves my question unanswered. Why was Hattusa rebuilt as the Hittite capital? And the follow-up question. Why did it remain the capital for almost the entire duration of Hittite history, despite the disadvantages of its doing so? In Chapter 5, I'll attempt to provide some answers to these questions.

Time

Let's now provide a time-setting for our tale. In my previous book, *Warriors of Anatolia*, I imagined a time machine that took us thirty-five hundred years back to the past.[12] We found ourselves in the last centuries of the Bronze Age – more specifically, in the period from the seventeenth to the early twelfth century BC[13] when Anatolia and various neighbouring regions were dominated, on and off, by Hatti, the kingdom of the Hittites. Our focus now shall be on a much shorter span of years – from the last decade or so of the fourteenth century to the first decades, six more or less, of the thirteenth. These decades provide the time frame within which our prince lived, prospered and eliminated or neutralized his opponents and enemies, winning for himself the highest office in the land and ruling this land for up to thirty years.

The kingdom's early decades

But before embarking upon his story, let's give it context by recalling some earlier episodes in his kingdom's history.[14] I've already referred to the refounding of Hattusa, probably by the first king called Hattusili, and its status as the capital of the fledgling kingdom of Hatti. Hattusili and his immediate regnal predecessor Labarna (his grandfather?) were early members of an elite family of Indo-European origin which maintained its control over Hatti throughout its history. They laid the foundations of the kingdom's rise to greatness by setting about the conquest of many of the smaller kingdoms, particularly in the eastern part of the Anatolian peninsula. Hattusili built further on his kingdom's power and reputation by regular campaigns of plunder and destruction in neighbouring Syria. His military exploits were capped off by his grandson and successor, Mursili I, who conquered and looted Aleppo, then marched his troops down the

Euphrates to Babylon. Which he also looted and destroyed. But these early Hittite campaigns were little more than smash-and-grab raids, with no attempt to establish permanent control over what they had left in ruins. What's more, military successes abroad were offset by factional disputes and infighting between various branches of the royal family. These shook it to its very foundations.

Rules of succession

Mursili was murdered and had his throne seized by his brother-in-law, Hantili. For the next seven decades or so, assassinations and coups continued to tear apart Hatti's ruling elite. The kingdom's very existence was threatened, especially as Hurrian tribes from the east hovered menacingly on the threshold of its core territory and indeed on the threshold of the capital itself. Finally, a man called Telipinu managed to get his bottom firmly planted on the throne and he issued a proclamation which established firm rules of royal succession.[15] A prince of the first rank, i.e. the son of a Chief Wife, will succeed his father on the throne. But, if there is no prince of the first rank, one of the second rank, i.e. the son of a concubine, will become king. And if there isn't one of these either, then a son-in-law will succeed.

The diplomatic route

Telipinu also managed to win back some of the kingdom's lost territories. But there was one major state originally subject to Hatti that he failed to recapture. Called Kizzuwatna, it lay in a strategically important region between the Anatolian peninsula and Syria. (Check it out on Map 1.4.) So, when brute force proved ineffective, Telipinu tried the diplomatic route and concluded a parity treaty with its ruler. Among other things, this treaty would help counter Hurrian aggression from the east. But it didn't always work and the self-interest of Kizzuwatna's rulers dictated with whom they sided – the Hittites or the Hurrians – and when. Despite this, the treaty marked a significant stage in the Hittite kingdom's development and was later to prove an instrument of great importance in the establishment and maintenance of the Hittite empire, which was largely held together by a network of alliances with the rulers of its subject states.

Leaving that aside, Telipinu's reign left no lasting achievements. He was followed by a succession of weak rulers, with further erosions of the status and military and political authority of the kingdom, which had long forfeited any claim it might once have had to being a major international power. About fifty years after Telipinu's death, the era of what is generally called the Old Kingdom came to an end, when its last king Muwattalli after assassinating his way onto the throne promptly got himself assassinated off it.

New beginnings and an existential crisis

Thus, dawned a new era, commonly called the New Kingdom or the Empire period (both terms are a bit arbitrary) when the first of several kings called Tudhaliya ascended the throne, conveniently left vacant by Muwattalli's involuntary departure. The first one or two Tudhaliyas carried out overwhelmingly successful campaigns in western Anatolia, against a powerful military coalition called (by modern scholars) the Assuwan Confederacy, and in Syria, against a Hurrian- or, more precisely, a Mittanian-led alliance of states.[16] Hatti, the kingdom of the Hittites, was once more back in the international arena.

But not for long. Within a few decades, the kingdom was again plunged into crisis when it was attacked and invaded by enemy forces, swooping in on the homeland from all around its borders. Hattusa itself was captured, looted and destroyed. The king at the time, another Tudhaliya (II or III, depending on how many Tudhaliyas there were[17]), managed to escape with his army and set up a temporary base on the eastern edge of the homeland at a place called Samuha. From here he planned the recovery of his kingdom, with the able assistance of a man called Suppiluliuma, perhaps one of his sons.[18] Indeed, as bouts of illness confined the king more frequently to his sickbed in Samuha, his leadership of his forces may have been increasingly delegated. Suppiluliuma became the principal architect and agent of the homeland's revival, driving the enemy forces from it and counter-attacking them in their own lands.

When death put an end to the old king's sufferings, probably even before he saw his restored capital, another Tudhaliya succeeded him, called Tudhaliya the Younger, perhaps his eldest son. Whatever the reasons for his being passed over for the royal mantle, Suppiluliuma felt deeply aggrieved, after all that he had done to win the kingdom back. His close supporters, many probably his comrades-in-arms, decided to take action. As Suppiluliuma lurked in the background, aware of what was about to happen but wanting to keep blood off his hands, daggers rained down upon the hapless new king, and Suppiluliuma mounted the throne. 'Et tu, Suppiluliuma', his predecessor might have said, or something similar in Hittite.

Rivals for power

As time would tell, the fact that Suppiluliuma did not actually hold one of the murder weapons was not enough to absolve him of guilt for the crime. But, in the meantime, he undertook the biggest challenge of his reign – the annihilation of Hatti's arch enemy, the kingdom of Mittani. After a long, hard-fought war lasting almost two decades, Suppiluliuma succeeded in demolishing the kingdom, rounding off his conquests by capturing the last Mittanian stronghold, the city of Carchemish on the Euphrates. We are now in the year 1326 or thereabouts. A rump kingdom called Hanigalbat was all that remained of Mittani, and Suppiluliuma promptly converted it into a Hittite puppet state.

Further threats were looming. Egypt had long involved itself in Syria with military occupations that sometimes proved fairly temporary. But it had now firmly entrenched itself in the Syrian region by establishing its rule over a number of city-states and petty kingdoms there. This sometimes brought it close to a military confrontation with Hatti, which had overlapping claims in the region. For the time being, however, an uneasy peace prevailed between the two kingdoms. Suppiluliuma was anxious to maintain this, especially while he was still fighting Mittani. Even so, sooner or later a clash was inevitable; and one was sparked off when a Hittite prince, Zannanza, sent to marry the widow of a dead pharaoh, probably Tutankhamun, maybe Akhenaten, was assassinated during his journey. Angrily dismissing the hastily installed new pharaoh's protests of innocence, Suppiluliuma ordered retaliatory raids on Egyptian territory in southern Syria. Many prisoners of war were brought back to Hatti as booty from the conflict.

Though a fragile peace was once more restored, the prospect of all-out war between the two kingdoms grew increasingly likely. What's more, another great power had emerged in the vacuum left by Mittani's fall – the kingdom of Assyria. Quick to gobble up most of the last remnants of the Mittanian empire, Assyria posed an increasing threat to Hittite subject territories both east and west of the Euphrates. There were now four Great Kingdoms of the Near Eastern world – Hatti, Egypt, Babylon and, Mittani's replacement, Assyria.

King by default

Suppiluliuma was succeeded by his eldest son, Arnuwanda, who died within a year or so from a plague brought back by prisoners from Suppiluliuma's southern campaign. Suppiluliuma himself had succumbed to this plague. There were three other surviving sons, but two of them were already committed to serving the kingdom as vice-regents, at Aleppo and Carchemish in Syria. That left only Mursili, perhaps barely out of his teens when kingship was suddenly thrust upon him. His youth and apparent inexperience provoked widespread uprisings amongst Hatti's subject and enemy states. But Mursili quickly proved he was up to the job, confounding his enemies, restoring order over his rebellious vassals, and bringing back to the homeland as war booty large numbers of prisoners, livestock and, probably, cartloads of treasure.

Still, plague continued to ravage the Hittite land, while Mursili was faced with another big problem – this one within his own household. It had to do with his stepmother, a Babylonian princess who had become Suppiluliuma's Chief Wife and adopted the Hittite royal title 'Tawananna' as a personal name. She had abused her authority by exercising despotic power over the palace household, stripping it of its treasures to lavish on her favourites, and introducing undesirable exotic customs into the kingdom. She was also suspected of causing the death of Mursili's beloved first wife. This last act was the final straw for Mursili. She was put on trial, found guilty, and banished from the palace.

After a generally successful reign, Mursili was succeeded by his son Muwattalli, the second eldest of four siblings, including two other sons and a daughter. His older brother Halpasulupi might normally have been first in line for the succession. But the rules of succession did not require a king to choose his first-born son as his successor. And, though we hear very little more of Halpasulupi, he, nonetheless, seems to have lived throughout his brother's reign and was made king of the eastern province of Isuwa, either by his father or his brother.[19] Muwattalli's reign is mostly remembered for two things, quite possibly linked. One was the shift of the royal capital to Tarhuntassa, the other was the outbreak of a hot war with Egypt.

The showdown with Egypt

The latter is defined by two battles at a place called Qadesh (more strictly, Qidš) on the Orontes river in Syria. Muwattalli's opponent in the first war was the pharaoh Seti I. Seti claimed a resounding victory. But it was not a conclusive one, for a few years later there was another, more famous, battle at Qadesh (in 1274 BC), this time between Muwattalli and Seti's son and successor, Ramesses II. Both battles were fought primarily over the disputed ownership of two states, Amurru and Qadesh, which lay in the border zone between the two kingdoms. Extending over one and a half days, the battle with Ramesses ended in a stalemate, though Muwattalli was the ultimate winner, for he won permanent possession of both Amurru and Qadesh. Not that you'd know this from the account of the battle left by Ramesses on the walls of five Egyptian temples. In these, the pharaoh claimed a glorious one-man victory over 'the fallen one of Hatti'.

With Muwattalli's death shortly after, the succession passed to his son by a concubine. This son is commonly known in Hittite literature by his birthname, Urhi-Teshub.[20] More later on the significance of this.

Introducing 'Hattusili'

And that brings us to the beginning of the story of 'the prince who stole an empire'. We cannot be sure what his birth-name was. Most likely, it was only when he ascended the throne as Great King of Hatti that he assumed the name Hattusili[21] – for reasons I'll discuss in Chapter 5. But, since I do not know what else to call him prior to his enthronement, I'll refer to him by his eventual throne-name, purely as a matter of convenience and long before he was actually entitled to use it.

*****

I've included this brief digest of Hittite history for three main reasons. Firstly, I hope it will provide a useful background to the life and times of our young prince and future king, especially for readers who are unfamiliar with Hittite history. My second reason is that I'll be referring to most of the characters and events of earlier periods in the kingdom's history to make some point or other about Hattusili's career. So, when I do, you'll know from the digest whom or what I'm talking about. My third reason is that at the end of it all I'll be asking some fundamental questions. What, if anything, is distinctive about the career of our prince and the king he was destined to become? What were his achievements and failures compared with those of his predecessors and successors? In what ways did his reign shape the course of Hittite history – in ways none of those who came before or after him ever did? Was he a Great King, literally, or merely one who occupied the throne on its inevitable progression to decline and extinction? By the end of the book, I hope I can provide at least partial answers to some of these questions.

2

Our Sources

The Chief Scribe, seated before the king, carefully unfolds from its wrappings a clay tablet, still damp and soft. Fitting neatly into the palm of his left hand, it is the draft of a treaty he has drawn up for the king's approval. The treaty is a pact between the king and a new vassal ruler installed by imperial fiat in one of the empire's subject states. The document formalizes the vassal's appointment. It imposes a raft of obligations upon him, including military support for the king when called upon and a local espionage service. Then follows a guarantee from His Majesty that he will protect the vassal and his rightful successors from any hostile action against them – as long as his treaty partner sticks by his oath to uphold the treaty's terms, sworn before the gods. Now follows a list of the divine witnesses, the gods, and the curses they will inflict upon the vassal and all his family, should he be foolish enough to violate his oath.

This is pretty standard stuff, found in many treaties, and the scribe has simply to incorporate their main clauses into the new treaty. But there is more to it than this. Most treaties start off with historical preambles. They provide important context for the treaties. Some extol the merits of the vassal's predecessors, especially their loyalty to the Hittite crown, and emphasize the new man's obligations to follow in their footsteps. Some tell of the hostilities of former vassals and warn the new one of the dangerous consequences of following in their footsteps. Some cover other topics as well. Scribe and Great King have already discussed what is required in this particular case, as well as what extra provisions are to be included in the body of the text, to ensure that all matters relevant to this vassal and his kingdom are covered.

The Chief Scribe has directed one of his junior clerks to retrieve from the archives all tablets containing the information he needs to complete his draft. This done, he requests an audience with the king, bearing with him his draft treaty, and ensuring that the clay on which it's inscribed is still soft so that corrections, additions and erasures can be made on it. The king listens carefully as the scribe reads the draft to him. Mostly, he nods in agreement. But at times he holds up his hand and stops the reader in mid-sentence. 'No! Remove that last bit! It's no longer relevant!' The scribe draws a line through the obsolete words. Or 'You've left out an important obligation this vassal must meet!' The king dictates what the obligation is, and the scribe notes it down in the margin of his text, his right hand a blur of stutters as his stylus presses small wedge-shaped signs into the clay.[1] Here and there the king requires minor changes to be made. These too are noted in the margins. The scribe then prepares a final version of the treaty, reads it to the king who endorses it with his seal, and the treaty is sent by special courier to the vassal. Its recipient doesn't seem to have any say in it at all. But if he's important enough, the treaty might not be inscribed on clay but engraved on bronze. Before it's despatched, a clay copy is made and assigned its appropriate place in Hattusa's archives.[2]

Our ancient written records

Our story is based almost entirely on surviving written records, mostly preserved on clay, which have a bearing on Hattusili's life and career.[3] In total, they provide one of the most wide-ranging sets of information we have of any Hittite king. Treaties concluded by Hattusili with his subject rulers, for example, give us important political and historical information about his reign, and some insights into how successfully his kingdom was managed. Of course, the most important treaty of all is the one he drew up with Ramesses II. We'll be discussing the treaty and its most significant implications in Chapter 8. I've already mentioned the importance attached to it today from the copy on display in the United Nations' headquarters.

Letters exchanged by the king with his foreign peers are highly instructive not only because of the information they provide about the king's relations with his fellow Great Kings, and about international affairs in general during his reign, but also because of the fleeting insights they provide into the personalities, emotions and occasional pettinesses of their authors. The most voluminous correspondence during Hattusili's reign are the letters that passed between the Hittite and Egyptian courts when the pharaoh was Ramesses – not only between the two Great Kings, but also between other members of their families.[4] And we should not fail to mention that Hattusili's Chief Wife was one of Ramesses' regular correspondents. Ironically, one of the best known 'letters' from Hattusili's reign, the so-called 'Tawagalawa letter' was probably not a letter at all. We'll have more to say about this in Chapter 12.

Prayers and hymns make an important contribution to our repertoire of Hittite texts. Often, they are uttered by a king, as the gods' deputy on earth, seeking to appease angry deities who have inflicted a devastating plague upon the land, or imploring one or more of them to smite the lands of their enemies with fever, pestilence, famine and other dire punishments. But some appeals to the gods are of a deeply personal nature – like the anguished but futile prayer of Mursili, father of Hattusili, for the recovery of his dying wife, Gassuliyawiya, and the prayers of Hattusili's own wife, Puduhepa, for her husband's recovery from one of his chronic illnesses, and Hattusili's plea to the Sun Goddess of Arinna to be absolved of any responsibility for the downfall of his stepgrandmother, Tawananna, for he was only a child at the time, and his stepmother, Danuhepa.[5]

Most significant of all is a text unparalleled in Hittite literature. I've referred to it briefly in the Introduction. Commonly known as the *Apology*, it contains an account of part of Hattusili's life and career, including his 'justification' for illegally seizing the throne from his nephew, the true king.[6] As we'll see, *Apology* is a modern and somewhat misleading title, as is the alternative title *Autobiography*. But whatever we call it (and for the sake of convenience we'll stick to *Apology*), this document tells us more about who Hattusili was as a person than all the bureaucratic records that provide most of our sources of information about his reign.

My own account of Hattusili's life and career will draw on all these sources of information (and more besides) and I'll sometimes include direct quotations from them. Of course, there is no substitute to reading the texts themselves, in full. And the ideal situation for you would be to have these texts right beside you as you read those parts of my book that refer to them. The good news is that almost all of them are still available, at quite reasonable prices, in the excellent Scholars Press series, published by the Society of Biblical Literature, Atlanta, GA. These include Gary Beckman's *Hittite Diplomatic Texts* (cited as *HDT*), Harry Hoffner's *Letters from the Hittite Kingdom*, Itamar Singer's *Hittite Prayers*, and *The Ahhiyawa Texts*, the book by Gary Beckman, myself and Eric Cline containing all texts referring to the (or a) Bronze Age kingdom of Greece (cited as *AhT*). All these books are accompanied by historical commentaries. Two of them, Hoffner's book and *AhT*, have the original text (in transliteration) on pages facing the English translation, like the Loeb Classical Library texts. In the Bibliography, you'll find full publications details of all the texts I refer to, with asterisks before the ones where these texts are translated into English.[7]

The only English version of the *Apology* that I know of, translated by the distinguished Hittite scholar Theo van den Hout, appears in the three- (now four-) volume anthology *The Context of Scripture* (*CoS*).[8] Substantial in size and scope, *The Context* contains translated texts, including many Hittite ones, from a wide range of Ancient Near Eastern civilizations. An investment in all volumes would be well worthwhile if you'd like a basic reference work for steeping yourself in the Ancient Near East and have the financial means to acquire it. But in my book, I'll assume you'll be relying almost entirely on what I tell you about the *Apology* and, with this in mind, I'll give you as much of its content as I can in my discussion of it.

Unfortunately, the great majority of our surviving texts are fragmentary. Both small and large bits of them are lost forever, though occasionally a missing piece of a tablet is found in the vast collection of unassigned fragments and fitted into its original place. But most of the tablets have gaps yet to be filled. If you do manage to get hold of any of the translations I've referred to, you'll generally find sections of them enclosed by square brackets. These sections are conjectural restorations by the translator. Sometimes the conjectures are self-evident – for example, in a standard introductory royal formula: *[Thus says] Tabarna, Muwattalli, Great King, King of Hatti, Hero; [son of Mursili, Great King, King of Hatti], Hero; grandson of Suppiluliuma, Great King, [King of Hatti, Hero].*[9] Sometimes the gaps are more difficult to fill, and translators have to rely on informed guesswork to suggest what's missing, with footnotes or endnotes to justify their conjectures.

One source I haven't yet mentioned is the monumental two-volume tome in German by the eminent Egyptologist, Elmar Edel.[10] It contains all the letters known to the time of its publication (1994) that were exchanged between the Hittite and Egyptian royal courts, all but one of them dating to Hattusili's and Ramesses' reigns. Unfortunately, a large proportion of the letters survive only as fragments, and Edel is what we might call 'unduly creative' in filling many of the gaps. The letters are an extremely important part of our repertoire of information about Hattusili and his times, especially his international relationships. I've devoted most of Chapter 9 to these letters; and, with the guidance of other scholars, like Harry Hoffner and Gary Beckman who have translated a small sample of them, I've exercised great caution in my use of Edel's often conjectural renditions.

The *Apology*, the letters and some of the prayers play a major role in this book, especially because of the modicum of flesh they put on Hattusili's bones, otherwise left bare by the impersonal bureaucratic records associated with his reign. With just an occasional exception, such bland sources of information are all we have left of other Great Kings of Hatti. Apart from an assassin and usurper, here and there, Hittite kings seem to have led rather colourless lives (when they were not away fighting), if we were to judge them solely from what's left about their reigns in state and temple archives. Our sources of information on Hattusili provide a partial response to this – even though they fall well short of providing a fully rounded picture of our prince and subsequent Great King in the manner of Shakespearian royalty or the cavalcade of emperors who enliven and often besmirch the chronicles of imperial Rome. But they do come up with a villain or two, now and then. The actual mechanics involved in recording what we know about Hittite kings, their subjects, their foreign peers, their gods, their laws, and their festivals are comprehensively dealt with by Professor van den Hout in his definitive account of Hittite scribal culture, *A History of Hittite Literacy: Writing and Reading in Late Bronze-Age Anatolia (1650–1200 BC)*.

Our modern sources

Which brings me to some general books on Hittite history and society. Oliver Gurney's *The Hittites* was for decades the standard work on the topic. First published in 1952, it reappeared in a number of reprints, all the way up to 1990.[11] If you already have a copy of this book, don't throw it away. Much of it is now out of date, but it still contains many wise, pertinent comments about Hittite history and civilization. Gurney's student James Macqueen followed in his master's footsteps with a book of his own in 1975, *The Hittites and Their Contemporaries in Asia Minor*, followed by a larger, revised edition in 1986.[12] Macqueen's book, too, has exceeded its use-by date but, if it is already on your bookshelf, I'd keep it there. It contains some still useful information on such topics as Hittite military organization, battle dress and armaments, daily life, art and literature, and religious beliefs and practices.

After six years in full-time university administration, I became increasingly frustrated with writing reports for bureaucrats and politicians on university matters that I knew would never be read – or, if they were, totally ignored – and decided to launch out afresh by writing books that I hoped at least a few people would read and perhaps enjoy. An invitation by Oxford University Press to write a new book on the Hittites was the final prompt I needed to take this step. Hence the genesis of *The Kingdom of the Hittites*. A first edition was published in 1998 and sold enough copies and received enough favourable reviews for me to write an enlarged and much improved edition in 2005. (You can safely throw the 1998 edition away if you have access to the new one.) I had made clear that this book was essentially a political and military history of the Hittites and, between the two editions, I wrote a complementary volume, *Life and Society in the Hittite World*, published in 2002.[13] Both books at the time of writing are still in print.

A more recent publication is Billie Jean Collins' *The Hittites and Their World*. Published in 2007,[14] this excellent account of both Hittite political and military history and Hittite society and civilization has aged little over the years, is affordable for the general reader and is warmly recommended. Also warmly recommended is Jürgen Seeher's *Hattusha Guide: A Day in the Hittite Capital*. As the title indicates, it is a guidebook, an indispensable companion if you're actually visiting the Hittite capital, written by one of the site's former directors of excavations. Even if you're not visiting the site, the book provides a concise account, well illustrated by plans, sketches and photographs, of the capital's layout and most important features.

Extensive new excavations leading to important new discoveries had been carried out by Dr Seeher's predecessor, Peter Neve. Dr Neve published a popular, also well illustrated account (in German) of the excavations while under his direction, in his book, *Hattuša: Stadt der Götter und Tempel*.[15] However, a number of his conclusions were considerably revised by his successor. Recently, a small section of the city's mudbrick walls has been rebuilt from scratch under Dr Seeher's direction, using the materials and the building techniques of the Hittites themselves. Seeher provides a fascinating account of the project in his book, *A Mudbrick City Wall at Hattusa*.[16]

Chapters on the Hittites contribute to a number of recent anthologies. These include the magisterial *The Oxford Handbook of Ancient Anatolia*, edited by Sharon Steadman and Gary McMahon.[17] Cited as *OHAA*, this volume contains many chapters on Hittite history and civilization, from the political to the social and cultural, from written records to archaeological remains. The most recent anthology devoted to the Hittite world is *Handbook Hittite Empire* (cited as *HHE*), edited by Stefano de Martino.[18] It is a comprehensive, up-to-date compilation of all aspects of Hittite history and civilization, with chapters on the peoples and languages of the empire, the governance of the subordinated countries, social stratification, religion and power, images of the Hittite king, the economy of the Hittite state, and many other Hittite and Hittite-related topics. Both this book and the *Oxford Handbook* are written for scholars and others deeply interested in a study of the Hittites. They are not inexpensive, but probably cost no more than a couple of tanks of petrol/gasoline and probably less than a couple of nights at a four-star motel or a bed and breakfast.

But if you're looking for a concise, inexpensive, recent book about the Hittites, you have two possibilities. There is my book *Warriors of Anatolia*, which contains brief chapters on the history, society, and civilization of the Hittite world. It was published in hardback in 2019 and paperback in 2023.[19] Secondly, in 2023, Reaktion Press published a book on the Hittites in its *Lost Civilizations* series (London: *The Hittites: Lost Civilizations*). Written by Damien Stone, it is only 45,000 words long (the series limit), but lavishly illustrated. While having nothing new to say about the Hittites, it provides a very useful introduction to them.

Let me now come to the few publications that deal primarily with Hattusili. First off the rank is Professor Horst Klengel's *Hattuschili und Ramses: Hethiter und Ägypter – ihr langer Weg zum Frieden*.[20] Published in 2002, and obviously accessible only to German-speaking readers, it explores such questions as what Hattusili and Ramesses actually looked like, the famous peace treaty and the events surrounding it, the Egyptian-related activities of Urhi-Teshub (the righful Hittite king overthrown by Hattusili) and the resulting tensions between Hattusili and Ramesses when Urhi-Teshub sought refuge in Egypt, what the palaces of the two Great Kings were like, and the marriage links between their families. Don't worry if you don't read German. The book is well and interestingly written but it contains little that you won't find in other books about the Hittites.[21]

In 2003, a symposium held in Leiden, Netherlands, was devoted to scholarly papers on Hattusili and his son, Tudhaliya. The proceedings of the symposium were published under the title, *The Life and Times of Hattušili III and Tuthaliya IV*, edited by Professor van den Hout.[22] Most of the papers are about Tudhaliya but, if you can get access to the book, there is one of particular relevance to our story. It's called 'The Urhi-Teššub Affair in the Hittite-Egyptian Correspondence', written by my dear friend, now sadly deceased, Itamar Singer. I'll have occasion to refer to it several times in later chapters.

The best summary to date of Hattusili's life and career is a chapter in the four-volume anthology *Civilizations of the Ancient Near East* (cited as *CANE*), edited by Jack Sasson and published in 1995. Entitled 'Khattushilish III, King of the Hittites', the chapter, written by Professor van den Hout, provides in the space of 6,000 words an excellent account of the career of Hattusili, from his early childhood to his final years, and contains much information about his family and the circumstances of his rise to Great Kingship.[23] On the negative side, the chapter is constrained by the compulsory word limit (as I know from writing a chapter for the same publication) and may be difficult to extract on its own without acquiring or having access to the entire (expensive) four-volume set.

Some digital sources

There's one other category of information I'd like to mention before concluding this chapter – film and television documentaries. Let me start with the well-known series, *In Search of the Trojan War*, written and presented by Michael Wood.[24] Yes, Hittites *do* play a role in the story of Troy (aka Ilion), even though Homer makes no mention of them in his *Iliad*. I'll come back to this in Chapter 11. But here I want to concentrate on just one small part of Michael Wood's presentation. In the fifth instalment of the six-episode series, Michael gives a splendid oration in the well-preserved theatre of the Roman city, Miletus (Greek, Miletos), on Turkey's western coast. The oration is in fact an adapted version of the famous 'Tawagalawa letter', referred to above and the chief subject of Chapter 12. Placing the oration in a Roman setting is an obvious, but acceptable, anachronism. I'm sure you'll agree if you've already seen the episode. I believe that the 'letter' was almost certainly composed by Hattusili himself (i.e. not by a scribe and then edited by the king). Millawanda (aka Milawata), the Bronze Age equivalent of Miletus, was the city where Hattusili ended up on his failed mission to capture an elusive, high-profile insurrectionist. Wood has complemented his television documentary with a book of the same title. It's well written, well illustrated, makes an attractive companion to the television series and has been revised and updated a number of times.[25]

On the subject of Troy, I took part in a BBC documentary, a few years later, called *The Truth of Troy*, directed by Aidan Laverty. Once again, the Hittites were given an airing, this time on a campaign ending up in Wilusa, the Bronze Age name of Troy/Ilion. The campaign was despatched by the Great King Muwattalli, brother of Hattusili and his predecessor-but-one on the Hittite throne. Budgetary constraints kept production costs of the documentary to a minimum, and filming the Hittite campaign march was restricted to model soldiers being moved from one region to another – by yours truly – on a large map set out on a board in the living room of the director's small London flat.

I was also involved, as an adviser and interviewee, in another BBC production, which still occasionally does the rounds on various digital platforms. With a primary focus on the Hittite capital, the production is called *The Dark Lords of Hattusha*. It's a snappy piece of work, using a range of scholarly sources of information on the rulers of the Hittite world and their capital, combined with the magic of digital technology. Just occasionally it's a bit loose with the truth, with a touch of exaggeration and over-simplification here and there. We can put that down to 'dramatic licence'.

But the award for the most thoroughly researched of all the documentaries on the Hittites must go to the Turkish director, Tolga Örnek. Called simply *The Hittites*, the film moves almost poetically through the annals of Hittite history from the first to the last of the Great Kings. The golden tones of the distinguished British actor, Jeremy Irons, the narrator, greatly enriches the story. Well-known Turkish actors hired by Tolga provide largely unspeaking, unmoving background roles to the narrative. But there are also scenes showing soldiers on the march – local lads hired by Tolga, kitted out in military uniforms and armed with Hittite spears, bows and arrows. For action sequences, including brilliant flashes of the battle of Qadesh, they were conveyed from one part of the capital to another, and from city to open spaces, by a couple of old Turkish buses. These had been brought out of retirement for the purpose. We used to refer to them as HABS – the Hittite Army Bus Service.

Tolga has since made several trips to Australia, the first to promote his Hittite documentary. He stayed with my wife and me in our Brisbane apartment on one of these occasions, and we had a number of chats about the amount of research he did to ensure as much authenticity as possible with all the costumes, the equipment and the settings for his film. Even the soldiers' tunics got special attention, woven as they were from natural fibres that he was assured by experts were grown in that period. This certainly beat the plastic-model soldiers used in *The Truth of Troy*. I have given Tolga's film special attention here for the reasons I've stated above, but also because Hattusili is among the standout figures in it. In Chapter 6 I refer to one of its most beautiful scenes, where the Great Queen Puduhepa bends lovingly over her husband's dying body and begs the gods that he yet may live.

I'm sure you are more skilful than I'll ever be in using digital technology and will have no trouble locating any of the above films and downloading them onto your laptop, iPad or smartphone. Let me then wish you happy reading – and happy viewing.

3

Benefactors of a Young Prince

A dysfunctional family

The prince was no more than a young child when his mother died.[1] His father Mursili had loved her dearly and deeply mourned her passing.[2] He held his stepmother, Tawananna, First Lady of the kingdom,[3] responsible for her death by using black magic (a traditional wicked stepmotherly thing to do). Tawananna was tried and found guilty, a verdict backed by the oracles, and sentenced to permanent exile. This was a relatively mild punishment, particularly since the oracles had prescribed her execution.[4]

Probably not much later, the king remarried and the young prince found himself with a new mother, called Danuhepa. With the banishment of Mursili's stepmother and the death of his first wife, Danuhepa would now have become the kingdom's First Lady. She brought to the marriage sons of her own[5] – and so was hardly likely to provide the prince with an acceptable substitute for his own mother. And, as we shall see (Chapter 5), the new First Lady was *apparently* not much better than her banished predecessor.

Despite his tender years, Hattusili must have been aware of the wiles and intrigues that entangled life around him in the royal court. There was much to learn from his dysfunctional family's nefarious activities. Maybe one day he would put what he learnt to good use. Besides, there was always the goddess Ishtar to justify – or be given credit for – whatever he did.

Divine patronage

Having Ishtar as your patron and protector was an honour of no small importance. Every king had a special deity whom he served above all others and who protected him throughout his life. A patron deity guided you through your everyday activities and was there with you on the battlefield, backed up by a host of other deities. That's what the prince's father Mursili tells us. His patron deity was the Sun Goddess of Arinna, goddess-in-chief of the Hittite world. She protected him in battle, along with all the other Hittite deities who ran before him into the battle's midst.[6] We do not know of any Hittite king who was killed in battle, despite the numerous campaigns in which warrior-lords like Mursili engaged. So divine protection seems to have proved effective, at least on the battlefield – well, that plus the probability that the king was in most cases protected from actual contact with the enemy by his bodyguard, the Golden-Spear Men, who must have formed a near-impenetrable barrier around him.

Back to our prince's patron deity, Ishtar. She had been an import into the Hittite world from more ancient civilizations further east. But she quickly assumed the role of one of the most formidable deities of the multitudinous gods in the Hittite pantheon. Noted primarily as a goddess of love, sexuality and war (these attributes are not all that far apart), she could assume many roles. All in all, she was the ideal patron for her *protégé* throughout his life. At least one of Hattusa's thirty-one temples must have been dedicated to her. And, unless the prince performed his priestly services at a cult-centre like Samuha in the homeland's buffer zone (see the next chapter) or carried out his priestly role without a special attachment to any of her temples, it's likely that he served the goddess in her temple (or one of them) in Hattusa. Perhaps here he performed her rituals and uttered prayers to her with appeals for the well-being of her devotees, the prospering of crops on lands administered by her temple, and the overthrow of her enemies. There were other duties to attend to as well when the need arose, like the washing, anointing and clothing of her statue in the temple's innermost sanctuary.

Literacy at the highest levels of the hierarchy?

A number of temples probably had their own scribal staff. No doubt many of these were priests whose clerical duties included the keeping of written records. These were records of prayers, rituals and other religious duties honouring a temple's deity, and accounts of the temple's business affairs, including the management of any lands the king had entrusted to its care and the revenue accruing from them.[7] Which raises the question of where the literate members of Hittite society acquired their ability to read and write. We have no evidence that the temples had their own scribal schools, like those of the Babylonian

Figure 3.1 Inscribing a clay tablet. Courtesy Tolga Örnek, from *The Hittites* (2003), [TV programme] Dir. Tolga Örnek, Turkey: Ekip Film.

world,[8] for training some of their young priests to become literate. But it is a possibility. And, if so, was our prince one of the recipients of this training? Let me chance my arm. I believe that Hattusili not only became a priest in Ishtar's service, and served her as such for a number of years during his childhood and early adolescence, but that, while he did so, he learned to read and write, a skill that would prove particularly useful to him during the years he occupied the Hittite throne.[9] But it was not necessarily in a scribal school, sacred or secular, that he acquired this skill.

This brings us to another important figure in our story. His name is Mittanamuwa, Chief Scribe of the kingdom. The significance of his role in Hittite affairs will become evident later. But we first hear of him when we are told that our ailing young prince was entrusted by his father to his care: *Mittanamuwa did his utmost for me and saved me from the illness. He was a man esteemed by my father and when he had saved me from the illness he honoured him for my sake as well.*[10] This information is provided by a separate document to the so-called *Apology* which tells us that Ishtar was responsible for the child's recovery, at least indirectly. On a practical level, the Chief Scribe may well have played a major role in the recovery. But his services to the young prince probably went a great deal further. More on this below.

In any case, we can be sure that Hattusili acquired two powerful benefactors in his childhood years – a formidable goddess in the Hittite pantheon and the Hittite kingdom's Chief Scribe.

The benefactors

Let's say a little more about each of these. First of all, the goddess. Like celestial rulers of many civilizations, Hittite gods, including personal patron deities like Ishtar, were active in all aspects of daily life. They gave lifelong protection to their devotees, and showered blessings upon them, so long as those so blessed proved worthy of their favours. They could also punish severely those who incurred their wrath. This was no more primitive superstitious fantasy than many would consider religious faiths today which unshakeably affirm the reality of the god or gods they worship, as attested by worshippers in cathedrals, mosques and synagogues. Hattusili had no doubt that throughout his life his patron Ishtar was literally by his side, supporting him in all his endeavours and ambitions, and protecting him from all threats, whether on the battlefield or in the conspiratorial circles of his own extended family.

Then there is Mittanamuwa. Directly or indirectly, I believe that the scribal profession played an important role in Hattusili's life; and Mittanamuwa was no small part of this role, from the prince's early childhood illnesses onwards. To begin with, ritualists, incantation priests, physicians and the goddess herself may all have contributed in some way to bringing Hattusili back from the brink of death. But I agree with Professor van den Hout that Mittanamuwa was the chief agent in the child's recovery. 'He must have known his way around the tablet rooms', van den Hout comments, 'and may even have impressed the king (Muwattalli) at times by quoting arcane texts from memory. The king probably counted on his special familiarity with these compositions that dealt with the adversities in life, the rituals, prayers, omens and oracles...'[11] Using his intimate knowledge of the tablet archives, including even the most arcane texts, Mittanamuwa could well have dredged up those recording earlier cases of the illnesses afflicting the child and the remedies that were most effective in curing them.

From Hattusili's first years onwards, I see a special bond developing between prince and mentor. And I believe that Mitannamuwa taught his *protégé* not merely the importance of acquiring for its own sake the ability to read and write, but the power such ability could confer upon its possessor. As Chief Scribe, Mittanamuwa was not simply the head of the king's scribal establishment. He must have been privy to some of the king's most confidential and most important dealings with his vassal rulers and royal peers, as well as members of his own court – and highly influential in the advice he provided the king on matters of state, on the conclusion of treaties, on correspondence with vassals and peers, and on a whole range of other matters to do with the management of the kingdom.

A king who could not read or write – and was thus unable to confirm or deny what he was told was written on a tablet – was largely dependent on the advice of scribal confidants who might use their knowledge in ways that were to their own advantage, and not always to their king's or the kingdom's. In sum, I suggest that Mittanamuwa showed that for a young man of ambition, particularly one of the royal blood, literacy could become a tool of great power – and that our prince acquired from an early age competence in the ability to read and write; this ability he used to acquaint himself first hand with the kingdom's most important recorded sources of information, both past and present, and to keep account of what he learned from them for the future fulfilment of his ambitions.

Soldier and priest

Mursili 'became a god' (in Hittite parlance, that means he died), about the year 1295 BC. In his final years he suffered what may have been aphasia, which left him unable to speak. We do not know whether he ever recovered. But he had made adequate plans for the succession and after his death the Crown Prince ascended the throne, adopting the throne-name Muwattalli, the second Hittite king to be so called. (It seems a strange throne-name to adopt, given that the first Muwattalli had seized the throne, more than a century earlier, by murdering its rightful incumbent, and occupied it only briefly before he himself was done away with.)

Acknowledging that his youngest sibling was specially favoured by one of the most important deities in the Hittite pantheon, Muwattalli must have ensured that he was trained from his early years for holding some of the highest offices in the land. This included military training – and that for the young prince meant exposure to actual battlefield conditions. Thus, more than two centuries earlier the first king called Hattusili, probably on his deathbed, ordered his officers to take his grandson and successor, Mursili (I) into battle while he was still a child.[12] So, too, Tudhaliya, *our* Hattusili's son and successor had already in his youth gained extensive campaign experience in military commands against the Hittites' long-term enemy, the Kaska tribes of the Pontic region.[13]

Almost certainly Hattusili himself had a similar battlefield apprenticeship, though our texts do not tell us this. Far from being incompatible with his role as a priest of Ishtar, his training as a war leader would have complemented it. After all, Ishtar in one of her roles was a warrior-goddess. In any case, all high-ranking members of the Hittite hierarchy had priestly responsibilities of one kind or another to discharge, all the way up to the king himself who was Chief Priest of the Hittite realm and the gods' deputy on earth. No doubt Muwattalli took precautions to ensure that his brother was adequately shielded against becoming a battlefield casualty during his military apprenticeship, whether from a sniper's arrow, a lucky spear thrust, or a successful enemy chariot charge. And divine intervention could always be counted on for backup support, if that ever proved necessary.

I suggest that by the time the prince was gaining battlefield experience, he had already acquired the ability to read and write, at least the cuneiform texts written

Figure 3.2 Suppiluliuma I. Courtesy Tolga Örnek, from *The Hittites* (2003), [TV Programme] Dir. Tolga Örnek, Turkey: Ekip Film.

in his own language.¹⁴ This skill he may well have used to read for himself the military achievements of both his grandfather, the great Suppiluliuma, and his father, Mursili, who had also distinguished himself on the field of battle. Mursili had written a biography of Suppiluliuma's military exploits, culminating in the destruction of the Mittanian empire.¹⁵ The biography survives in clay copy fragments, but we know from these that the primary text was inscribed on tablets of bronze. Very likely the tablets were set up in Suppiluliuma's mausoleum (all trace of which, like the mausolea of other Hittite kings, has disappeared), to which members of the royal family and other privileged persons had access, primarily to perform periodic sacred ceremonies in the deceased king's honour.

I believe that the prince used his access to study carefully the contents of the tablets, which included not only his grandfather's successes, but also his failures, both diplomatic and military, and the kingdom's near extinction during the reign of Suppiluliuma's predecessor, Tudhaliya III. The prince's own father, Mursili, also recorded his military achievements, in two sets of documents we call the *Annals*, one set covering the first ten years of his reign, the other the whole of it.¹⁶ Clay copies of large portions of the *Annals* survive. I think it likely that their primary texts, too, were inscribed on bronze and set up in the king's mausoleum.

For a modern reader, these documents make for pretty boring reading. They are primarily catalogues of campaigns undertaken (mostly bare of the sort of narrative details we find in the works of the later Classical historians, like the *Anabasis* of the fourth-century BC, military commander Xenophon), of battles won and occasionally lost, and, particularly in the case of the *Annals*, statistical records of the numbers of transplantees¹⁷ brought back to the homeland as booty. But they are not meant for the enjoyment, information, inspiration or titillation of a wide reading public like the works of the Classical writers.

While they may serve to demonstrate the credentials of their authors as victorious warrior-lords, I see them primarily as reference guides for later generations of rulers and other holders of high military office, who must have consulted them when making preparations for their own military campaigns. These and other documents would have provided our young prince with a valuable working knowledge of the constituent parts of the empire, the difficulties his predecessors had experienced in maintaining their control over them, particularly those parts that were prone to rebellion, the costs and rewards of military campaigns outside and often far from the homeland, and the effectiveness or ineffectiveness of diplomatic efforts to bring peace and stability to the imperial system with minimal need for military intervention.

Let me stress once more that we have no actual evidence that our prince learned to read and write, either in his childhood years or at any later period in his life. But I believe that he very likely did. And I'll suggest further reasons for this in a later chapter.

Our story resumes

On his death, Mursili passed to his son Muwattalli an empire that was reasonably stable. Yet the newly installed king inherited several major problems his father had left unresolved, especially in the empire's peripheral regions. In the west, Mursili's early campaigns of conquest had established his hold over the wide spread of the Arzawan lands, consolidated by his treaties of vassalhood with their rulers. His removal from the conquered lands of large numbers of livestock and prisoners of war had provided a welcome boost to the homeland's food supplies and relatively small population. But the lengthy period of peace and stability enjoyed by Hittite subject territories in the west was coming to an end, as the region became increasingly fractious and prone to insurrection.

This was due in part to an activist called Piyamaradu, who sought to destabilize the Hittites' western states and may for a time have established control over one of them.[18] This was the kingdom of Wilusa, Homeric Troy's historical counterpart, in the northwest of the Anatolian peninsula. Of particular concern to Muwattalli was that Piyamaradu appeared to have the backing of a Greek kingdom called Ahhiyawa in Hittite texts. He may well have feared, not unreasonably, that the Ahhiyawan king was preparing to carve out territory of his own in western Anatolia, using Piyamaradu as his proxy. A military expedition despatched to Wilusa wrested back control of the vassal state and Muwattalli subsequently confirmed its allegiance by drawing up a treaty of vassalhood with its current ruler, Alaksandu.[19] But Piyamaradu escaped capture and continued to harass Hatti's western states; apparently with ongoing encouragement from the king of Ahhiyawa, whose support of the rebel might well have forewarned of expansionist plans of his own in the region, likely to provoke a confrontation with the Hittites over control of the region's westernmost territories. More on this in Chapter 12.

Hattusili had multiple problems to deal with when he eventually mounted the throne. A Greek king lurking menacingly in the background was but one of them.

4

The Prince Goes to Court

The ill-fated governor of the Upper Land

On first impressions, why would anyone want to govern a place like this? Called the 'Upper Land' in Hittite texts, it lay on the eastern fringe of the Hittite homeland, near the source of the Marassantiya River (Classical, Halys; Turkish, Kızıl Irmak) which bounded much of the home territories. It served as a kind of buffer zone against threatened invasions of core Hittite lands especially by predatory peoples across the Euphrates in the east and southeast. Its main urban centre was probably a city called Samuha, which lay at the eastern tip of the region near the Turkish village of Kayalıpınar, forty kilometres west of the modern Turkish city, Sivas. During the dark days of the reign of Tudhaliya III,[1] our prince's great-grandfather, Samuha had become the king's temporary headquarters when he'd been forced to abandon his capital Hattusa, before it fell victim to invading forces from around the homeland and burnt to the ground.[2]

Inconvenient though Samuha's lack of centrality may have been to the rest of the Upper Land, it was probably here that the region's governor was installed, in a reasonably comfortable palatial structure first built for Tudhaliya in what may have been his last days. The king had fallen ill in the city and may have died before he could leave it. From its archaeological remains, we can conclude that Samuha had a relatively rich cosmopolitan life and that a cult of the goddess Ishtar flourished within it.[3] Indeed, one of the most important temples of the Hittite world recently discovered in the city was almost certainly dedicated to the worship of Ishtar. Much of the rest of the Upper Land may have been a fairly desolate region – though current impressions of it could change as continuing archaeological investigations bring other sites to light – and the threat of enemy incursions was an ever-present one. Even so, being governor of the region with a base in Samuha was perhaps not such a bad job after all.

So it was that a man called Arma-Tarhunda was appointed to govern the Upper Land. The appointment was very likely made by Hattusili's father, Mursili, a cousin of the appointee. Such nepotistic preferment was not uncommon in the doling out of royal favours, and most members of the royal family, at least the male ones, could expect to be awarded a prominent position within the kingdom's hierarchy, either in the army or civil administration or in a priestly role, or in all three. As it turned out, Arma-Tarhunda quite liked his job as governor of the Upper Land, which probably did combine all three roles. How effective he was in any of them we do not know.

In any case, it seems that he was unceremoniously dumped from his position by Mursili's son and successor, Muwattalli, some time after Muwattalli ascended the throne. The king's brother, young Prince Hattusili, now got the job of governing the Upper Land. Perhaps he'd already served there as a priest of Ishtar in the goddess's cult-centre at Samuha. In any case, it seems that many were not well pleased with the appointment. And the sacked governor himself was furious. We shall hear more about him and the actions he took presently.

The missing years

But, first, we should note a gap in the record of Hattusili's career. The narrative moves forward abruptly, from the time of his dedication to Ishtar's service as a child to the death of his father Mursili and the accession of his brother Muwattalli; and, immediately thereafter, to his appointment as an army commander of the highest rank. This was the rank of GAL MESHEDI, literally, 'Chief of the Bodyguard', one of the most prestigious posts in the imperial administration. In theory, the title designated the chief of the elite bodyguard of spearmen who protected the king.[4] In practice, the man who bore this title was the most important and most powerful commander in the Hittite army after the king. The prince leaves us in no doubt about this when he says: *I became army commander in front of my brother. My brother installed me as Chief of the Royal Bodyguard.*[5] He was no more than twenty, give or take, at the time.

By his military achievements so far, Hattusili must have proved himself worthy of the appointment and capable of exercising it. Close as he was to his brother, Muwattalli would hardly have entrusted him with the post if he had not already demonstrated a high order of military skills and achieved significant successes on various fields of battle. So there must be a lot that Hattusili has passed over in the *Apology* leading up to the appointment. He does, however, tell us that, following the court case, his brother delegated to him command over all Hatti's forces, and with them he conquered every one of the kingdom's enemies. (Maybe there's just a touch of hyperbole here.)

A victim of the 'hate factions'

But, before informing us of these conquests (with specific details to be provided on another tablet), the prince tells us about the fallout from his appointment as governor of the Upper Land: *When people saw the recognition of Ishtar and my brother's benevolence towards me, they envied me. Arma-Tarhunda, son of Zida, and other people as well began to cause me harm, they were evil to me, and defeat hung over me. My brother Muwattalli summoned me 'to the wheel'.*[6] Hattusili is claiming that he was the hapless victim of a hate campaign by the Arma-Tarhunda faction and its supporters because of favours bestowed upon him by his brother and the goddess Ishtar.

Such a claim deserves to be treated with some cynicism. Behind his facade of victimhood, we see (I believe) a fiercely ambitious young man who was ruthless in his pursuit of power and almost certainly conspired to have Arma-Tarhunda removed from the governorship of the Upper Land so that he could take his place. Rule of this region and the experience he gained from it may have been an important step towards consolidating his position as the second most powerful man in the kingdom. The fact that someone else was currently the Upper Land's governor was a mere inconvenience that could easily be disposed of.

But not so easily, as it turned out. The prince may well have made himself a prime target of one of the periodic outbursts of rage that erupted within certain factions of the royal establishment and their aristocratic supporters. However, he gives us scant information about the hostility he incurred on this occasion and the reasons for it. His account is too clogged up with telling us, repeatedly, of Ishtar's benevolence towards him and the protection she provided against any form of evil that threatened him, whether it be an ill-disposed deity, the contrivers of an unjust lawsuit or any of the illnesses that regularly befell him.

Summons to His Majesty's court

We don't know what the prince means when he says his brother 'summoned him to the wheel'. But there is general agreement that he's referring to some sort of judicial process. That assumption may be supported by a reference soon after to 'an evil lawsuit', if the two statements can be connected. Interestingly, there is another reference to a wheel in a Hittite judicial context. This occurs in two clauses from the canonical collection of two hundred laws.[7] Clauses §§197–8 refer to a case where a husband finds his wife *in flagrante delicto* with her lover. He can kill them both without penalty if he does so immediately. But he can also bring them to the king's court and ask that his wife's life be spared. The catch is that, if his appeal is successful, her lover's life must be spared also. Alternatively, if the cuckolded husband requests the death penalty for both of them, 'they shall roll the wheel'. This section ends with the king deciding whether both of the guilty pair shall live or die.

The two references to a wheel, in a legal context in at least one case, suggest that both are somehow connected. We should perhaps avoid the temptation of thinking that the object in question was some kind of wheel of fortune, with the outcome decided by a spin of it, leaving the gods, or a particular god, to decide the outcome. But that may be close to what actually happened in this case (with the wheel almost certainly weighted in the prince's favour).

Let me hazard the following reconstruction. The prince, wanting the governorship of the Upper Land, has accused its present incumbent Arma-Tarhunda of corruption, mismanagement and general unfitness to rule – and he has Ishtar to back him up. Muwattalli accepts that the allegations are valid, and Arma-Tarhunda is stripped of office and forced to make way for the prince. Arma-Tarhunda requests an audience with the king, protests that the charges against him are fabricated, and demands that the matter be resolved by due legal process. Muwattalli agrees and the litigants face off in a court of law. This will be held in what is literally called 'the palace gate'. City gates, often a place where trade markets were set up, may well have provided a venue for trials of citizens of a lower social order. 'Gate' was then a term traditionally used for a place where justice was dispensed, but when 'palace' was attached to it, the venue must have been a court for trials presided over by the king himself and conducted somewhere within the palace.

This, I suggest, is what Arma-Tarhunda requests and is granted. But the outcome of the contest is hardly surprising. Muwattalli as Supreme Judge of the Hittite world presides over the case, hears the evidence and decides in favour of Hattusili. It might be a stretch too far to suggest the king himself was party to the trumped-up charges (in my reconstruction) which saw Arma-Tarhunda off. But, of course, Hattusili gives the credit to Ishtar for the decision in his favour. It is she who makes clear that her *protégé* is innocent of all charges. And who could question the outcome of a trial when it is a divinely endorsed one – and by such a formidable deity?

A dogged pursuit for justice

But that's not the end of Arma-Tarhunda. He was nothing if not persistent in his pursuit of justice. Unfortunately for him, to no avail. Every line of appeal he was granted failed. There was but one option now open to him. And he took it ... By this time, Muwattalli had consolidated his control over the kingdom's upper regions and appointed Hattusili to rule them – no longer merely as their governor but as their king. (However, we'll still call him 'the prince' until he achieves his ultimate goal: Great Kingship over the whole land of Hatti.)

His base was a city called Hakpis, located somewhere to the north of Hattusa (at modern Amasya?). After Muwattalli's shift of the royal capital to Tarhuntassa, hostile northern tribes, sensing that Hattusa's loss of status would seriously weaken the kingdom's defences, had made opportunistic attacks upon the homeland territories. The *Apology* informs us that order was eventually restored with the defeat of the enemy tribes in a series of campaigns conducted by both Muwattalli and Hattusili. It was then that Hattusili was installed by his brother as king in Hakpis, from which he ruled the northern half of the kingdom.[8]

But he was probably still in Syria managing the Damascus region in the aftermath of the Qadesh campaign (see Chapter 6) when Arma-Tarhunda renewed his action against him, allegedly resorting to the dark arts of witchcraft and sorcery when due legal process had failed him. The *Apology* tells us that: *when Arma-Tarhunda ... saw the benevolence of Ishtar, My Lady, and my brother towards me, (he) with his wife and son began to cast spells over me, because they were not successful in any (other) way. Even Samuha, the city of the goddess, he filled with spells.*[9] So what forms did the casting of spells take, and how seriously were they taken?

The resort to witchcraft

We have four references to witchcraft in our Hittite texts. The first occurs in the last clause of the Telipinu Proclamation. (I referred to this document in Chapter 1.) There we are told that the procedure for dealing with it is that: *all matters must be cleared of (it). Whoever within the family knows witchcraft, you must seize him from the family and bring him to the palace gate* (i.e. the royal court). *But whoever does not bring him, for that man a bad end will come.*[10] That is to say, all places and activities infected by someone who has cast spells must be thoroughly purged of the evil, and part of the purging process is bringing to justice the person or persons guilty of the offence.

The fact that the case is to be tried by the highest court in the land, presided over by the Great King himself, highlights the gravity of the offence. And we're warned that anyone who attempts to conceal the offender will come to an unspecified 'bad end'. That sounds ominous, but Hittite justice is far from impartial. The punishment for the crime will depend on the status of the guilty person or persons and the actual nature of the witchcraft in each case. The judge must take all this into account when deciding on the sentence in the event of a guilty verdict.

In Hittite law, an act of sorcery is committed if a person performs a purification ritual on someone else and then dumps the remains of the ritual in another person's house instead of on incineration heaps.[11] Again, the case will be heard by the king (or his representative) who will decide on the appropriate penalty. Another clause in the laws covers a more malevolent form of black magic. Here, sorcery is declared when a clay image is formed for magical purposes, and no doubt with evil intent.[12] This is a common form of magic in many civilizations, both ancient and more recent. Linked with it is the case of a person killing a snake and speaking someone else's name. Once more, this is intended to have some evil effect on the victim.[13] For this act of sorcery there is a fixed offence. If you are a free person and found guilty, you are fined forty shekels of silver – a fairly large amount if you are from the lower classes. But that is better than being a slave whose penalty for the offence is death.

So we now come back to Arma-Tarhunda. To judge from the *Apology*, he and his wife and sons were prolific spell-casters. Not only did they target the prince, but also the entire cult-centre of Samuha, Ishtar's special city. What form these spells took isn't specified. But their actions at least had the effect of having Arma-Tarhunda's case reopened in the royal court. Possibly Arma-Tarhunda was appealing against a verdict of guilty handed down to him by a lower court. The previous verdict was upheld by the king, who had then to deal with the charges of witchcraft brought against the whole of Arma-Tarhunda's family.[14] The sentence the king imposed on them was the confiscation of all Arma-Tarhunda's property and its transfer to the prince. He also put the family at his brother's mercy by letting him decide what their personal fate would be. For so serious an offence the death penalty could not be ruled out. Indeed, as we have noted, there were laws giving even a cuckolded husband the power of life or death over his wife and her paramour.

But the prince was prepared to be merciful – at least to Arma-Tarhunda. He had lost his case and his property, and that, the prince considered, was punishment enough. Especially since Arma-Tarhunda was a blood-relative and now an old man. As a further show of clemency, the prince restored half his property to him. But mercy had its limits. Arma-Tarhunda was separated from his wife and sons who were exiled to the island of Alasiya (Cyprus).

We do not know the precise nature of the spells Arma-Tarhunda allegedly cast on the prince and his patron deity's cult-centre. A series of black magic rituals of some kind were no doubt involved, and this must have necessitated a counter-series of white magic rituals, especially in the city of Samuha, to dispel their power. Smoke, the stench of the blood and burning flesh of sacrificial victims, and the incessant, dirge-like wailing of incantation priests and priestesses must have filled the city for days on end before the cult-centre was declared pollution-free and fit for the arrival of fresh batches of pilgrims.

By the way, one of Arma-Tarhunda's sons had apparently taken no part in his family's witchcraft activities. His name was Sippaziti. Muwattalli reminded his brother of the man's innocence, and no further action was taken against him. It was a just decision. But it left at large a member of Arma-Tarhunda's family whose unspoken desire for revenge against the prince on his father's behalf remained unsatisfied. He would join with others in seeking to destroy the prince. That part of our story has yet to come.

5

Unseating the Rightful King

Ishtar took me as a prince and elevated me to kingship. (Thus) I became Great King.[1]
(In other words, I was . . .)

The Prince Who Stole an Empire

The king is dead. Long live . . .?

News of it must have resonated throughout the Hittite word, indeed through much of the entire Near Eastern world. Muwattalli, Great King of Hatti, the ultimate victor in the battle of Qadesh, was dead. But our surviving texts give us no information about how, when or why he died. His brother, Hattusili, makes just a passing reference to his death in the words: *When my brother became a god.* As we've already noted, this was the standard euphemism for a king's death since, like the Romans of later times, the Hittites believed that, after shuffling off this mortal coil, in some cases departing it precipitously, their kings joined the ranks of the gods. Hattusili gives us the news, almost incidentally, in the context of his preparations for installing a new Great King on Hatti's throne.

Let me provide some background to what must have been a momentous event in the kingdom. Muwattalli's death probably occurred just two or three years after the Qadesh conflict. He was in his early fifties then, ten years or so older than Hattusili, his youngest sibling. Death by natural causes, such as a heart attack or stroke, or by an accident, cannot be ruled out, and the rigours of the Qadesh campaign may eventually have taken their toll. We know of no later campaigns led by Muwattalli in which he could have lost his life. Maybe there's a more sinister explanation closer to home – a poisoned chalice or an assassin's dagger. But that is pure speculation, and we have no indication of any plot to unseat and assassinate the king. Very likely his death came as much as a surprise to Hattusili as to anyone else.

The enthronement of Urhi-Teshub (Mursili III)

In his *Apology*, what Hattusili tells us happens next comes as a further surprise. Here, in the *Apology*, are his own words: *Since my brother had no legitimate son, I took up Urhi-Teshub, his son by a concubine, and appointed him Lord of Hatti... And thus Urhi-Teshub became Great King of the Hatti Lands, while I was king of Hakpis.*[2] I'll have more to say about the nature, purpose and validity of the *Apology* in Chapter 7 but, for now, let's focus on these words, for they mark a significant turn of events in the kingdom's history.

First of all, they give the clear impression that Hattusili claimed sole credit for declaring his brother's son, Urhi-Teshub, the next Great King and appointing him to his father's throne. This is misleading for several reasons. It's inconceivable that Muwattalli had not named Urhi-Teshub his successor, probably well before his death. He may even have made him co-regent for a time, though we have yet to find clear evidence of this, e.g. on seal impressions bearing both names.[3] In any case, Muwattalli almost certainly proclaimed Urhi-Teshub his successor before the Qadesh engagement, the most dangerous military confrontation of his career. He could not be sure of surviving it or avoiding capture by the enemy. In Hittite as in other royal successions, there would always be an heir on standby, even if the heir were only a child at the time of his succession, and a regent appointed to rule until he came of age. Urhi-Teshub's succession must have been guaranteed long before Hattusili had anything to do with it.

The self-appointed kingmaker claims that his nephew was not his brother's 'legitimate' offspring, merely the son of a concubine. But that was no bar to his appointment to the throne, which fully accorded with Hittite tradition. The rules of royal succession laid down by King Telipinu two centuries earlier still applied: *Let a prince, a son of the first rank, become king. If there is no prince of the first rank, let him who is a son of the second rank become king.*[4] That is to say, the son of a concubine – 'a son of the second rank' – was eligible for the kingship if his father and predecessor had no son by a Chief Wife. And Urhi-Teshub was undoubtedly the son of a concubine. At least Hattusili got that bit right.

But this raises an obvious question. Why was there no 'son of the first rank' to occupy the throne? Maybe the answer is that Muwattalli's Chief Wife had no sons. But I think it more likely that Muwattalli had no Chief Wife, at least in a formal sense. And to make sure the succession stayed in Muwattalli's line, one of his concubine's sons inherited the throne. Now we know of only two sons of Muwattalli, Urhi-Teshub and Kuruntiya.[5] Perhaps they were born of the same mother, perhaps different ones. The former became heir to the throne, the latter was entrusted to his uncle Hattusili's safekeeping – for reasons we'll come to presently.

But to raise a follow-up question. If Muwattalli did *not* have a Chief Wife, why not? The probable answer is that either he hadn't gotten around to finding a partner of suitable status upon whom he felt he could safely bestow the title before his death, or that he had no intention of declaring *anyone* his Chief Wife. This seems more likely to me, given Muwattalli's direct experience of the abuse of power by the two most recent Chief Wives: his stepgrandmother, the Babylonian Tawananna and, in his view, the new Tawananna, his stepmother Danuhepa. Far better to avoid repeating, yet again, a bad experience by not giving precedence to *any* of his second-rank wives – refusing to elevate one above the rest – or looking for someone else he could make Chief Wife. Incidentally, the title 'Tawananna' seems to have fallen out of use not much later.[6] That was almost certainly due to the stigma now attached to it, courtesy of the Babylonian Tawananna, and apparently Danuhepa as well.

In fairness to Hattusili, he was probably needed in the royal capital Tarhuntassa to endorse personally his nephew's enthronement. Despite Telipinu's pronouncement and Muwattalli's undoubted confirmation of Urhi-Teshub as heir to the throne, the appointment of a concubine's son to Great Kingship may not have been favourably received by the populace at large or by the kingdom's elite elements, regardless of there being no son of the first rank available. After all, this was the first time the 'second-rank son' provision had ever been put to the test after its inclusion by Telipinu in the succession rules. As the senior member of the royal family, Hattusili was the most appropriate person in the kingdom to declare Urhi-Teshub the new *Great* King and have his declaration respected. The appropriate time to formalize this declaration was at the new king's coronation ceremony.

Clearly, Hattusili had to be present for such an occasion. Let us suppose this scenario:

Hattusili has been but a few short months back in his northern kingdom. After his earlier successes in imposing rule by military force over the region, he has now, at his brother's command, turned to resettling and refortifying abandoned cities there. This is a major part of his remit – after expelling the enemy forces occupying and ravaging Hittite territory, to repopulate the whole of the northern kingdom, and thus buffer it against invasions from the north, particularly by the Kaskan enemy.

In the midst of this, a messenger arrives with urgent news from the south. Muwattalli is dead. Hattusili needs to get to the royal capital Tarhuntassa as quickly as possible. He hastily assembles a bodyguard, perhaps made up, paradoxically, of Kaskan warriors who had fought with him at Qadesh.[7] Hattusili sets off with his small army, reaching Tarhuntassa by forced marches in less than a month, or if they come by chariot, within a matter of days.

He arrives to find a city still in a state of shock at the Great King's death. What is to happen next? Will a mere nonentity, born on the wrong side of the royal blanket some might argue, now become Hatti's Great King? Hattusili summons a meeting of the local grandees in the Audience Hall of the palace Muwattalli had newly built for himself. Hattusili's bodyguard is always at hand to ensure his personal safety, and obedience to his commands. Their master is now the *pro tem* ruler of the empire by divine consent, particularly Ishtar's.

In this role, he has just one main function to perform – the endorsement of Urhi-Teshub and his anointing as the new Great King. The gods have approved his appointment, and it's a perfectly legitimate one according to the traditional succession rules. Of course, well before his death Muwattalli must have made clear to his brother, and perhaps to many of his high-ranking officials, that he wanted Urhi-Teshub to succeed him, probably because there was no one more suitable in his direct family line. But by giving the appointment his personal stamp of approval, Hattusili creates the impression that it is one of his own making. In the long term, this will be to his political benefit, as he has no doubt planned.

In much of what I've just said, I'm seeking to provide a bit more context for a pivotal event in the history of the kingdom. This event is treated in the barest detail in our sources, notably the *Apology*. As I've already promised, I'll be talking later about the nature, purpose, and reliability of this document – and the appropriateness or otherwise of the title bestowed by modern scholars upon it. Let me now simply say that it is just as questionable for what it *does not* tell us as for what it does. With perhaps one major exception, Urhi-Teshub appears to have done little to justify the high authority vested in him, certainly nothing in the tradition of his great warrior-forefathers. To be sure, his brief reign gave him scant opportunity to establish a creditable track record – at least to judge by the few documents that have anything to say about him in the surviving tablet collections. But I should not be at all surprised if Hattusili had personally checked and 'cherry-picked' the records after his nephew had lost his throne, ensuring that any reflecting positively on his reign were ground into dust.

Adoption of an illustrious throne-name

But Urhi-Teshub seems to have started off with high ambitions. On his accession, he adopted the throne-name Mursili, though he continued to use his original name alongside it.[8] Mursili was one of the most revered names in the history of Hittite kingship. The first king of this name had achieved legendary status by conquering the almost unconquerable Aleppo in Syria. He had then marched his troops hundreds of miles down the Euphrates to Babylon, capturing, looting and destroying the city, and bringing to an end the royal dynasty of Hammurabi. The second Mursili was the new king's grandfather. By his numerous campaigns of conquest, particularly in the western and northern parts of the kingdom, and by the bounteous spoils he brought back from them, in livestock, prisoners and the treasures of looted cities, he ensured that his name too would be revered during the kingdom's remaining years. It was in this illustrious company that the new king, Mursili 'III' sought to find his place.

But here's the surprising thing. Among the surviving texts that actually refer to Mursili III after his enthronement, few actually call him by this name. Well, perhaps it's not so surprising when we discover that most of these texts were authored by Hattusili (some by his son and successor Tudhaliya). And most of them have to do with Mursili's activities in exile after Hattusili had seized his throne. In fact, if it were not for the discovery of the seals bearing Urhi-Teshub's throne-name, we'd never have known for sure what this name was.[9] It's as if Hattusili set out to deny that Urhi-Teshub was ever a Great King, despite the fact that he had endorsed his enthronement, and despite the fact that even a dethroned Great King apparently had the right to retain his throne-name. Hattusili's refusal to respect his, and to continue to refer to his nephew simply as Urhi-Teshub, could be seen as an attempt to erase from all memory, living and historical, the fact that Urhi-Teshub ever occupied the throne that was illegally taken from him. And playing up his alleged illegitimacy might also be useful, despite the fact that Urhi-Teshub was the son of an official second-rank wife and NOT illegitimate – quite different to a son conceived from a king's roll in the hay with one of the local lasses. Having said all this, I'll follow scholarly custom and call Mursili III only by his birth-name in all future references to him. Rather unfair to the poor man.

But we are now getting well ahead of our story again.

Hattusa: the capital once more

At the outset, the fledgling ruler seems to have had a harmonious and productive relationship with his uncle, who must have been highly influential in winning for him the support of the empire's chief dignitaries and military officers. The coronation gave the final stamp of approval to his legality. How much wider initial support was for his kingship is not known to us. But the battle-hardened warrior Hattusili, also well versed in the skills of diplomacy and imperial administration, must have proved an invaluable mentor to his nephew – as well as a willing one for his own ends.

And that brings us to the most significant event in Urhi-Teshub's reign (before the one that ended it) – the transfer of the royal capital back to Hattusa, within no more than two decades after Muwattalli had moved it to Tarhuntassa. One of our texts briefly reports the event in these words: *He (Urhi-Teshub) removed the gods from Tarhuntassa and restored them to Hattusa.*[10] The return of the kingdom's chief gods and ancestral spirits to the former capital meant that Hattusa was once again the administrative, political and spiritual centre of the empire. All other parts of the capital's bureaucratic establishment, most importantly, its tablet collections, and the military personnel, craftsmen and labour forces deemed necessary to defend and sustain the capital, must have accompanied the gods as they were re-established there.

What were the reasons for returning to the old city? The few sources that briefly mention this event are no more helpful in explaining it than those referring to Muwattalli's shift of the capital to Tarhuntassa in the first place. Probably the first shift had at least something to do with preparations for the forthcoming conflict with Egypt. But there were other advantages as well. Though we have yet to find any trace of the city of Tarhuntassa, we can be pretty sure that the land of Tarhuntassa occupied a large part of south-central Anatolia extending to the shores of the Mediterranean. If so, the central kingdom had a coastline for the first time in its history, and thus the potential for becoming a sea power.

The new capital also probably allowed easier access to its Syrian subject states, arguably the most important of its dependencies, and thus to its viceregal kingdoms whose rulers held sway, in the name of the Great King, over most of the Syrian vassal rulers. Very likely, face-to-face meetings between the Great King and his vice-regents were more conveniently and quickly arranged from the southern capital than from the old capital in the north. Added to that, life for all, from the king to the lowest peasant, in a land with a generally mild climate, must have been far more pleasant than in the homeland atop the Anatolian plateau with its often harsh, freezing winters and hot, dry baking summers.[11]

Despite such drawbacks, I believe that Urhi-Teshub decided to re-establish Hattusa as the central kingdom's capital fairly early in his reign, at a time when relations with his uncle were still warm, and both worked together in a kind of mentor-student relationship as the new king was finding his feet. But so long as Tarhuntassa in the south remained the capital, with Urhi-Teshub seated upon its throne, while Hattusili sat in Hakpis as ruler of the empire's northernmost regions, regular communication between the pair must have been seriously hampered by the distances between them, and face-to-face meetings relatively rare.

There were, however, two main reasons surpassing all others for shifting the capital back to Hattusa – at least, in my opinion. They can be summed up in two words: *image* and *tradition*. With its massive walls, its large temple complex, dominated by the vast sprawling sanctuary of Hatti's two chief deities, and its imposing royal acropolis, Hattusa was the physical symbol of the might and power of the Hittite empire. Shimmering in the hot summer's haze, radiant in its coating of snow on fine winter days, or glimmering in ghostly luminosity in the winter's gloom, it possessed a kind of mystique, an Oz-like splendour that was unparalleled in the Near Eastern world. And it was the city of the mighty Hittite kings of the past, and perhaps even the final resting place of some of them. A hastily built new capital in the south could be no match for this. Urhi-Teshub probably had many supporters among the empire's nobles for taking up residence once more in Hattusa, and certainly among the priestly fraternity, insofar as they counted separately from the nobility. And the statues of the gods taken by Muwattalli from Hattusa and relocated in Tarhuntassa were once more restored to their rightful homes.

Almost certainly Hattusili was happy with the move, and may indeed have initiated it. (In fact, he later acquitted himself in his prayer to the Sun Goddess of any part in the move to Tarhuntassa.[12]) It gave him closer contact with his nephew, and he must have welcomed the likely shift to the homeland of a substantially greater part of the empire's defence forces. These could now more readily be called upon to assist in maintaining peace in the northern regions he ruled. At the same time, Tarhuntassa would not be neglected. It would become a third viceregal kingdom of the empire, along with the kingdoms of Carchemish and Aleppo in Syria. And it would come to be ruled by Urhi-Teshub's brother, or half-brother, Kuruntiya.

But let's not get ahead of our tale yet again.

A rebuff to Assyria

Mursili III, aka Urhi-Teshub, reigned for just five years. At some time in this brief period, relations between uncle and nephew began to sour. In Urhi-Teshub's perception, his uncle was turning from mentor into puppeteer. So, increasingly, the second-rank son seems to have made decisions and engaged in actions without Hattusili's knowledge or approval.

To illustrate, let me begin with a somewhat controversial case. It concerns a letter written by an Assyrian king to the king of Hatti. Unfortunately, we don't have the letter itself – just a remnant of a draft response to it, with the name of the writer and the addressee both missing. (Isn't that just the way with so many of our Hittite letters?) We can be fairly sure from other evidence that the Assyrian king was Adad-nirari I, who'd been gobbling up former territory of the now defunct Mittanian empire east of the Euphrates. Of the three possible authors of the letter, Muwattalli, Urhi-Teshub and Hattusili, the latter two are considered the more serious contenders.[13] Basically, what we have of the response indicates that the Assyrian had written in conciliatory terms, referring to his conquests and claiming Great King status as ruler of his emergent empire. But he goes further, assuming brotherhood with his correspondent. This provokes a furious response:

You conquered by force of arms and have become a Great King. (Of that there is no doubt.) *But why do you keep speaking about brotherhood? ... Why should I write to you about brotherhood? ... Do those who are on bad terms usually write to each other about brotherhood?* (Again) [W]*hy should I write to you about brotherhood? Did the same mother give birth to us? Neither my [grandfather] nor my father wrote to the King of Assyria [about brotherhood]. And you must stop writing to me [about brotherhood] and Great Kingship. [It is not my] wish!*[14]

Let me provide some background for this outburst. Throughout the Late Bronze Age, the supreme rulers of the Near East and Egypt addressed one another as Great Kings. This was an acknowledgement of the power each exercised over a large swath of territory and the array of subject states and their vassal rulers within it. Four kings were acknowledged in this way – the pharaoh of Egypt, the Great King of Hatti, and in southern and northern Mesopotamia, respectively, the Great Kings of Babylon and Mittani, up until the Mittanian empire's destruction by Suppiluliuma. This acknowledgement was complemented by the Great Kings' entitlement to address one another as 'my brother', as they all did except for the kings of Hatti and Mittani. These latter two Great Kings were pretty much in a constant state of war until the collapse of the last remaining Mittanian strongholds in the 1320s BC. Now, Assyria was aggressively filling the power vacuum left by Mittani's demise – all the way up to the left bank of the Euphrates – in the process, absorbing the last remnants of the Mittanian empire that had but recently become Hittite puppet states.

Hittite subject territory in Syria was by this time no more than a river's breadth away from the triumphal Assyrian forces. But the Assyrian commander-in-chief, Adad-nirari had sent a conciliatory letter to his Hittite counterpart, claiming his conquests had won him Great King status, and now requesting recognition as the Hittite king's 'brother'. Let me stress that we know this not from the letter itself (which has not survived) but from the fragmentary draft Hittite response. This leaves no doubt that there is a clear distinction between acknowledging a Great King and accepting his entitlement to being called 'my brother'. Strictly speaking, the latter was purely a term of courtesy, but it was an important one, implying close diplomatic links between two Great Kings – from regular exchanges of correspondence, gifts and diplomatic embassies, to marriage alliances between the royal families, to the conclusion of treaties of alliance, like the 'Eternal Treaty' later drawn up between Hattusili and Ramesses.

The author of the response to Adad-nirari's letter had no choice but to acknowledge the Assyrian's claim to Great King status. The facts spoke for themselves. But he strenuously objected to being called his 'brother', with its presumptuous implication that the pair had diplomatic and personal links of the kind I've just mentioned. Adad-nirari was treated as an arrogant upstart, seeking to insinuate himself into the exclusive 'Club of Royal Brothers'[15] before being accorded peer status by the other Great Kings and demonstrating a willingness to comply with the protocols membership of such a 'club' entailed.

These protocols were entirely informal. But they played a major role in maintaining a relatively high level of peace and stability between the international powers throughout the 500-year history of the Late Bronze Age. With the exception of almost constant warfare between Hatti and Mittani, there were only two occasions in which Great Kingdoms of the era engaged in major conflicts between themselves. (We'll say more about one of these in Chapter 8 and the other in Chaper 13.) Of course, there were many other military campaigns fought by the Great Kings. But these were either against rebel states, or occasionally against proxy states of other Great Kingdoms, or tribal groups like the Kaska peoples, or small independent enemy kingdoms.

So who wrote the Hittite response? Though as I've noted, several different authors have been proposed, I support the view that it was Urhi-Teshub, some time after he'd become Mursili III. From many years of experience, Hattusili was not merely a battle-hardened warrior, but must also have become well schooled in the arts of diplomacy and statecraft. It is inconceivable that a man of his skills and experience would have replied in such an intemperate and provocative way to the Assyrian king, who was seeking to assure the man he dared call 'brother' that he intended no threat to Hittite territory.

That did not, of course, mean that Assyria would never pose such a threat. (And it was indeed to become an increasing menace to Hittite territories west of the Euphrates.) But, for the time being, it would have been wise to take the Assyrian's letter at face value, or at least to have used more diplomatic language in responding to it. The response as we have it is much more likely to have emanated from a fledgling Hittite king, puffed up with his own newly acquired importance and determined to rebuke anyone who tried to presume on this, fellow king or otherwise.

Further, he not merely rejected the request of brotherhood. Adad-nirari was clearly using the term figuratively, but his correspondent deliberately misconstrued it as a claim by the Assyrian of being a true blood-brother – and mocked him for it. Let's suppose that the letter was first drafted at a time when relations between Urhi-Teshub and his uncle were still cordial. If Urhi-Teshub had run the draft past his uncle, Hattusili would almost certainly have urged him to delete the surviving passage from the final version, or at least substantially modify it. But, if relations had already soured between the pair, then Urhi-Teshub may have sent it unchanged in his response to the Assyrian's letter. Later, Hattusili may have suffered some blowback from this response – as we shall see.

The reinstatement of Benteshina

In what were probably the first years of his reign, Urhi-Teshub reversed a number of decisions taken by his father. He may have done so with his uncle's support – and in some cases probably at his instigation. Of course, the most important of these was the transfer of the capital back to Hattusa. Others included the reinstatement to his vassal throne of Benteshina, former ruler of Amurru. This was one of the disputed border states that had ignited the conflict between Muwattalli and Ramesses. Formerly subject to Hatti, Amurru had been forced by Ramesses' father Seti I, then pharaoh, into vassalage to Egypt. With Egyptian forces massing on his border, Benteshina had no option other than to defect to Egypt. But once Muwattalli had restored his control over the vassal kingdom, he unfairly punished Benteshina for disloyalty, removing him from his throne and banishing him from his kingdom. Yet things didn't work out too badly for the disgraced vassal. He had a warm, enduring friendship with Hattusili, who persuaded his brother to let him spend his exile in Hakpis, capital of Hattusili's northern kingdom. Then, after he became king, Urhi-Teshub restored him to the throne of Amurru. We can probably give Uncle Hattusili credit for this.[16]

Downfall and restoration

Recall from banishment and restoration of status by Urhi-Teshub bring to mind the curious case of the Hittite queen Danuhepa. I've already mentioned that she was the second wife of Muwattalli's (and Hattusili's) father Mursili. He'd married her probably not long after the death of his first wife, and accorded her the status of Chief Wife. This we can conclude from seal impressions in which the names Mursili and Danuhepa appear together, and references to the queen and her 'ruination' in Hattusili's prayer to the Sun Goddess of Arinna.[17] But we hear absolutely nothing more about her during Mursili's reign. And where she came from in the first place remains a mystery. However, her name pops up again on seal impressions jointly with Muwattalli's after Muwattalli succeeded his father. In the time-honoured tradition we assume that she continued to be the empire's First Lady after her husband's death, with all the powers that that entailed.

Now, I'll need to do a little reconstructive work here, to fit what we know about Danuhepa into a plausible scenario. To do this, I'm relying particularly on what we learn from Hattusili's prayer to the Sun Goddess. Danuhepa's exercise, and possible abuse, of the powers and privileges her office entailed seem to have contributed to an increasingly fraught atmosphere in the royal household. Perhaps she was already proving troublesome in her husband's reign. But matters came to a head after his death. At first, Muwattalli respected the position she occupied, and the ways in which she exercised her authority. But as the conflict with Egypt drew closer, he feared the growing dysfunction of the royal household he would leave behind when he led his forces into Syria, especially since he couldn't be sure he'd ever return. Matters were further complicated by the fact that Danuhepa had sons of her own. From a marriage outside the Hittite dynasty? Could their mother have sought to pave the way for one of them ending up on the throne by removing any obstacles in the way to it, including Muwattalli's own sons?

Muwattalli had probably by now designated Urhi-Teshub as Crown Prince and successor to the throne. But as we've noted, the king had at least one other younger son, a lad called Kuruntiya, Urhi-Teshub's brother or stepbrother. A later text tells us that (while he was still a child) Muwattalli entrusted his upbringing to Hattusili,[18] presumably to ensure his safety. This would no doubt have meant sending him to Hakpis, seat of Hattusili's kingdom in the far north, where he would be well away from any plots and conspiracies in the royal capital.

Back in Hattusa, Muwattalli solved his Danuhepa problem by putting her on trial in the palace, and stripping her of all her powers. She was accompanied in her downfall by her sons, and all her supporters, both lords of the land and more lowly followers. Hattusili so informs us in his prayer to the Sun Goddess but doesn't say what Danuhepa was supposed to be guilty of, or whether she and her supporters were actually sent into exile. I have guessed that all this happened before Muwattalli set off for Qadesh. He wanted to make sure all his affairs were in order first.

That's not the last we hear (or rather see) of Danuhepa. Her name pops up again on seal impressions alongside the name of Mursili III, throne-name of Urhi-Teshub. We can conclude that, once again, Urhi-Teshub overturned an important action taken by his father and reinstated Danuhepa as queen of the empire. But, from here on, all is silence about her. Perhaps she simply faded quietly away as Urhi-Teshub's reign approached its end. Perhaps documents pertaining to her during Urhi-Teshub's reign have been lost – or were destroyed by Hattusili for fear they might incriminate him in the proceedings taken against her. Perhaps there were *two* Danuhepas who together spanned the reigns of Mursili II, Muwattalli and Mursili III (Urhi-Teshub). If there were only one, perhaps she was still alive in Hattusili's reign. All these possibilities have been proposed and discussed.

All we can say with some degree of certainty is that there is more than a whiff of illegality about her treatment, particularly by Muwattalli, though we don't really know what this was. The fact that Hattusili protests so vigorously to the Sun Goddess that he was in no way implicated in her downfall suggests that the charges against her may have been trumped up. His agreement to take Kuruntiya into his safekeeping was perhaps part of a deal with Muwattalli to provide security for a possible back-up successor to the throne before the king risked making his move against the queen and her supporters, who may have been numerous, and depriving them of all their power.

Meanwhile, the relationship between Urhi-Teshub and Hattusili increasingly deteriorated as the young king asserted his independence from his uncle, and no doubt continued to overturn decisions and nullify actions taken by his father. His restoration of Danuhepa to Great Queenship probably rankled mightily with Hattusili, despite the likelihood of its being 'divinely sanctioned'. And, as Urhi-Teshub's five-year reign entered what was to be its final period, his uncle found himself increasingly marginalized from participation in the empire's affairs.

How the nephew might have perceived events

Let's look at the situation from Urhi-Teshub's point of view, in the context of my reconstruction of the events of the period. As the young king found his feet and grew more confident in ruling his empire, he no longer needed mentoring by his uncle. But not only did Hattusili refuse to accept any reduction of his role in managing the empire, he became an increasing threat to his nephew's continuing occupancy of its throne. Nor is there any doubt that he had the military muscle to seize it, using the troops already under his command, including, probably, a redoubtable Kaskan force which had pledged its loyalty to him.

Well aware of the danger his uncle now posed, Urhi-Teshub sought to offset this by depriving him of his chief centres of support in the north. First, he took from him all the regions once depopulated but resettled by Hattusili and made subject to him during Muwattalli's reign. They were now directly subject to the Great King, and – in theory at least – no longer took their orders from Hattusili. Yet, hoping his actions would not provoke retaliation from his uncle, Urhi-Teshub left him with his two most prized possessions: Nerik, holy city of the Storm God, whose reoccupation and restoration, claimed by Hattusili, embedded one of the most precious jewels in the crown of Hattusili's career;[19] and his capital Hakpis, the latter perhaps now a kingdom much reduced by Urhi-Teshub in the territory over which it held sway.

But this was not enough. Hattusili's anger and sense of injustice grew ever greater. And Urhi-Teshub became ever more fearful that his uncle was mustering support to seize his throne. He met this threat by depriving him of both Nerik and Hakpis – in effect stripping him of all his powers, including his command of all the northern region's military forces. He left him with a single fortress, not even named in the text. It was a mere token gesture, a gross insult to the man who was once not only king of Hatti's upper regions but his brother's partner in the rule of the empire. Now, this man was little better than the fairytale 'King of the Castle'. Once more he was just a prince of the royal line.

A mini civil war and an empire stolen

Yet, according to his own account, Hattusili continued to act with restraint. Though he may have refused to give up the territories he still controlled in Hatti's upper regions, he sought to have the whole dispute resolved by a judicial process, presided over by Ishtar and the Storm God of Nerik. If such a trial did take place, I'm not sure how exactly it would have been conducted. But, doubtless, it would have been rigged in the prince's favour. How could it have been otherwise when the divine presiding judges, nominated by Hattusili, were to be his patron deity Ishtar and a Storm God deeply indebted to the man who had restored his most important sanctuary? The offer of a trial was rejected as Hattusili knew it would be. He was merely seeking the high moral ground, by making a show of attempting to resolve the dispute by legal (and divine) process rather than by force. Resort to the latter had now become inevitable. As the abortive negotiations took place, with communications by letter, Urhi-Teshub must initially have stayed securely protected in his well-fortified palace in Hattusa, while Hattusili remained firmly entrenched, probably in Hakpis, in the north.

Uncle and nephew were now in open conflict. The result was a brief civil war – the only such war in Hittite history. Hattusili tells us about it in the *Apology*. Sadly, his account is frustratingly light on actual detail, gap-riddled, heavily biased and entangled in constant and (for us) irritating interventions by the goddess Ishtar. She it was who allegedly provoked the conflict by appearing to Hattusili's wife Puduhepa in a dream, foretelling that her husband would become a Great King, and that she, the goddess, would personally lead his forces to victory. Throughout the conflict, Ishtar continued to be a powerful presence, rallying in yet another dream some of Hattusili's loyal officers, who'd been sacked by Urhi-Teshub before the outbreak of hostilities and were now assured of their master's victory.

But Urhi-Teshub put on a courageous, if quixotic, show against an opponent far more skilled and experienced than he in the arts of war. Here is my reading of the actions the young king took. Instead of continuing to hunker down in his capital, awaiting the arrival of his uncle's forces, Urhi-Teshub boldly took the initiative, marching north with the aim of flushing his uncle out of his stronghold there before he had a chance to assemble an army of his own. After gathering what forces he could, in and around his capital and in the southern part of the homeland, he marched eastwards to the region called the Upper Land where he reinforced his army with troops stationed there who remained loyal to him. Then he set out for Hakpis, capital of the northern kingdom, which (in my reconstruction) Hattusili refused to surrender, or else reclaimed when war with his nephew was declared.

Very likely the hard core of Hattusili's army was a contingent of Kaskan troops. He refers explicitly in his narrative to the support of Kaskans who had initially been hostile to him. I suggest that this was a particular group of Kaskans who'd been won over from their own people and remained fiercely loyal to the pretender alone, not to the empire or its current ruler. Perhaps first recruited by Hattusili and accompanying him to Qadesh, they had provided their paymaster with a formidable bodyguard and military force, rather like the fearsome German praetorian guard who served as the personal militias of many Roman emperors. Hattusili's victory over his nephew may well have been due largely to his Kaskan forces.

Theoretically, Urhi-Teshub could have called on the support of his vassal rulers. There were standard 'mutual defence' clauses in the treaties drawn up by Great Kings with their vassals. The king guaranteed military support for a vassal if his rule, or the rule of any of his rightful successors, was endangered by rebellion or enemy attack; the vassal gave a similar undertaking to his overlord if his overlord's position was imperilled, an obligation which also covered the king's legal successors on the throne. In fact, there was little chance that a vassal ruler would ever attempt to fulfil such an obligation, even if he had the inclination and the resources to do so. Royal coups were generally over and done with before news of them ever reached the vassal states.

In this case, however, word had probably spread through the provinces some time before the coup that the Great King was under threat from a member of his own family, who sought the throne for himself and was prepared to fight a war to assert his claim. Yet it's unlikely that any of the vassal rulers were able, even if willing, to provide material support to the Great King in the events unfolding in the homeland. One of them, Masturi, king of the Seha River Land in western Anatolia, fell back on the debunked claim that Urhi-Teshub did not warrant acknowledgement as a Great King. 'Should I protect a (mere) second-rank son?' he protested.[20] But the western states were too far away, and the conflict likely to have been too short, for their rulers to have made any difference, one way or the other.

Urhi-Teshub had to rely totally on whatever support he could gather within his homeland territory. This was not enough. And any plan of action he may have had when he left Hattusa ended in failure. It was a David and Goliath contest of sorts – except this time Goliath was the victor. Outclassed and probably outnumbered by his battle-hardened uncle's army, Urhi-Teshub's forces were quickly driven into retreat, to the northern region's easternmost limits. Here they took refuge in the city of Samuha, no doubt a still strongly fortified city as it must have been when it had served as the headquarters of Hattusili's great-grandfather Tudhaliya III.[21] Urhi-Teshub was finally penned up in the city, 'like a pig in a sty',

Hattusili reports, while graciously giving Ishtar the credit for this final indignity inflicted upon the brave but now vanquished ruler of Hatti.

Faced with the prospect of a long siege, which he could ill afford, both politically and militarily, Hattusili probably negotiated terms of surrender with Urhi-Teshub. In return for giving up the city, the deposed king was promised both his life and his freedom. He would not suffer death or imprisonment, but was granted an 'honourable exile'[22] in a subject state called Nuhashshi. This was a region in northern Syria, east of the Orontes, where he was was put in charge of a few cities – an appointment probably amounting to little more than a sinecure. Initially, he may have complied with these terms of surrender but not for long. The throne of Great Kingship was no longer his. But it's far from the last we'll hear of him.

The 'civil war' was probably a brief affair, a series of skirmishes fought primarily between the main supporters of each of the protagonists, rather than an extended, more widespread conflict with the horrific casualties that frequently characterize such encounters. Following the defeat and capture of his nephew, Hattusili now proceeded to Hattusa to claim his long-coveted prize. No doubt he arrived in the capital under heavy guard and with limited fanfare. He was conscious that the populations of the capital, the homeland regions and the empire remained divided in their loyalties.[23] And he was fully aware of the mammoth task he faced in uniting all beneath his rule and establishing his credibility as the new Great King of Hatti. Diplomacy, not force of arms, would be essential to achieve this.

Now for the difficult part

'You know how to win a victory, Hannibal, but you do not know how to use it.' These are the words allegedly spoken to the Carthaginian leader Hannibal by his lieutenant Maharbal, after Hannibal's rout of the Roman forces at Cannae in 216 BC; Hannibal had failed to follow up his victory by marching immediately upon Rome. Winning a victory was often the easier part of a military enterprise; successfully following up on it, the more challenging part.

Hattusili's task was made more difficult by the fact that Urhi-Teshub, like Rome, remained free and ready to enter the fray once more. In the past, Hittite usurpers had seized power by despatching their predecessors with a quick thrust of a knife blade or a nod to a hired assassin. But a king like Urhi-Teshub was more problematic. He had lost his throne by being bumped off it after losing a war with his successor. Members of the royal family who lost favour with the

Great King, sometimes for egregious offences they had committed, like the Babylonian Tawananna, had their lives spared and were simply banished somewhere, generally within the empire's limits. Such was Urhi-Teshub's fate; he was sent into exile in the land of Nuhashshi and given some administrative duties to perform there, in the hope that he'd behave himself and quietly fade into obscurity. But Urhi-Teshub was determined *not* to go quietly.

Great King Hattusili

In the meantime, his successor must have been formally installed as Great King in a coronation ceremony in Hattusa. And it was *then*, I believe, that he officially assumed the throne-name Hattusili. We have no idea what name he was given at birth, the name by which he may have been known right up until his occupancy of the throne. But he probably had little doubt about what throne-name he would adopt. The first Hattusili had achieved legendary status in the kingdom. He it almost certainly was who resettled the old abandoned city of Hattus, calling it Hattusa and naming himself after it. He had embarked on military ventures far from the homeland, establishing Hatti for the first time as an international power by his repeated, lucrative plundering campaigns in Syria, and on at least one occasion across the Euphrates. The name 'Hattusili' was a revered one in the kingdom, and our Hittite prince no doubt hoped that some of its lustre would rub off on him when he assumed the name on his accession.

According to the usual sequence of Hittite kings, this Hattusili is generally numbered the third of that name. Unfortunately, the Hittites do not provide us with an actual kinglist, as the Egyptians do. We have to make this list up for ourselves, from conclusions we draw from the texts. Fortunately, we can compile a fairly complete list, though the task is more complicated by the fact that several kings sometimes shared the same throne-name. Thus we know for sure that there were two Suppiluliumas and three Mursilis (including Urhi-Teshub). And we generally list our Hattusili as the third of that name. But there's a lot of doubt, and there has been much scholarly debate, about whether there was ever a *second* Hattusili. 'Hattusili II' remains a kind of phantomatic figure who has yet to convince us that he ever existed. To avoid confusion with our numbers, however, we generally accept that he did exist, if only so that we do not have to call our Hattusili anything other than Hattusili III.

And Hattusili left his subjects in no doubt that henceforth the royal succession would remain firmly in his direct family line. He made this clear in an oath directed particularly to those who'd taken sides with Urhi-Teshub in the contest for the throne: they must henceforth pledge allegiance only to the king's sons of the first rank – those sons he had sired by his Chief Wife Puduhepa.[24] The sweetener in the oath was the general amnesty Hattusili now proclaimed for all his subjects, supporters and opponents alike. All would now be united – as one people. That was the grand new vision. Was it realised?

6

'And She Gave Us the Love of Husband and Wife'

After Qadesh

The prince is growing increasingly restless as he completes yet another inspection of Damascus and its associated territories. Following the Qadesh engagement, his brother King Muwattalli has made him temporary administrator of the region until it's handed back to the Egyptians. The prince obeys his brother's orders without question. But he frets at his enforced stay there, far from his own domain in the lands of northern Anatolia. Hattusili had imposed his control over this once almost ungovernable region. But now messengers from the north report that it is again descending into chaos and is once more under threat of enemy attacks. Those deputizing for the prince send desperate appeals for his reassertion of authority there. But what can he do while he is stuck in Damascus?

Muwattalli, too, is made aware that the empire's northern kingdom is becoming dangerously ungovernable, and belatedly despatches orders for his brother to leave Damascus and return home. Despite signs that his health is once more deteriorating, the prince wastes not a second in preparing for his journey. A large bodyguard is assembled. Some of the regions they'll be passing through are infested with bandit gangs that will pay no heed to the party's royal status. Constant vigilance and a heavily armed force are essential for the prince's protection. This slows the party's progress. Regular stops must be made to allow scouting parties time to scour nearby hill and desert country that conceal the bandits' favourite lairs.

Progress is made even slower when the prince makes a detour to the city of Lawazantiya, lying southeast of Hattusa in the land of Kizzuwatna. Lawazantiya is an important cult-centre of the goddess Ishtar, and the prince decides he must pay homage and make offerings to his divine patron there. Perhaps he is acting on instructions from the goddess herself – and these he dare not defy. The long, hazardous journey takes a heavy toll upon the prince. He looks old and frail when he enters the cult-city, though he is still only in his early forties. Despite his weariness, he seeks an immediate audience with Lawazantiya's Chief Priest Pentipsharri, who introduces his daughter to him. She is a tall, slender, graceful woman, though barely in her mid teens. And she flouts royal protocol by looking directly into the prince's eyes, instead of casting hers downwards.

So far, the prince has managed to keep his frail health from disabling him. But now a fever seizes upon him. He becomes very pale, his body shakes violently, he sweats profusely and his knees begin to buckle. Again in defiance of royal protocol, which prohibits a mere commoner from touching a royal person, the priest's daughter hastens to his aid, and supports him against her young, strong body. Carefully, she lays him upon a couch. Everyone else she orders to leave the chamber, including the prince's own physicians and incantation priests. The room is soon empty, except for the prince, the priest's daughter and her handmaiden. There is something in the woman's manner that commands instant obedience. An order is given. The maid leaves the chamber and quickly returns with a chalice containing a potion which her mistress has brewed herself.

Gently, the young woman presses the chalice to the prince's lips. He manages a few sips, and sinks back into his pillow. His tremors gradually subside, his sweating ceases and a healthy colour returns to his cheeks. He falls into a deep, restful sleep. When he awakes, his eyes slowly open to see the young woman's face directly above his as she kneels beside him.

'Who *are* you?' he asks.

'My name is Puduhepa, sir', she replies.

'You are very beautiful, Puduhepa', he says.

'Thank you, sir. Do you wish to marry me?' she asks.

He raises himself on one arm and looks closely at her. She looks closely back at him. 'Yes,' he replies, 'but I should tell you I already have several wives.'

'Shall I be your Chief Wife, sir?'

Once more, he looks closely at her. 'Yes,' he replies.

'Then I will marry you, sir, and we shall be partners for life. Equal partners.'

And, thus, the goddess Ishtar gave them the love of husband and wife.

The prince's Damascus command,[1] and his return to his kingdom via Lawazantiya, where he met (and married) Puduhepa are recorded in our texts. The other details, including the prince's eagerness to return home from his Syrian command, and his dialogue with Puduhepa, are my own invention. No other reason for the prince's detour to Lawazantiya is known other than what Hattusili tells us himself, about his desire to pay homage to the goddess Ishtar. Of course, we might dispel as fantasy the notion of a divinely inspired 'love at first sight' meeting between the prince and the priest's daughter, and their Ishtar-endorsed marriage. Formidable a young woman though Puduhepa may have been, the marriage was almost certainly pre-arranged by mere mortals, with or without divine consent. Nor can we rule out the possibility that Puduhepa had been well prepped for her first encounter with the prince. But let's not be too cynical and spoil a good story.

The Hurrian factor

For practical, strategic, political or perhaps purely cultural reasons, King Muwattalli may have decided that a union between his brother and Puduhepa was a desirable one. Somehow, he had become acquainted with Pentipsharri and his daughter, and perhaps he even made a pilgrimage to Lawazantiya to pay homage at Ishtar's shrines. Lawazantiya was an outlier in the Hittite world, near the eastern fringe of the vassal state Kizzuwatna. But it was an important place of pilgrimage and worship. And its culture was predominantly a Hurrian one.

Population groups of Hurrian ethnicity made up the bulk of the Mittanian empire destroyed by Suppiluliuma. But Hurrian culture survived the empire's fall, and indeed flourished in its wake, as reflected in its growing presence and influence in Hittite mythology, art and religion. Pentipsharri was High Priest of the Hurrian pantheon's chief deities, the divine couple Teshub and Hepat, equivalent to the Hittite Storm God and the Sun Goddess of Arinna. Puduhepa was also a priestess in Hepat's service, her theophoric name an outward sign of her dedication to the goddess. And especially after she became High Priestess of the Hittite empire, one of her chief projects was to spread the recognition and worship of the most important Hurrian deities throughout the realm, facilitating this by syncretizing (i.e. amalgamating) them with the most important Hittite deities.

Nor did she ever forget that her Hurrian origins lay in the land of Kizzuwatna. At Fraktin in south-central Anatolia, 50 kilometres southeast of modern Kayseri, there is a rock relief, depicting the royal couple. The figures are badly weathered (or, in Puduhepa's case, perhaps not finished). But inscriptions naming them have left us in no doubt who they are. On the left side of the panel, Hattusili is shown making a libation to the Storm God (standing to his left). This part of the scene appears on the front cover of this book. On the right side of the panel,

Figure 6.1 Fraktin monument. Puduhepa and Hepat. Courtesy Hannah Bryce.[2]

Puduhepa pours a libation to the goddess Hepat, who is seated to her left. Next to Puduhepa, on the right side of the relief, and just barely visible, are the words *Puduhepa, daughter of the land Kizzuwatna, beloved of the gods*.[3]

Puduhepa's new home

Let us return to Lawazantiya and the prince's and his bride's nuptials there. We have only Hattusili's *Apology* to tell us about their marriage, and the information we can glean from the text has gaps in it and is chronologically confusing. So I'll try to reconstruct the events as I see them, filling in some of the gaps, sorting out the chronology – and daring to be wrong.

With the end of the wedding ceremonies and festivities, the newly married couple spend some time in Lawazantiya, making a home for themselves there. For awhile, Hattusili seems to have given little thought to his northern kingdom. Perhaps he has appointed new deputies who have stabilized the region sufficiently for him to delay his departure from the peace and

tranquillity of the Hurrian cult-centre. While there, he very likely immerses himself in Hurrian culture. It is to play a large part in his life ahead. And the couple's time in Lawazantiya is perhaps long enough for Puduhepa to give birth to the first of their many children.[4]

Some time before his brother's death, Hattusili returns to his northern kingdom. A horse-drawn, canopied carriage has been prepared for the royal couple and their child (if they have one by then), though husband and wife travel some of the way by chariot, side by side. They visit Hattusa on their way. Puduhepa is pleased to see the legendary former capital and sacred city of the Hittites, and her husband welcomes the opportunity to visit once more his long-time mentor and friend Mittanamuwa, still Hattusa's Chief Administrator.

Within just a few years of Muwattalli building his new capital at Tarhuntassa, there are signs of decay in parts of the city. Some of the temples have been abandoned and are being demolished, the ground beneath them being cleared for settlement by relatively humble residential dwellings. The relocation of temple priests and ancillary staff to Tarhuntassa explain the former capital's loss of status as the empire's sacred centre. But a dwindling population is mainly responsible for the increasing decline of the once great city. Many of the homeland's able-bodied survivors of the Qadesh conflict have been permanently located in and around the new capital, to provide the region with an effective labour and defence force. Hattusa and the homeland regions, especially the northern ones, have been starved of resources to ensure this.

Mittanamuwa has given the hard facts to the royal couple, for we can assume that from now on Puduhepa is involved at the highest level in discussions concerning the empire's security and general well-being. The prince has been warned not to expect a grand reception on returning to his kingdom in the north, after so long an absence from it. And it may well be that he departs Hattusa on his own, leaving Puduhepa in the Chief Scribe's care until he has personally overseen the restoration of his kingdom's security before taking his new wife and the rest of his household there.

He wasted no time, now, in setting about this task. With the limited resources available to him, Hattusili expelled the enemy forces from his lands, especially the ever-predatory Kaskan invaders, restored order within these lands, and refortified their cities against further attack. Among his northern cities, two were of particular importance. The first was Hakpis, in effect designated by Muwattalli as capital of the northern part of the empire, and the seat of Hattusili's rule. The second was Nerik. Dedicated to the worship of the Storm God, it was one of the most sacred centres of the Hittite world and, after centuries of enemy occupation, it had been restored to Hittite control – an achievement claimed by Hattusili, as we have seen. Both cities lay near the empire's northern periphery, and their security against enemies both north of and within the frontiers required constant vigilance. No doubt garrisons of armed forces, kept on round-the-clock standby, were stationed close to or within each of them.

But it was not just external enemies Hattusili had to worry about. Even Hakpis itself 'turned hostile' to him, he tells us.[5] He doesn't say why. Whatever the reasons, the mere mention of rebellious activity in his own capital illustrates the volatility of the whole region over which he held fragile sway. Ironically, Hattusili sent in Kaskan troops to restore order in his capital. I imagine these were Kaskans whose services he had bought; many may have been part of the contingent he took to Qadesh, and were probably counted by Ramesses amongst the Hittites' mercenary forces.

When peace and calm have been restored in Hakpis, work is resumed on making the city fit for occupation by Hittite royalty. As in other centres of the kingdom, at least one building must have served as a palace, or could be converted into one. Hattusili orders the kingdom's finest craftsmen to make it as comfortable and as grand-looking as possible for the reception of his queen. When all is in readiness, Puduhepa is summoned to the city. She has a potentially dangerous journey, despite Hattusili's belief that he has gained full control of his kingdom. Nevertheless, probably with the protection of a heavily armed escort, she arrives safely. A special coronation ceremony is held, with much feasting and entertainment by and for the city's population, as Hattusili and Puduhepa are installed as 'King and Queen of Hakpis'. We don't know how many, if any, of the rest of Hattusili's household of concubines and their offspring join them in Hakpis. But Puduhepa may well have commanded their presence. She can't control them from afar, and the concubines are, after all, an important part of her husband's breeding stock.

A throne shared

In the years to come, Hattusili would enjoy, and benefit from, a partnership of many years with his Hurrian wife. In many ways, it was an equal partnership. Puduhepa shared not only her husband's bed, but also, metaphorically speaking, his throne. Once Hattusili had assumed the mantle of Great Kingship she became, as his Chief Wife, High Priestess of the Hittite realm. This gave her enormous influence over the conduct of the kingdom's religious affairs, the conduct of many state festivals, the reshaping of Hittite religion to incorporate many Hurrian traditions and, most importantly, the amalgamation of the Hittite and Hurrian pantheons.

In the secular sphere she was also highly active. I have no doubt that her husband discussed with her many affairs of state – those involving the administration of the homeland, the management of the vassal rulers and relations with the king's foreign peers, rulers of the Great Kingdoms of Egypt, Assyria and Babylon. From early in her marriage, she appears to have become involved in judicial proceedings, if we can so conclude from her appearance with her husband in his prolonged legal battle with his relative Arma-Tarhunda,[6] and from her apparently increasing role in dispensing justice, sometimes judging legal disputes in the vassal states, even on very minor matters. Thus, she presided over a case brought before her court, probably after her husband's death, by a shipowner in Ugarit who accused the defendant in the case of wilfully damaging his vessel. She found the defendant guilty and ordered him to make full compensation to the plaintiff.[7] What is particularly significant about this case is that she wrote about it to the king of Ugarit and signed her letter with the seal, 'My Sun'. This was the royal title assumed by the Hittite Great King. Its use by Puduhepa indicates that she was granted full authority to act on his behalf. This authority continued after his death during at least the early part of his successor Tudhaliya's reign.[8]

And, as we shall see, she was to play a prominent role on the international stage, especially in Hittite relations with Egypt. Her husband corresponded regularly with the pharaoh Ramesses, and so did she. (More on this in Chapter 9.) Indeed, like her husband, she called the pharaoh 'my brother',[9] a form of address which reflected parity status with her husband in their correspondence with other Great Kings. That is also clear from a number of important documents jointly stamped with the seals of Hattusili and Puduhepa. Not a mere formality, as is evident from two documents formalizing Kuruntiya's kingship – in effect his viceregalship – in the land of Tarhuntassa.[10] In these documents, Hattusili and Puduhepa jointly made the appointment and jointly determined the obligations, restrictions and concessions which it entailed.

Puduhepa was almost certainly involved in all stages of the negotiations between her husband and Ramesses leading up to the conclusion of the 'Eternal Treaty' which bound the two Great Kings in a permanent political and military alliance (see Chapter 8). Though she is not named in the text of the treaty, either the 'Hittite' or the 'Egyptian' version of it, she appeared as her husband's co-signatory in impressions of their individual seals stamped on a silver tablet of the 'Hittite' version, now lost.[11] These impressions make clear that the Hittite Great King and Great Queen were not merely husband and wife. They were equal partners in the monumental task of ruling an empire and maintaining peaceful relations with their international royal peers. Puduhepa regularly corresponded with Ramesses in the diplomatic and personal exchanges that passed between the royal courts in the lead-up to the treaty, and especially in later years when in her role as royal matchmaker she arranged at least the first of two marriages of Hittite princesses to the pharaoh.

Though the Great King and Queen of Hatti shared in many of the political and administrative affairs of the kingdom, one thing they did not share were the rigours of military campaigns. Puduhepa may well have taken part in councils of war. But she stayed at home tending to the kingdom's domestic affairs and religious observances, and managing the royal household while her husband went off on campaign (which probably didn't happen very often). Prominent though she deserves to be among the great queens of Ancient Near Eastern tradition, she was no Sammu-ramat, the mother of the Assyrian king Adad-nirari III, who accompanied her son on his military campaigns and became the historical prototype of the legendary Semiramis. Nor on this measure was she comparable to the Palmyrene queen Zenobia, renowned as a hunter and fierce warrior, who went with her husband on his military expeditions and became a great military leader in her own right after his death. Puduhepa was better off keeping the home front in order.

A marriage bed shared

In the scenario I created at the beginning of this chapter, Hattusili informs the young priestess that he already has several wives. We have evidence of this in a letter Puduhepa later writes to Ramesses telling him that, when she entered the palace in Hattusa for the first time, she found already installed there a number of princesses and their offspring. Very likely, these princesses were her husband's existing wives, and the children were his.[12] More strictly, these 'wives' should be called concubines, since none of them appear to have been granted the status of 'Chief Wife', a title only Puduhepa could claim. They had probably been relocated in Hattusa for safekeeping under the supervision of Mittanamuwa when Hattusili left his northern capital to join his brother at Qadesh. My suggestion that

Hattusili visited Hattusa on his way home to Hakpis not only afforded him the opportunity of seeing once more and consulting with his old friend and mentor Mittanamuwa, but also the opportunity of resuming his conjugal relations with his other 'wives' there.

Puduhepa may not merely have accepted such reunions but positively encouraged them. It really didn't matter how many new chicks these conjugal visits produced, just so long as she continued to rule the roost. Besides, Ishtar had ensured that Hattusili and Puduhepa had chicks of their own, and the males among them could expect to occupy the most privileged positions in the royal hierarchy, including a place in the royal succession. Nevertheless, we should not downplay the status of a concubine's sons in the succession stakes, at least by default if a king failed to produce offspring by his Chief Wife. Let me stress this once more. The succession principles laid down by the sixteenth-century king Telipinu made perfectly clear that the Great King's son by a concubine could succeed to the throne if the king's Chief Wife failed to provide a son and heir – or if there were no Chief Wife. As we've noted, Hattusili's stigmatization of his brother's son and successor as illegitimate grossly misrepresents the truth.

All this seems to fly in the face of Hittite morality in general. Marriages below the level of the topmost royalty appear to have been strictly monogamous (*if* we can so judge from the silence of our texts about any other sort below the level of royalty). Indeed, some of the harshest penalties prescribed in what is sometimes called the Hittite Law Code (really a hodgepodge of two hundred laws somewhat randomly assembled) were imposed upon persons found guilty of adulterous relationships, including sometimes the death penalty.[13] But at least on the matter of polygamous relationships, the king was above the laws that applied to ordinary mortals. Indeed, his regular servicing of a household of concubines, when he was not away fighting or on one of his religious pilgrimages, might be considered a duty rather than a leisure activity.

A brood of royals

We've noted that the Chief Wife of the king traditionally enjoyed substantial power in the Hittite world well beyond the palace establishment, especially in her role as the kingdom's High Priestess. She also had a powerful domestic role as manager of the palace household and all its functions, including supervision of the royal brood of sons and daughters spawned by the king, whether these were her own children or the offspring of concubines. In time, when the princesses were considered to be of marriageable age, probably in their mid-teens, she was responsible for choosing those most suitable to be wed to husbands of approved status.

Occasionally, the king's sons were married to the daughters of important vassal rulers. But, generally, political and military alliances were consolidated by marriages between a king's daughters and his foreign peers. My imagined scenario at the end of this chapter suggests how harrowing the experience might have been for a princess chosen for this purpose. In all such arrangements, Puduhepa played a leading role. She was the Hittite world's supreme matchmaker[14] – a responsibility which involved both careful choice of the proposed spouse as well as astute diplomacy and bargaining skills in seeing the arrangement through to a successful conclusion.

An abundance of sons and daughters served a number of purposes. Most importantly on the male side, they ensured that the throne had a king's successor of his own blood to sit upon it after his father's death. Beyond that, any sons of the king might serve as his authorized representatives on trade and diplomatic missions to foreign rulers. All were no doubt obliged to undergo military training to equip them for their place among the king's officer class, sometimes as divisional leaders, sometimes as commanders of their own campaigns. Fresh supplies of such officers became all the more important after the battle of Qadesh which, according to Egyptian records, resulted in high casualties among the officer classes on both sides.

Tawananna – a title stigmatised

If her husband died before her, the Chief Wife continued to exercise the role of Hatti's First Lady until her own death. Her status in the kingdom, for most of its history, was defined by the title 'Tawananna'. In Hittite tradition, this was thought to be the name of the first Hittite queen. It was not always an honourable title. As we've seen, several Tawanannas were accused and found guilty of abusing their privileged position – including Suppiluliuma's Babylonian wife and Mursili's second wife, Danuhepa – and stripped of their powers. The potential for abuse of power was there for Puduhepa as well. Indeed, by the extension of her activities into the kingdom's political and judicial affairs, with her husband's approval, if not by more broadly based assent among the kingdom's elite, she must have had many opportunities to exceed the bounds of her authority by indulging in a range of corrupt practices, like her disgraced predecessors. But there is no evidence to suggest that this ever happened. She no doubt proved a very formidable figure in the kingdom, and her wrath may have been feared by those who tried to question her authority. However, as far as we can tell, she always seems to have acted in what she believed was her husband's and the kingdom's best interests.

Things may have changed after Hattusili's death. In any case, the title 'Tawananna' sank into obscurity. The abuse of power associated with it by Suppiluliuma's Babylonian wife ensured that, henceforth, it became politically undesirable for the title to be openly accorded any of the Babylonian's successors. There is just one further fleeting reference to its being used – in this case probably, but not certainly, of Puduhepa.[15]

Prayers for a beloved husband

What does seem beyond doubt is that the working partnership between Hattusili and Puduhepa was underpinned by a deep, abiding, lifelong love for each other. This is most evident in Puduhepa's prayers addressed to the Sun Goddess of Arinna (Hurrian, Hepat) and to the underworld goddess Liliwani (Lelwani). She pleads with the Sun Goddess for the health, well-being and long life of her husband. So, too, she pleads with Liliwani, asking her to intercede with the major deities to grant that both she and her husband will enjoy together long years, months and days.[16] Her prayer to Liliwani ends with another appeal to the goddess, and a vow: *If you, Liliwani, my lady, will speak favourably [to the gods] and will keep your servant Hattusili alive and grant him long years, months, and days, I shall come and make for Liliwani, my lady, a silver statue of Hattusili, as big as Hattusili himself, with its head, its hands and its feet of gold.*[17]

Hattusili's chronically weak constitution gave Puduhepa good reason for her concern. One specific ailment from which the king suffered was called 'fire-of-the-feet' in a plea she made to the goddess Ningal. She offered ten flasks of gold set with lapis lazuli if the ailment was quickly cured.[18] I have been informed by neurology specialists that the king was suffering from an incurable disease called peripheral neuropathy. This can make walking (or even standing) extremely painful – as I can attest from personal experience. It's like stepping through or standing in a bed of hot coals. For a king who spent much of his life travelling, his ailment must have been an almost intolerable burden, especially as he aged. Other votive prayers tell us of an eye illness which afflicted the king. Ramesses sent him some medicines to help alleviate the condition.[19]

Given that Hattusili must have been well into his forties and perhaps in his early fifties when he became Great King, already old for that time, it is understandable that Puduhepa, many years his junior, expressed such concern for his health. Of course, part of her concern was for her own well-being should her husband die. For there is no doubt that she shared the hostility which Hattusili continued to experience (as indicated in her prayers) from enemies he had made as far back as the time when his brother was Great King; very likely this hostility intensified after he'd seized the throne. In any case, I have not the slightest doubt that the bond between Hattusili and Puduhepa was of a deep, personal, intimate nature and that they shared a genuine, abiding love for each other. Puduhepa's prayers encapsulate both this love and the fears for her future after her husband's death. In these prayers we see expressions of 'the love and loyalty of this queen, who always lived under the threat of losing her beloved husband'.[20]

I was privileged to take part in a film called *The Hittites*, directed by the distinguished Turkish film director, Tolga Örnek. Among its many memorable re-enactments, there is one in which a grieving Puduhepa, still in her prime, leans over the couch of her dying husband and whispers to him prayers of comfort and hope. This is one of the film's most poignant scenes, accurately portraying, I believe, the close, warm, loving partnership between the king and his queen – a partnership that was now so soon to end with the old man's passing.

A Hittite bride for the pharaoh

We began this chapter with an imagined scenario. Let's end with one. It's built around the draft of a letter Puduhepa intended to send to Ramesses,[21] some time after peace between Hatti and Egypt had been settled, and preparations for a royal wedding were underway – or appeared to be.

Her Majesty, Queen Puduhepa, angrily paces up and down the Reception Hall as the scribe reads to her a letter from His Majesty, Ramesses, Pharaoh of Egypt. He translates into Hittite as he does so. The letter is written in Akkadian, the international lingua franca of the time.[22] It is included in a bundle of royal correspondence sent from Egypt by members of Ramesses' family who communicate regularly with their counterparts in Hattusa. Hatti and Egypt are now at peace. Well, not quite, as Her Majesty's furious response to the pharaoh's letter shows.

The 'Eternal Peace' treaty had been been concluded almost thirteen years earlier, and the formal peace between the two Great Kingdoms has held firm. It just needs a marriage alliance to put the finishing touches to it. Ramesses wants a Hittite bride, and Hattusili and Puduhepa are anxious to give him one. The last couple of years have involved lots of toing and froing between the royal courts. Negotiations over the terms of the marriage have been protracted, and at times acrimonious. Responsibility for them on the Hittite side is handled by Puduhepa. Royal matchmaking and marriage arrangements lie strictly within her province, which accounts for her frequent correspondence with Ramesses over a suitable Hittite bride for him.

And now it seems that final agreement is within sight on all matters related to the marriage. Officials have come from Egypt as the pharaoh's representatives to complete the deal. First, they need to check out the proposed bride. Puduhepa has chosen her from one of her husband's multitude of progeny and presents her to the Egyptian officials. She has grace, poise, elegance and beauty. Surely all her bridegroom could want. But his officials scornfully reject her. 'She's too old! Why, she must be twenty if she's a day!'

Well, it was worth a try, Puduhepa thinks, especially as the girl will soon be beyond the age for marrying anyone worthwhile – even a petty king or vassal ruler.

Her Majesty now brings out a second candidate. The officials look her up and down and then nod approvingly. This is more like it! The girl has all the qualities of her elder stepsister, but another quality besides. She has just turned fifteen, barely out of childhood. That will make His Egyptian Majesty happy! But just to be sure, the officials demand inspection of her in the minutest detail. This means she has to strip naked, and she stands there shivering, terrified and humiliated as the officials' eyes roam slowly over her whole body, including its most intimate parts. Confirmation of her virginity may also be required. They must make absolutely certain that their royal master will be pleased with his new bride. Because if he's not, they will answer for it with their heads.

The girl finds little comfort in her stepmother's words that she will be garbed in the finest robes and bedecked with the most precious jewels. Closeted within the confines of the palace for all her fifteen years, the world outside is an unknown and terrifying place – even the immediate surrounds of her own world, let alone one thousands of miles away where she is to be married to a man more than four times her age whose language she cannot speak. But that is of small moment in the context of the much more important world of the affairs of state.

Then there is the matter of the dowry to accompany the bride or be sent on ahead of her. The pharaoh insists that it is agreed to by his representatives, item by item. Puduhepa has a condition of her own. She demands that the bride be given the status of Chief Queen over all the pharaoh's other wives.[23] Ramesses has anticipated this condition and given his officials his consent. It will, of course, mean an even larger dowry.

So, of what does this dowry consist? Probably not gold, at least in its raw state. That would be like carrying coals to Newcastle (if you will forgive the anachronism). The mines of the pharaoh produce gold in abundance, prompting one foreign king's belief that it lies everywhere on the ground in Egypt, like dirt, just waiting to be picked up – a belief as naive as Dick Whittington's that the streets of London were paved with gold.

But there are many other items both large and small that make up the dowry, the latter including exquisite miniature art pieces – statuettes of both human and animal figures made of precious metals, jewel-encrusted goblets and daggers, and gold and silver libation vessels shaped like the foreparts of bulls and stags. On a larger scale, a herd of cattle, a flock of sheep and a group of slaves help complete the dowry, and perhaps also some fine quality horses bred from stock plundered from the plains of northwestern Anatolia or the now defunct kingdom of Mittani in the east.

So everything is now agreed, and the pharaoh awaits his new Hittite bride with increasing impatience. He communicates this to Puduhepa in a succession of increasingly blunt demands for her fulfilment of the marriage contract.

'Where is my bride? Why have you not yet given her to me?'

And, even more importantly, 'Where is the dowry? Why, Your Majesty, are you welshing on your part of the agreement? Why the delay?'

The queen reacts angrily. 'Surely, my brother, you have heard of the fire in Hattusa that has destroyed many of the items intended for the dowry. Why don't you ask Urhi-Teshub since you have him there with you?'

This is a sneer, mocking the pharaoh's constant assurances that he has no knowledge of the the dethroned king's whereabouts. One of the worst insults of all is to accuse a brother-king of outright lying! But lighten up, Ramesses. You will find that your new bride is well worth the wait, comparable as she is to the Near Eastern world's greatest royal beauties, whether they be Assyrian or Babylonian or the daughters of any other king.

But then Puduhepa piles on another insult. It's not really the bride that Ramesses is interested in. It's the dowry that he wants to get his hands on. Greed, not the desire for a beautiful bride that will cement the bonds between the two kingdoms, is what really lies behind the pharaoh's impatience.

The fate of the Hittite bride

Whether a final version of this letter was ever sent to the pharaoh and, if so, whether it was toned down and expressed in more diplomatic terms, we shall never know. In any case, a complete dowry was finally assembled and sent to the pharaoh's palace, along with the young bride. Happily, Ramesses was delighted with her and for a time she became a pleasurable distraction from his affairs of state. The Egyptian name bestowed upon her was Maat-Hor-Neferure, which means 'One who sees Horus, the Visible Splendour of Re'. We don't know what her Hittite name was. Nor do we know whether she was ever accorded the title of Chief Queen, though that position was now vacant since Ramesses' Chief Wife Nefertari (aka Naptera), who had corresponded regularly with Puduhepa, had died before the Hittite princess arrived in Egypt.[24] Perhaps it was her death that had prompted Ramesses' request for a Hittite bride.

Eventually – perhaps quite quickly – His Majesty tired of his beautiful new princess. There cannot have been much they had to say to each other, even if they'd been able to communicate verbally. The princess soon disappeared from the royal scene, sent to live in the pharaoh's harem at the oasis settlement called Faiyum, on the the fringes of the Western Desert.[25] Hittite officials sent to Egypt to ensure that Ramesses fulfilled the promises he had made about his bride could not even find out where she was. But what could they or Hattusili or even Puduhepa do about it?

A few years later, Ramesses asked for another Hittite bride. And he got one!

7

'Uneasy Lies the Head...'[1]

A restless exile

Hattusili was not the first usurper to seize Hatti's throne. But he had the unique distinction of doing it without assassinating his predecessor. He simply stole the throne from his nephew by defeating him in a mini civil war, and then packing him off to Syria. But Urhi-Teshub had not the slightest intention of abandoning what was his rightful inheritance, and quickly set about getting himself acknowledged, or reacknowledged, as Hatti's Great King, a third Mursili. For a time, then, the Hittite empire had two Great Kings. Or so it must have seemed to other Great Kings and lesser foreign rulers, as well as to the empire's own subjects.[2] Hattusili soon realised that he had made a serious mistake in setting his nephew up in the land of Nuhashshi in Syria. While it kept him well away from the centre of power in Hattusa, it placed him closer to the other three Great Kingdoms – Babylon, Assyria and Egypt.

Indeed, he had scarcely set foot in his new home before he began conspiring against his uncle. Without doubt, secret agents of the king had been placed in Nuhashshi close to his nephew and now swiftly reported back to the king that Urhi-Teshub was up to something with the Babylonians and was planning to travel to Babylon.[3] We don't know what Urhi-Teshub was actually supposed to be up to, and Hattusili probably didn't either. He may have been seeking no more than Babylon's continuing recognition of him as Hatti's Great King. But any communication Urhi-Teshub had with the Babylonians could rightly be regarded as sinister in intent – as also a communication he had with the Assyrian king Shalmaneser I.[4] At least Hattusili knew that his intelligence system was working. Anyhow, Hattusili put a stop to the Babylonian jaunt before it got started, removing his nephew from Nuhashshi and relocating him 'alongside (or across) the sea'.

This must have been somewhere on the eastern or southeastern Mediterranean coast, perhaps on the coast of Amurru,[5] or, if the relevant phrase means 'across the sea', perhaps on the island of Cyprus, where Arma-Tarhunda's wife and one of his sons were already in exile. Arma-Tarhunda's other son Sippaziti, whom Muwattalli had declared innocent of his family's previous actions against Hattusili, had joined forces with Urhi-Teshub in the civil war, had had his property confiscated, and was made to 'cross the border as well'.[6] This could mean that he accompanied Urhi-Teshub to his new place of exile. Maybe 'crossing the border' means crossing the sea to Cyprus, where they joined Sippaziti's mother and brother. The expression could also mean that Sippaziti was forced to relocate to an adjacent Syrian state, quite separate from where Urhi-Teshub was now sent. But Cyprus remains my best guess.[7]

Hittite kings occasionally laid claim to Cyprus as a subject state, though the claim had little substance to back it up. Nevertheless, the island served as a useful dumping ground, theoretically, for overthrown royals, and probably other disgraced members of the Hittite aristocracy. But, if Hattusili really did send the ex-king there as a second place of exile, it's difficult to understand why. After all, the south coast of Cyprus was but a short merchant-vessel journey from the Egyptian coast. And Urhi-Teshub was soon on board ship. He could seek asylum in Egypt, and pharaonic support for reclaiming his throne. Even if the odds were against that happening, Egypt offered plenty of places for a refugee to disappear into – until the time was ripe for his reappearance.

Hattusili seeks validation

Apart from having to contend with the problems of an elusive ex-king, one of Hattusili's first tasks was to convince both his foreign peers and his own subjects that *he* was now the rightful occupant of Hatti's throne. In the words of Stefano de Martino, 'The deposition of Muršili III and Hattušili's coup d'état shattered the prestige of the Hittite royal house, as well as the stability of the network of political relations that had been established with its subordinated polities and other foreign countries. Hence, Hattušili III tried to strengthen his power, affirm his legitimacy, and establish strict relations with the outer world.' De Martino goes on to discuss Hattusili's decrees, commenting that these 'are the clearest proof of the king's communicative ability, and of the intersection of governance, devotion, and securing consent'.[8]

Most importantly, in his bid to secure the support of his subjects, he needed to win overt acknowledgement of his new status from his brother kings. His seizure of the Hittite throne made him acutely aware of the correct observance of international diplomatic protocol in seeking to establish his legitimacy as the Great King of Hatti. The snub he'd already suffered from Adad-nirari I, Great King of Assyria, demonstrated that this would be no easy task. Adad-nirari had failed to acknowledge Hattusili's coronation, by sending one of his ambassadors to represent him along with the customary coronation gifts. Hattusili angrily reminded him of this: *When I assumed kingship,* he wrote, *you did not send an ambassador to me. It is the custom that when kings assume kingship, the kings, his equals in rank, send him appropriate greeting-gifts, clothing fit for kingship, and fine oil for his anointing. But you did not do this today.*[9] Adad-nirari had pointedly refused to recognise Hattusili's ascension to the throne of Hatti.[10] Very likely he was the same Assyrian king (unidentified) who, according to one of Ramesses' letters, had said to Hattusili: *You're no Great King, just a substitute for one!*[11] So, despite Hattusili's claim in the *Apology* of being readily accepted by 'the kings who were my elders',[12] acknowledgement by his royal peers as Hatti's legitimate Great King was in most cases probably slow in coming and only reluctantly conceded.[13]

But Hattusili's fortunes received a positive boost from Assyria's southern neighbour. Not long after his accession, Hattusili had pulled off an important international diplomatic coup by establishing a pact of friendship and alliance with Kadashman-Turgu, Great King of Babylon (*c.* 1282–1264 BC[14]). He drew up with him some sort of pact or accord which had all the hallmarks of a treaty.[15] This in itself was a Babylonian acknowledgement of Hattusili as Hatti's Great King. Hattusili even persuaded Kadashman-Turgu to break off his diplomatic ties with Egypt. Hittite-Egyptian relations had yet to be rebuilt after Qadesh, so Hattusili must have been delighted with his Babylonian alliance, especially as Kadashman-Turgu promised to provide him with troops and chariotry if he made war on Egypt. Hattusili had apparently threatened the pharaoh with military retaliation for his refusal to extradite an 'enemy' who had fled from Hatti and sought refuge in Egypt. This unnamed enemy was almost certainly Urhi-Teshub. But the threat was surely no more than sheer bluff. Hattusili now had neither the intention nor the capacity to fight another war with Egypt, even a limited one. His Babylonian 'treaty partner' was well aware of this, and his offer of military support must have been purely tokenistic.

But the alliance served its purpose in other ways. Very likely Kadashman-Turgu sent a delegation to Hattusa to take part in Hattusili's coronation celebrations, with 'fine oil for his anointing' and an array of gifts that befitted the occasion – all that the Assyrian king had conspicuously failed to do. And such a delegation, replete with a large military escort, would have provided an impressive spectacle for Hattusili's subjects, especially those living in the homeland, as it made its way to the royal capital and processed through it to be received with much pomp and ceremony at the palace by the Great King himself. This is my imagined reconstruction of the Babylonian delegation's arrival and reception in Hattusa. If I am right, such a spectacle would have been a clear visual manifestation, to the aristocracy and common folk alike, that Hattusili had won important international recognition as Hatti's rightful king – even if at this stage from only one of his foreign peers.

A new regime in Babylon[16]

It all seemed too good to last – and it was. Within a year or so of his pact with Kadashman-Turgu, Hattusili received disturbing news from Babylon. His 'treaty partner' had died and been succeeded by his son Kadashman-Enlil, who quickly restored diplomatic relations with Egypt. Worse still was a report that the new king was strongly influenced by his powerful vizier Itti-Marduk-balatu, leader of a powerful anti-Hittite faction in the Babylonian court.

This was a major challenge to Hattusili's diplomatic skills. A harsh response to Kadashman-Enlil's failure to renew his father's close relationship with his Hittite counterpart was hardly likely to restore harmonious relations between the Hittite and Babylonian royal courts – especially in view of the already mounting hostility towards Hatti in Babylonian court circles. Indeed, a letter ill-advisedly worded might only have served to strengthen Kadashman-Enlil's links with Egypt. Because of the potential threats posed by both Egypt and Assyria to Hittite subject territories in Syria, Hattusili must have set great store on cultivating good relations with the new Babylonian king.

So he wrote to him in measured terms, reminding him of his father's peace accord with the new regime in Hattusa, and mildly reprimanding him for his failure to renew and maintain this accord. He begins his letter by bestowing the customary blessings upon his addressee's household, wives, infantry, horses, chariots and everything else in his land. But then it's time to get down to business. Firstly, he reminds the young Kadashman-Enlil of the close ties he, Hattusili, had with his father, each promising that whoever lived longer would protect for the rest of his life the progeny of the other. This is why, Hattusili says, he had written to the noblemen of Babylonia threatening to come to the kingdom and conquer it if its king and his rightful successors to the throne were not protected by their own subjects. He would also provide the country with military assistance if a foreign enemy threatened to attack it or there were some other threat to its security.

All this information, he says, should already be recorded on tablets. Have they not been filed (in the Babylonian archives)? Perhaps the young Babylonian king has no knowledge of them, because he was too young for them to be read out to him when they arrived. Hattusili blames his vizier *whom the gods have caused to live far too long, and in whose mouth unfavourable words never cease*[17] for misrepresenting Hattusili's intentions towards him and his kingdom. These would have been perfectly clear if the young king had been provided with the record of Hattusili's peace agreement with his father. I suspect that for diplomatic reasons Hattusili is seeking to provide the new Babylonian king with a plausible excuse for not responding earlier to his overtures, and to leave the way open for him to do so now. I very much doubt that Kadashman-Enlil did not already know the contents of the tablets to which Hattusili refers, and that he knew that Hattusili knew that he knew. It was all part of a diplomatic game.

We learn further from the letter that in the months that followed Kadashman-Enlil's accession, there were spasmodic and sometimes acrimonious exchanges of correspondence between the Hittite and Babylonian courts. The Babylonian vizier wrote to Hattusili accusing him of interfering in his country's affairs and of treating his king's subjects as if they were subjects of Hatti. Then for a time communications from Babylon abruptly ceased. When they resumed, probably after repeated demands from Hattusa for an explanation, Kadashman-Enlil informed his royal brother that hostile Syrian desert tribesmen called the Ahlamu had made travel to Hattusa too dangerous, even for his own messengers. And the Assyrian king had denied his messengers the right to travel through Assyrian territory to reach their destination. However, in one of the letters that did get through, the Babylonian king complained that his merchants were being killed in Amurru and Ugarit, Hittite vassal states. Responsibility for dealing with such crimes had been delegated to Hatti's vice-regents in Carchemish and Aleppo. But the ultimate responsibility was the Hittite Great King's, and Kadashman-Enlil wanted to make sure that the offenders were brought to justice.

Hattusili responds to these complaints and excuses one by one. I suggested in Chapter 3 that he had learned to read and write during his early years, perhaps under the mentorship of the kingdom's Chief Scribe. And I think it possible that the king's long, well-argued, and wide-ranging letter was inscribed on clay tablets by Hattusili himself, at least in draft form. He cursorily dismisses the Babylonian's excuse that he had stopped writing to Hattusili because of the risks posed to his messengers by Syrian desert tribesmen or by the Assyrian king's refusal to allow the messengers passage through Assyria. Surely his royal brother has military forces adequate to deal with such threats and ensure the messengers' safety? Moreover, continues Hattusili, his own messengers pass repeatedly through Assyrian territory without problems. Perhaps the truth of the matter is that his royal brother's evil vizier has talked him out of communicating with Hattusa. As for the alleged murder of Babylonian merchants in Hittite territory, the assassins will be captured and punished according to Hittite law. Hattusili will deal with the matter himself if his royal brother sends him the relatives of the dead merchants so that he can personally investigate their claims.

The tone of the letter is often patronizing, and some of the Hittite king's statements seemingly border on the absurd. As if, for example, Babylon should go to war with Assyria for denying its messengers right of passage through its territory! But in these words there lies an implicit warning – at least to my way of thinking. The refusal to grant this passage reflects festering tensions between Assyria and Babylon which were later to culminate in an Assyrian invasion of Babylonia; whereas the granting of such rights to Hittite messengers reflects kingdoms seemingly at peace with each other. Kadashman-Enlil should thus be well aware of the consequences of alienating the ruler of Hatti, whose kingdom *apparently* enjoys friendly relations with Babylon's hostile northern neighbour.

Some requests and an embarrassing admission

There are other matters of contention that are dealt with in the letter. But then Hattusili changes tune with a couple of requests. One is for the Babylonian to send him 'tall stallion foals'. The previous animals he and his father had sent were of good quality, but too short, and the supply of horses to Hatti needs constant replenishment because the older animals are unable to survive the rigours of the harsh Hittite winters. The second request is for the loan of a sculptor to make statues for Hattusili's family quarters.

Hattusili also had an embarrassing admission to make. Babylonian as well as Egyptian medical science was much respected in the Hittite world. And Kadashman-Enlil had agreed to Hattusili's request to lend him one of his physicians. Unfortunately, the poor man fell ill and died while on loan, despite all efforts to save him. What made this all the more embarrassing was that Muwattalli had also been sent a physician from Babylon, almost certainly just on loan as well. But it seems that he proved so valuable to his Hittite hosts that Muwattalli bribed him to stay, providing him with a fine mansion and marriage into the royal family. Hattusili claims in his letter that he protested strongly about Muwattalli's 'detention' (more accurately, 'retention') of the doctor Babylon had sent him. Obviously he wanted to make it clear that the second physician really *had* died in Hatti, and it was for that reason alone that he had failed to return home.

There are large gaps in what remains of the letter. If you do manage to read a translation of it, you'll find lots of square brackets, which enclose bits that have been restored. But enough of it survives to make it one of the most fascinating and informative pieces of correspondence from the Bronze Age world. It's clear throughout that Hattusili is speaking as a highly experienced older man to a relative novice in the ways of the world, especially the world of intrigue and conspiracy within palace circles, and the contests for political and military supremacy in the wider world.

But, from reprimand and warning, Hattusili quickly turns to more positive aspects of the relations between the two kingdoms. He notes that the man he is now pleased to call 'my brother' 'has become a grown man' and enjoys hunting. The first part of this observation implies that Kadashman-Enlil was a mere youth when he succeeded his father, with the further implication that he then lacked the sound judgement he now has. The second part shows interest in the king's leisure activities; the reference to hunting is a complimentary one, for this is traditionally the sport of kings. And Hattusili's request for the loan of Babylonian doctors and sculptors is partly intended to reflect a further warming in relations between the two kingdoms, though the bribing of one of the doctors to stay in Hatti, and the death of the other there may well have temporarily strained these relations.

We do not know what response, if any, Kadashman-Enlil made to the letter. In any case, it should be seen within the context of a much more formidable test of Hattusili's diplomatic skills: ratcheting down tensions with Egypt and finally establishing a peace accord with the man who had been his and his brother Muwattalli's arch enemy, the pharaoh Ramesses.

Back to the *Apology*[18]

Let's return now to the document that's provided us with most of our information about Hattusili up to this point. It's the document I've already referred to several times as the *Apology* or *Autobiography* of Hattusili. It takes us from:

(a) Hattusili's childhood illnesses; to
(b) his adoption by the goddess Ishtar as her priest and the lifelong protection and guidance she has provided as his patron deity; to
(c) his court cases with a hostile branch of his family; to
(d) his military successes; to
(e) his 'appointment' of his nephew Urhi-Teshub as Great King; to
(f) Urhi-Teshub's shift of the capital back to Hattusa; to
(g) the growing tensions between uncle and nephew culminating in civil war; to
(h) the defeat, capture and exile of Urhi-Teshub; to
(i) the ascension of Hattusili to Great Kingship.

Next, we have a brief account of Hattusili's alleged recognition as Great King of Hatti by other kings, his alleged expansion of his empire by annexing additional territories to it, the appointment of Muwattalli's other son Kuruntiya to the throne of Tarhuntassa, now an important viceregal kingdom within the empire, and the Great King's dedication of his son Tudhaliya to the service of Ishtar.

Incomplete though this account is as an 'autobiography', and a highly biased one at that (what autobiography isn't?), it provides a relatively comprehensive account, at least by Hittite standards, of Hattusili's career up to his seizure of the Hittite throne, and provides a number of important pieces of information about his reign. The *Apology* is the more common name by which the document is known. But the term is not used in its usual modern sense as an expression of regret for some wrongdoing. Far from it! It's derived from the Classical Greek word *apologia*, which means a speech given *in defence of* one's actions. The most famous example of an *Apologia* in the Classical Greek sense is the one delivered by Socrates in Athens in 399 BC before a 500-strong jury of his fellow citizens, in response to charges of impiety and corrupting the city's youth. As recorded by Plato, it is a robust oration in defence of freedom of speech and thought. But the booing, jeering, so-called democratic jury frequently drowned out the accused man's words and he had often to stop his speech to plead for silence. Not surprisingly, he was found guilty as charged and executed.

Except in name, the Hittite *Apologia* (a title bestowed on the document in 1935 by the Hittite scholar E. H. Sturtevant) is in no way comparable to the Socratic one. Its primary purpose, so it seems, is to give Hattusili a platform for justifying his seizure of the Hittite throne. On the assumption that this is the case, how valid is the justification? From both a moral and a legal perspective, the usurper's action is clearly indefensible. Let me stress yet again that there is no doubt that Muwattalli had intended his son Urhi-Teshub to succeed him,[19] a decision he'd probably taken before the battle of Qadesh, and had very likely entrusted Hattusili with the responsibility of ensuring his decision was honoured. Hattusili's claim that he himself had made the decision as well as putting it into effect wilfully distorts the truth.

As for the coup, there is no suggestion in the *Apology* that Urhi-Teshub ever endangered the kingdom by abuse of his royal powers or incompetence in exercising them. The only justification Hattusili provides for his action is that Urhi-Teshub stripped him of his northern kingdom and virtually all his authority. That is to say, Hattusili's justification for his coup and the civil war which led up to it was purely personal – his dispute with Urhi-Teshub and the gradual erosion and loss of all his powers. He had been sacked by his own nephew, on whom he claims to have bestowed the Great Kingship of Hatti!

We should, of course, take into account another side of the picture. In my mind, Hattusili quite literally believed he was guided throughout his life by the goddess Ishtar, that it was she who had saved him from death as a child, saw to his rise to the top ranks of military leadership as his brother's partner in power, and ultimately paved the way for his accession to the Hittite throne. All this was pre-ordained once he had entered the goddess's service and become her devoted *protégé*. In everything he did, including his seizure of the throne, he was acting as Ishtar's agent. This was really all the justification he needed for his actions. There are many examples in history, both ancient and modern, of leaders and entire peoples who commit acts which would otherwise be deemed illegal or beyond the norms of morality, or straightout atrocities, in the unquestionable belief that they are carrying out their god's or their gods' commands.

The *Apology*'s audience

So, who was the *Apology*'s intended audience and how widely was the document circulated? To address the second question first, we know that multiple copies were made on clay,[20] and probably because of the importance Hattusili attached to it, on bronze as well. And it's generally assumed to have been composed in the latter part of his reign, at least no earlier than the treaty he concluded with Ramesses in 1259 BC, possibly near his reign's end.[21] The intended audience, I suggest, were those most highly placed among the king's subjects: the top-ranking political and military personnel in the land, like those assembled by the ailing first Great King called Hattusili to hear his appointment of a new heir to the throne. Our Hattusili had already spent the early years of his reign establishing his credibility as Great King among the kingdom's grandees, and also, as we shall see, among all his subjects, as well as contemporary foreign kings, from whom he sought acknowledgement as their royal peer.

But, if the *Apology* was intended primarily to justify Hattusili's seizure of the throne, why would he have chosen a much later date to compose and distribute it? Was there a critically important time for him to do so? Let me suggest one: the time leading up to his formal announcement of the man he had now chosen as Crown Prince, successor to his throne.

Hattusili's successor

This brings us, first of all, to someone we've already met, just briefly – a somewhat enigmatic character who was to play a major role in the last decades of the empire's existence. His name is Kuruntiya. He was the son of Muwattalli and a younger brother or stepbrother of Urhi-Teshub. Muwattalli had entrusted him to Hattusili's safe-keeping, probably not long before the Qadesh episode. He was probably still a child, or barely out of childhood at the time, and was very likely whisked away to his guardian's then capital, Hakpis, in the far north. Muwattalli may well have sought to keep him safe from any machinations within his own court, especially during his absence on the Qadesh campaign. It's possible that Urhi-Teshub accompanied his father on this campaign. There were always expectations that a Crown Prince would succeed his predecessor as an already experienced warrior, even though such experience could put his life at risk. Qadesh provided an ideal opportunity for Muwattalli's successor to be blooded on the field of battle, with the risk that he might never return from it. Nor might his father.

Muwattalli had placed his complete trust in his brother and I believe that, in assigning the young Kuruntiya to his protection, he did so on the understanding that, in the event of both his own and Urhi-Teshub's deaths, Hattusili would preserve the rightful royal line of descent by appointing Kuruntiya to the throne. Of course, Hattusili also fought at Qadesh, and must have made special arrangements for Kuruntiya's safety during his absence. As it happened, all three – Muwattalli, Urhi-Teshub and Hattusili – survived the conflict. And, after his father's death probably just a couple of years later, Urhi-Teshub became Hatti's next Great King, through the agency of Hattusili and in accordance with his father's wishes. So far, so good. But Hattusili's coup changed everything.

A later text, the famous Bronze Tablet inscription,[22] tells us that Kuruntiya bonded closely with Hattusili's family. We have no indication, however, that he played any part in his brother Urhi-Teshub's decline and fall. For that matter, we have no idea of any activities in which he engaged during these turbulent times. There is a gap of ten years or more in our information about him – between the time when Muwattalli entrusted him to his brother's safe-keeping and his re-emergence as Hattusili's 'appointee' to the kingship of Tarhuntassa. (We shall follow this up in Chapter 10.) Of course, though this was a prestigious appointment, it fell well short of the Great Kingship of Hatti. As the son of Muwattalli, Kuruntiya had a legitimate claim to the throne, especially if his brother Urhi-Teshub was no longer in a position to reclaim it. But Kuruntiya seems not to have been a contender for the highest office in the land – at least not yet.

In any case, there's no doubt that Hattusili was determined to keep the succession in his own direct family line. First of all, he may have appointed as his successor Nerikkaili, perhaps his oldest son. His name commemorates Hattusili's reoccupation and restoration of Nerik, the most famous cult-centre of the Storm God. Nerikkaili appears in several documents with the title *tuḫkanti*, generally regarded as the title of the Crown Prince, and he seems to have played a prominent role in the kingdom's affairs. But his succession was not guaranteed, and he could be set aside in favour of another of the king's sons if circumstances warranted it.

And that is what happened when he was replaced by Tudhaliya, Nerikkaili's brother, or more precisely half-brother, as successor to the throne. (I am *assuming* that it was in fact Nerikkaili who preceded Tudhaliya as Crown Prince.) Tudhaliya had one distinct advantage over Nerikkaili, which put everything else in the shade. Nerikkaili was probably born before Hattusili met and married Puduhepa and was likely to be the son of a concubine, if Hattusili had no Chief Wife then.[23] Puduhepa assumed the role of Chief Wife of the king from the very outset of the royal marriage. The 'validity' of their offspring was beyond question, and Tudhaliya may well have been their first-born.[24] Whether or not he was, Hattusili set aside the heir presumptive and appointed Tudhaliya in his place.[25] No doubt he did so with no small urging from Puduhepa.

Let us remember that Puduhepa was many years younger than her husband, probably about twenty-five years younger, and could expect to outlive him by a significant margin, especially as his death seemed likely to be hastened by one or other of his illnesses. If so, she would as Chief Wife continue to reign over the royal household and exercise other important functions in the Hittite world at large, most notably the office of Chief Priestess of the realm. She had, in fact, enhanced the status of Chief Wife by becoming virtually her husband's partner in power. Their joint seals on the treaty concluded with Ramesses is just one example of this. If Nerikkaili had succeeded his father as king, her powers would theoretically remain unchanged. But recent history had demonstrated the toxicity that could blight the relationship between a king and his stepmother after his father's death, with the stepmother being the one to lose out – whether or not she deserved it. This is part of my thinking that Puduhepa may have played some role in her husband's decision to replace Nerikkaili with Tudhaliya as successor to the throne.

As far as we can tell, Nerikkaili, if he'd been the Crown Prince, accepted his loss of status with good grace. At least there is no reported evidence to the contrary. Indeed, he may not have wanted the job in the first place. But this is sheer speculation. He may well have felt aggrieved at being dumped from the succession. If so, Hattusili apparently decided not to tell us this, perhaps destroying any records that did. In any case, the discarded heir continued to serve his kingdom in a number of important civil and diplomatic roles, as well as cementing a major strategic alliance by marrying an important vassal ruler's daughter. Perhaps Nerikkaili was happy to accept his diminished role in the kingdom's affairs. But this is purely an argument from silence. Maybe there's a story behind all this we simply know nothing about.

The *Apology*'s ultimate purpose?

Once Hattusili had made the decision to appoint Tudhaliya as his heir, the timing of his announcement of it may have been of critical importance. This brings us back, once again, to the *Apology*. I've suggested that the document was intended primarily for an audience of the land's most important officials (though it may, of course, have been read out to a much wider audience as well) and then preserved on tablets of bronze as well as clay. The original was perhaps lodged in the king's mausoleum, referred to near the end of the document.[26] And we've already noted the likelihood that it was composed in the latter part of Hattusili's reign, at least some time after the Hittite-Egyptian 'Eternal Treaty'. By this time, all the events recorded in the document were well and long known and there was nothing new that it had to offer – except, I suggest, for its closing sections. These begin by announcing the dedication of the king's son Tudhaliya to the service of Ishtar: *I handed over to you as your servant my son Tudhaliya. Let him administer the house of Ishtar! I (am) the servant of the goddess. Let him be the servant of the goddess as well! ... Whoever in future opposes the son, grandson (or) offspring of Hattusili and Puduhepa, may he fear Ishtar of Samuha above (all) the (other) gods!*[27]

Muwattalli had dedicated his brother to Ishtar's service and, with her protection and guidance (according to him), he had risen to the highest office in the land and continued to prosper in the years to follow. Everything up to this point in the *Apology*, just before Hattusili's last words, serves as a reminder of what he had achieved throughout his life and career, from his illness-plagued childhood onwards. For this he gives all credit to Ishtar. The *Apology* is not so much a personal justification or celebration of his achievements, as a reminder of Ishtar's constant guidance and support that assured their attainment.

This prepares the way for the king's final declaration. Tudhaliya will now become Ishtar's chief representative, the 'administrator of her house'. He will be dedicated to her service and she will ensure his protection throughout his life just as she has protected, and continues to protect, his father. And, by the grace of the goddess, the succession is firmly implanted in their family line. It is now divinely sanctioned. To my way of thinking, the ultimate purpose of the document is here revealed. Muwattalli had dedicated his brother to Ishtar's service and, with her protection and guidance, he had risen to the highest office in the land. Now, Hattusili's closing words suggest, implicitly, that the dedication of his son Tudhaliya to the goddess's service will pave the way for *his* accession. Henceforth, the descendants of Hattusili and Puduhepa will be under the goddess's protection. In other words, Hattusili is preparing his subjects for the announcement of Tudhaliya as the new Crown Prince, thus confirming the retention of the royal succession within his direct family line.[28]

The reference to Ishtar of Samuha at the very end of the *Apology* is perhaps intended as a reminder of the fate of Urhi-Teshub whose capture in Samuha spelt the end of his kingship. But not of his determination to get his throne back. Hattusili's declaration of divine backing for himself and his successors may have convinced some of his subjects. But he still had enemies aplenty who were far from reconciled to his claim that the throne now belonged to the Hattusili-Puduhepa firm. And we haven't heard the last of Urhi-Teshub's brother Kuruntiya.

8

The Eternal Treaty

The Aftermath

It was afternoon on the second day. The heat was stifling, the stench intolerable, the air alive with the drone of millions of flies gorging on the banquet spread before them. The pharaoh, having declared himself the victor, had mustered what remained of his four army divisions and begun the long march back to his homeland. Left behind were those tasked with identifying and burying their comrades-in-arms. On a slightly elevated mound within the plain, the Great King Muwattalli, Commander-in-Chief of the Hittite army, stood with his brother surveying the scene. 'I think we won', he said as he watched the

Figure 8.1 The battle of Qadesh. Courtesy Tolga Örnek, from *The Hittites* (2003), [TV Programme] Dir. Tolga Örnek, Turkey: Ekip Film.

departing Egyptian troops. His brother gazed out over the blood-drenched plain, littered with the mutilated corpses of thousands of dead warriors, Hittite and Egyptian alike. Some had limbs hacked off, others had been impaled on spears, others lay crushed beneath the wreckage of overturned chariots. Some of the horses had yet to die, their limbs flailing in agony in their death throes. 'I think nobody won', said his brother.

Scuttling crablike amongst the bodies were dozens of gowned Egyptian tally clerks, totting up the numbers of their own and the enemy slain. Some carried bags which they filled with sliced-off enemy hands, to help verify the count – until they were driven from the field by furious fusillades of Hittite spears and arrows.

The new Hittite chariot technology had seemed so good in theory. Chariots designed to hold three men – a driver, a fighter with spears and arrows, and a shield-bearing defender of the driver and fighter. Surely more than a match for the two-crewed chariots that led the Egyptian forces into battle. And to begin with, it seemed to work. The sudden, chariot-led, Hittite charge had caught by surprise and almost broken apart the pharaoh's crack first division as it began setting up camp, near the field of battle and too far ahead of the other three Egyptian divisions for them to help repel the enemy attack. The pharaoh himself had come close to capture and death. Victory could have been so much more quickly achieved by Muwattalli's forces and their casualties so much lighter – but for the breakdown of discipline in the Hittite ranks as they exulted in a battle too easily won, diverted too readily by the prospect of the loot to be plundered from the enemy camp. The timely arrival of reinforcements for the pharaoh's beleaguered forces ensured that the battle had barely begun. And the three-man Hittite chariots proved too slow and too difficult to manoeuvre, toppling their crews who were then rapidly picked off by the archers of the lighter, faster and nimbler, two-man Egyptian vehicles.

All that day and the following morning, Hittites and Egyptians speared, hacked and fired their arrows into one another until exhaustion set in. Muwattalli proposed an end to the hostilities and Ramesses agreed. Though the pharaoh had finally gained the upper hand in the conflict, he had failed to take Qadesh. And it seemed there were hardly enough warriors left – on either side – for any more fighting. Both commanders may have claimed victory. But words similar to those uttered a thousand years later by the Greek king Pyrrhus as he surveyed his battle losses after defeating the Romans at Asculum (279 BC) might have passed through their minds: 'Another such victory . . . and we are undone.'

The battle had been fought primarily over two disputed territories: Amurru, a once (and probably still) bandit-infested land lying between the Orontes and the Mediterranean; and the tiny principality of Qadesh. Control over these territories had fluctuated between Hatti and Egypt. And, even if Ramesses had finally gained the upper hand in the conflict, Hatti was the ultimate victor since the pharaoh had tacitly ceded control over the contested territories to his arch enemy Muwattalli, 'the Fallen One of Hatti'. As the pharaoh's army retreated, Muwattalli's forces swept south, extending their conquests up to and including the Damascus region, formerly subject territory of the pharaoh.

Hattusili, king of the Hittite empire's northern realm, was the brother who stood alongside Muwattalli in my reconstruction of the battle's aftermath. He must have played a major role in the conflict, as leader of the troops he brought with him from his northern kingdom and of other troops assigned by Muwattalli to his command. No doubt his skills and experience as a seasoned warrior contributed significantly to any successes won by the Hittites in the battle itself. No doubt, too, he played a major role in consolidating Hittite rule over the territories won, or won back, from the pharaoh in the ultimate success of the campaign.

The curious absence of Qadesh from the *Apology*

I've referred to the Qadesh engagement at some length for the paradoxical reason that in his *Apology* Hattusili makes no mention of it. At least no direct mention. There is just a passing reference to 'the Egyptian campaign' and nothing at all about the principal battle of this campaign. Hattusili merely says: *Now when my brother went to Egypt, I led for him on campaign to Egypt the troops and chariots of those lands I had resettled, and I commanded the troops and chariots of the Land of Hatti under my charge in front of my brother.*[1] The showdown at Qadesh was undoubtedly the single most important event of the Hittite campaign against Egypt, indeed the prime reason for it. And in another text Hattusili claims his side won the battle. (More on this in the next chapter.) But nowhere in the *Apology* does he refer specifically to the Qadesh engagement, let alone a claimed Hittite victory. How do we explain this omission?

I believe it was deliberate and carefully considered, not just Hattusili passing rapidly and incompletely over an episode that he thought had little relevance to his main narrative. The large body of troops of which he had command – this much at least is evident from the *Apology* – almost certainly indicates the importance of his contribution to the campaign's crucial battle. Why did he not highlight this in his narrative, just as he highlighted other military achievements of his career? Distinguished performance at Qadesh would surely have helped consolidate his credibility and authority as a Hittite Great King.

I can think of several reasons for his downplaying the Egyptian episode. (And to misquote Groucho, if you don't like these, I have others.) Let me suggest one in particular. It has to do with diplomacy. If the document has been correctly assigned a date some time after the 'Eternal Treaty' was concluded, or even before then while negotiations were still underway, Hattusili apparently decided it was best not to reopen old wounds by any triumphalist assertions about the battle. Both sides had claimed victory and for a time there had been some acrimonious exchanges in correspondence between Hattusili, now Hatti's Great King, and Ramesses about which side had won. In one of his letters complaining that Ramesses had given Urhi-Teshub asylum in Egypt, Hattusili had made a veiled threat of military action if Urhi-Teshub wasn't extradited, rhetorically asking the pharaoh if he'd *forgotten the days of the enemies from the Land of Hatti*.[2] Ramesses could hardly mistake the inference. His correspondent was clearly referring to the Hittite claim of victory at Qadesh – and threatening Egypt with further military action if it held on to Urhi-Teshub. Of course, it was pure bluff, as both Hattusili and Ramesses well knew. But the pharaoh's pride was ruffled. He could hardly let the matter pass without a stinging rejoinder:

I penetrated, as a matter of fact, into the midst of the enemy from the Land of Hatti and struck the enemy, when the army of Muwattalli, King of the Land of Hatti, came together with the many lands that found themselves with him. . . . And the King of the Land of Hatti fell upon me with his army and all lands that were with him. But I brought about his defeat quite single-handed, although my army was not with me, and my chariots were not with me. And I led the enemy from these Lands of Hatti and brought them into the Land of Egypt.[3]

It was all very well for the pharaoh to try unruffling his pride with such a response. But resurrecting memories of the battle and claims of who won and who lost could have proved a serious obstacle to establishing a lasting peace between the two protagonists and former rivals for power in the Syrian region (Hattusili now taking his brother's place). Best to let the matter drop. And subsequent letters that passed between the royal courts maintained a 'Don't mention the war' silence about the conflict, as if both sides had tacitly agreed to refrain from any further reference to it.

Let me take this a step further. I think it likely that the pharaoh was one of the recipients of the *Apology* – that its author not only provided copies to all his leading officials, including his vice-regents, but also to his fellow Great Kings (in an Akkadian version, of course). I've already referred to Hattusili's eagerness to win diplomatic recognition from his peers. And this must have applied particularly to the pharaoh of Egypt, whose acceptance of him as the true Great King of Hatti counted most of all. Perhaps for his sake, in particular, Hattusili has considerably downplayed the Qadesh campaign, almost to the point of omitting it altogether.

But the campaign did not immediately end the threat Ramesses posed to Hatti's subject states in Syria. Not long afterwards, in the eighth and ninth years of his reign, the pharaoh conducted two further expeditions deep into the Orontes valley, to the north of Qadesh and up to the eastern frontier of Amurru. These campaigns placed virtually all the Hittites' Syrian territories at risk. Their timing might well have been prompted by news from Hattusa that the Hittite throne had suddenly been left vacant by the death of Muwattalli. And the replacement of the battle-hardened warrior-king by his young and probably inexperienced successor Urhi-Teshub may have induced the pharaoh to try his hand once more at extending Egyptian control over much of Syria, including Hatti's vassal states.

Yet, inexplicably, Ramesses did not follow up these campaigns. He once more withdrew from the north, so that Aba, the Damascus region, again became his northernmost Syrian possession. I should like to think that intensive Hittite diplomatic activity, in which Hattusili figured prominently, played some part in curbing the pharaoh's military ambitions in Syria. And perhaps the stream of correspondence between the royal courts of Egypt and Hatti, which began when Hattusili became Great King, did help reconcile Ramesses to the status quo in Syria after Qadesh. But, of course, the pharaoh's decision not to persist with his Syrian ventures may have been based on other factors of which we have no knowledge.

The 'Eternal Treaty'[4]

These events serve as a prelude to what we might consider the defining event of Hattusili's career: the conclusion of a treaty with Ramesses. The treaty was finalized in the year 1259 BC, fifteen years after Qadesh. There were two versions of it: one, an Egyptian version sent to Hattusa; the other, a Hittite version sent to Ramesses' capital Pi-Ramesse. Here is the preamble, translated into Akkadian, of the version sent by the pharaoh to Hattusa: *[The treaty which] Ramesses, [Beloved] of Amon, Great King, King [of Egypt, Hero, concluded] on [a tablet of silver] with Hattusili, [Great King], King of Hatti, his brother, in order to establish [great] peace and great [brotherhood] between them forever.*[5] Though the preamble's last words seem to limit the peace accord to the lifetimes of its signatories, it later becomes clear that the treaty is to remain in force during the reigns of the Great Kings' successors and thus have no time limit. Hence it is commonly referred to as the 'Eternal Treaty', because the Kingdoms did remain at peace 'forever' – until the collapse of the Hittite empire, just seven decades later.

The similarities between the different versions of the treaty on most matters, and despite some complexities in their relationship, indicate close collaboration between representatives of the Great Kings in drafting the treaty. There must have been much toing and froing by these representatives between the royal courts to present their respective Majesties with proposed amendments, additions to and deletions from the draft documents before final agreement was reached. After what may have been several years of negotiation and haggling, two independent versions of the treaty were prepared, one in the Egyptian court, one in the Hittite court. The Egyptian version was translated into Akkadian,[6] the international diplomatic language, and sent to Hattusa. Three fragmentary clay copies of this document were found in Hattusa's archives. The Hittite version, after being composed in the Hittite (strictly, Nesite) language, was translated into Akkadian, and then once more into Egyptian. This was the language used when it was carved in the Egyptian hieroglyphic script on the walls of the temple of Karnak and, in a more abbreviated form, on the Ramesseum, the temple of Ramesses.[7] Both temples are located near modern Luxor, ancient Thebes, Egypt's traditional capital.

So, the version of the treaty found in several fragments in Hattusa is a translation in Akkadian of the original Egyptian text; and the inscription carved in the Egyptian hieroglyphic script on the walls of two temples in Egypt is a translation, mostly, of the original Hittite text. In keeping with all this, I'll henceforth call the version found in Hattusa the 'Egyptian version', and the version carved on the temple walls in Egypt the 'Hittite' version. I hope this isn't confusing.

Engraved on silver

The final text of each version was inscribed on a tablet of silver, for presentation by the representatives of each Great King to his treaty partner. This no doubt occurred within the context of a major diplomatic mission from the Egyptian to the Hittite royal court and vice versa, accompanied by a rich array of gifts to demonstrate to the world how much the royal brothers esteemed and loved each other. (The value and nature of the gifts were likely to be carefully assessed and given the tick of approval before the diplomats who presented them, as part of the treaty package, were allowed to return home.) Metal seems to have been commonly used as the writing medium for the originals of important Hittite documents, like the biography of Hattusili's grandfather Suppiluliuma. Surviving now only on clay tablet fragments, the original of this document was inscribed on bronze tablets. (We learn this from information provided by one of the clay fragments.) And bronze was the metal used for inscribing a treaty between Hattusili's son and successor Tudhaliya and one of the Hittite viceroys, Kuruntiya, King of Tarhuntassa; the original bronze tablet has survived and is referred to a number of times in this book. Bronze was a prestigious writing material. But silver was a step above it and thus more appropriate for treaties between two Great Kings.

Hattusili may well have considered the conclusion of peace with Egypt his most important achievement as Hatti's Great King – and, if so, quite rightly so. Treaties on such an international scale were extremely rare in the Bronze Age. There was a painful reminder of an earlier Hittite-Egyptian treaty which Suppiluliuma had violated by attacking Egyptian subject territory. This was identified as one of the causes of the plague that devastated the land of Hatti for many years,[8] from the last days of the reign of Suppiluliuma, who himself fell victim to it along with his eldest son and first successor, Arnuwanda, and through much of the reign of his second successor Mursili. Hattusili had no intention of repeating his grandfather's mistake.

The presentation of the silver tablet at the Hittite royal court by a diplomatic mission from Egypt, with all the pomp and ceremony likely to surround such an event, would have helped underscore the importance of Hattusili's achievement in the eyes of his subjects. Many of these would still have had recollections of the heavy casualties inflicted on their fellow citizens at Qadesh just fifteen years earlier. And tensions had continued to simmer between the two kingdoms, erupting in occasional skirmishes with the prospect of escalating once more into a full-scale war. In fact, the likelihood of that happening was virtually zero. But fear and anxiety are powerful emotions often at odds with reality. These emotions could finally be set at rest. For now there was tangible evidence that there would be a lasting peace between the two great powers. The silver tablet stamped with the pharaoh's seal was a guarantee of this.

The Egyptian tablet on display?

But how could the tablet be effectively displayed? To be sure, many copies of it could be made on clay and widely distributed, with perhaps some copies being translated into Hittite. The latter might be despatched to the king's western vassal rulers, who had scribes able to read Hittite but not Akkadian. The upper echelons of the Hittite administration must all have become familiar with the treaty's contents, and perhaps public readings of the document were presented to gatherings of all the king's subjects.

But what about the original? Where was it displayed? I cannot imagine that it was simply squirrelled away in the palace or temple archives, occasionally to be retrieved and dusted off when the king or some authorized official wanted to see it. Viewing the real thing would have had much greater impact than merely seeing a copy of it (think Magna Carta, a first folio Shakespeare etc.), and this must have required it to be on regular, if not constant, display, even if only for a small number of privileged viewers. Where was this display likely to have been? To judge by other tablets, notably the Bronze Tablet, whose dimensions are 35 by 23.5 centimetres, it was only a small object, about one-and-a-half times the size of this book. You could easily hold it in the palm of your hand (if you have a large hand). How do you make such a small object, even one fashioned from silver, visually impressive enough to reflect its enormous international significance? The answer has to be by the context you provide for it.

I have in my mind's eye an image of a small chamber deep within the labyrinthine complex of Hattusa's Great Temple. The archive rooms of the temple contain many treaties – originals, copies, drafts – concluded mainly between Hatti's Great Kings and their vassal rulers. They are systematically shelved and catalogued for easy retrieval whenever there is a need for consulting them. But the tablet inscribed with this treaty is special. The chamber where it is housed is a sanctuary, dedicated to the gods by whom the treaty's signatories have sworn oaths to uphold its provisions. These oath-gods will ensure that the provisions are honoured for all time – and that any who violate them will suffer dire punishments. Maybe hymns to the oath-gods and the signatories' chief deities are recorded on tablets there, or inscribed on the sanctuary's walls. Maybe ritual sacrifices are offered there. But the sanctuary is largely bare, save for its centrepiece. This is the silver tablet, suspended at eye-level on two silver chains above a bronze plinth, centrally located so that both sides of it can easily be seen and read. Its polished surfaces gleam amidst the

tiny fountains of oil-fuelled light encircling it, giving it a radiance that makes it stand out against the sanctuary's darkened surrounds.

How close were the two versions of the treaty?

I shan't speculate on where the silver tablet sent to Egypt from Hattusa was located, because that is largely irrelevant. It's made so by the fact that the Hittite version of the treaty was carved on the walls of two temples for everyone to see. It's our good fortune that the temple of the god Amun at Karnak in Thebes contains a complete translation of the Hittite version (and a bit more besides) and is the one we'll be referring to here. Inevitably, the passage of the Hittite version through three languages (Hittite → Akkadian → Egyptian) has resulted in minor changes to some of its clauses, and there are a few small differences in perspective between the two versions.[9] But overall, the two versions show little variation. The Hittite version carved on the Egyptian temple walls has, in fact, proved very useful for filling in a number of gaps in the fragmentary Egyptian (the Akkadian-translated) version found in Hattusa. We can thus add to the Egyptian version the treaty's preamble, its final sections listing the curses and blessings imposed or bestowed upon those who violate or honour the treaty, and a description of the seals of the Hittite signatories, Hattusili and his Chief Wife Puduhepa; these, the Hittite version tells us, were stamped upon the silver tablet sent to Egypt.

The one major difference between the two versions is that the Hittite one inscribed in Egyptian hieroglyphs contains an introductory section which has no counterpart in the Egyptian version sent to Hattusa. This was clearly added to the Hittite text by Ramesses *after* the original had been agreed to by both negotiating parties and signed off by Hattusili and Puduhepa. Now, introductory sections quite commonly preface Hittite vassal treaties, often to provide historical context for the treaties; sometimes they praise a vassal ruler for his past loyalty, sometimes they remind him of one or more of his predecessors' violations of their obligations, and the Great King's benevolence in forgiving them. The vassal rulers had no say in the terms and conditions of the treaties imposed upon them by their overlord. But treaties between royal peers required agreement to all their provisions by both parties. Yet Ramesses had composed an introductory section for the Egyptian translation of the treaty's Hittite version, *apparently* on his own initiative and without his royal brother's consent. He then had it carved in stone on the temple walls before his royal brother could do anything about it, even if he ever knew about it.

To be fair to Ramesses, the usual pharaonic display of hyper-inflated rhetoric is reasonably muted in his add-on introduction. Even so, it's not without a large dollop of pharaonic self-glorification, with a claim of pharaonic supremacy over all foreign countries (including Hatti, by implication).[10] If Hattusili had been given the chance, he would no doubt have objected to the whole section and demanded its removal. He would certainly have objected strongly to one sentence, in particular, if it has been correctly interpreted: that the treaty process had been initiated by him when he sent his envoy to the pharaoh *to beg for peace*.[11] A statement like this would have gone down well with the pharaoh's subjects; the Great King of Hatti was presented as a *supplicant* for peace rather than as the pharaoh's equal partner in establishing the accord. But we may be doing Ramesses an injustice. It's a matter of nuance. The statement could mean that Hattusili *requested* a formal treaty rather than *begged* for one.[12] And it is indeed very likely that Hattusili did take the initiative in setting the peace process in motion.

An endorsement of Hattusili's successor

Both versions of the treaty contain standard and near-identical non-aggression clauses, guaranteeing that the treaty partners will remain at peace with each other. Then follow 'defensive alliance' clauses, in which each partner promises to provide military aid to the other, in the event of an attack on it by a third party. This applies to both external and internal enemies, the latter including rebel uprisings by a treaty partner's own subjects. Such clauses are standard fare in a treaty. But then comes an interesting extra provision in the Akkadian text found in Hattusa (a reminder that this is the Egyptian version of the treaty) to which there is no corresponding clause in the Egyptian hieroglyphic text, that is to say, the Hittite version.[13] This provision confirms the succession of Hattusili's son after his father's death and commits the pharaoh to sending him military aid in the event of an 'offence' by any of his own subjects against him. Ironically, the Egyptian version preserves this stipulation, but the Hittite version does not. Was it mistakenly omitted when the text was copied onto the temple walls? Or was the omission deliberate?

The death of a Hittite king frequently resulted in a period of instability before his successor was firmly installed on his throne. But Hattusili may well have feared – and with good reason – that retention of the succession in his direct family line was far from secure. At the time of the treaty, his reign was less than two decades old, and memories of his illegal seizure of the throne remained fresh in the minds of his adversaries. Especially those members of the extended royal family whose long-standing hostility to the usurper did not diminish with the passing years. And the righful king Urhi-Teshub, who was still entitled to his throne-name Mursili, remained at large, having eluded all attempts to capture him.

There was, besides, his brother Kuruntiya, vice-regent of the kingdom of Tarhuntassa. Kuruntiya had been a loyal *protégé* of Hattusili his uncle, and had developed a warm friendship with Tudhaliya his cousin, Hattusili's son. But how tempting would a bid for Great Kingship be if the Hittite throne suddenly became vacant? Hattusili was after all now in his mid-fifties – old for that time – and a chronic sufferer of ill health. The throne was an increasingly faint heartbeat away (or so it seemed) from becoming vacant.

Of course, Ramesses' ability to provide timely military support to Hattusili's appointed successor if suddenly called upon was virtually zero. By the time any such support could be mustered, even if Ramesses ever had the slightest intention of mustering it, a coup and all the consequential blood-spilling would be well and truly done with before Egyptian military support could get within weeks of the royal capital. The clause in question was purely symbolic. It did little more than provide the pharaonic stamp of approval to the right of royal succession by Hattusili's son and descendants. This on its own may have helped consolidate support, at least among Hatti's elite elements, for the *permanent* shift of the succession to Hattusili's direct family line. Ramesses had already endorsed Hattusili as the rightful king of Hatti, probably not long after his accession. The treaty took this endorsement a step further. The pharaoh was now acknowledging the right of Hattusili's descendants to sit upon the throne of Hatti forever.

The extradition of fugitives

A relatively large part of the treaty is devoted to the extradition of fugitives from the territory of one kingdom to the other. The provisions are mostly confined either to single fugitives or to groups of two or three. One clause in the Egyptian version, however, raises the possibility of a mass movement of refugees from Egypt to the land of Amurru in Syria, then under Hittite control.[14] In this case, the treaty stipulates, the king of Amurru must pack the fugitives off to his sovereign lord in Hattusa, who will return them to the pharaoh. (It seems a rather roundabout way of doing things.)

Though these clauses deal purely with hypothetical instances, and such extradition clauses are standard in Hittite vassal treaties, the treaty partners almost certainly had specific cases in mind when the treaty was drawn up. During the time Amurru was under Egyptian control, part of its population may have been forcibly transplanted to Egypt, especially a part that rebelled against Egyptian rule and fought for their country's independence. Then permanently resettled in Egypt, they may well have sought to escape their bondage and return to their own country. It would now be incumbent upon Hattusili and Benteshina, his subject ruler in Amurru, to help put a stop to this. Perhaps for this reason the relevant clause in the treaty was inserted at the pharaoh's demand.

This is just a suggestion, with no surviving historical episode to back it up. On the other hand, the clauses referring to the extradition of individuals, whether of high or low status, were almost certainly initiated by Hattusili with a specific case in mind: the flight of Urhi-Teshub from his place of exile in Syria. As we've already noted, Urhi-Teshub had no intention of fading into obscurity. From the time of his overthrow and banishment, he was determined to get his throne back. He remained a constant threat to his successor by seeking support for his restoration from the kings of Assyria and Babylon and, especially, from the pharaoh when he fled Hittite territory to Egypt. Here he almost certainly sought asylum with Ramesses and was granted it for a time – to Hattusili's (and Puduhepa's) fury. If he were still in Egypt when the treaty was finalized and he could be caught, the pharaoh would be bound to extradite him. Very likely, he had left Egypt by then. He was still somewhere at large, but no longer the pharaoh's problem.

A wishful piece of ideology

I mentioned in the Introduction that the replica of a large fragment of the treaty sent to Hattusa was set up outside one of the entrances to the UN Security Council Chamber in New York City. It remains on display there as a symbol of peace among the nations of the world for all time. This wishful piece of ideology goes well beyond the purpose of the original treaty. Though declarations of eternal peace and brotherhood figure prominently in the early sections of the document, in its actual details it is mainly concerned with establishing a mutual defence alliance between two major Bronze Age powers, against either a foreign aggressor or local uprisings within one or the other's kingdom. As its extradition clauses also indicate, the treaty is essentially a series of pragmatic agreements between Hattusili and Ramesses, totally devoid of any broadly-based ideology of peace encompassing all peoples and nations for all time. It's as much about war as it is about peace – an almost Orwellian concept.

What were the treaty's real aims?

So, what really was in it for each of the treaty partners? I've already suggested that it provided pharaonic endorsement for the Hittite royal succession in Hattusili's family line. Given the Hittite populace's apparent acceptance that there was only one dynasty from which its kings would be drawn, any dissent over who actually occupied the throne was largely confined to members of the extended royal family and those upon whose support they could call. In such elite circles, the backing of the pharaoh for an incumbent and his appointed successor probably carried no small weight.

More importantly, Hattusili was faced with the constant prospect that tensions with Egypt, if left unresolved, could escalate once more into full-scale war. To what extent did the loss of Qadesh, and particularly Amurru, rankle in the pharaoh's mind? Should he assemble another large army from the millions of subjects at his disposal and march north to retake these states? And perhaps much more of Hittite-controlled Syrian territory besides? If he did, Hattusili knew he no longer had anywhere near sufficient resources to mount an effective resistance. Besides, he needed to preserve what resources he did have to deal with mounting problems in the west; and even more threateningly from across the Euphrates. A treaty with Ramesses would ease his fears, at least for the time being.

So what was in it for Ramesses? Not a great deal, first impressions might indicate. I've suggested that, if Hattusili initiated the peace accord, Ramesses could extract some propaganda value from it by representing the Hittite as a mendicant suing for peace. This would confirm Ramesses' boast that he had won the battle of Qadesh. But, as a whole, he does not use the treaty for anti-Hittite propaganda purposes. The truth probably is that because of other interests and concerns, like his massive building projects and his problems with enemies further up the Nile and either side of it, he had lost interest in his Syrian ventures; he was content to leave Aba, the region of which Damascus was the main urban centre, as the northern limit of Egyptian subject territory. The treaty would help quell any ambitions Hattusili's successors might have to push Hittite territory further south, unlikely though such ambitions were.

And now we must consider the elephant in the room. I am not the first to suggest this, but a likely incentive for both sides to formalize a defensive alliance was the emergent power across the Euphrates, the kingdom of Assyria in northern Mesopotamia. Assyria had quickly occupied the vacuum left by Suppiluliuma's destruction of the Mittanian empire, swallowing up the remnants of the empire, some of which had been for a time ruled by Hittite-controlled puppet-kings, and extending its rule all the way to the Euphrates. The weakly defended Hittite territories across the river offered a tempting prize for a line of aggressive Assyrian kings, from Adad-nirari I (c. 1295–1264 BC) onwards. If, after winning control of all territories in northern Mesopotamia east of the Euphrates, the Assyrians turned their attention westwards, they might easily sweep up the Hittite subject states in northern Syria, and then set their sights on Egyptian territories in southern Syria and Palestine. Perhaps this was an important reason for the Hittite-Egyptian defensive alliance – to present a united front against an Assyrian threat. In this respect, at least, the treaty would have had more than symbolical value. And, just as in modern times when an alliance is concluded between two or more partners in response to a perceived threat from a specific but unnamed enemy, so, too, no reference is made to any such enemy in the Hittite-Egyptian treaty. An alliance of limitless duration may well be prompted by a specific threat but, for diplomatic reasons, and to cover future eventualities, no reference is made in the treaty to a particular enemy.

As it happened, the Assyrian king of the time, the highly aggressive Tukulti-Ninurta, conducted no known military operations west of the Euphrates but turned his attention southwards to the kingdom of Babylon and to a series of campaigns against the Babylonian king, Kashtiliash IV. Hatti and Egypt were thus spared any confrontations with Assyria. Could an important reason for the Assyrian's decision to refrain from campaigns across the Euphrates be this: he considered the risks of all-out conflict with the treaty partners' combined forces too great to be sustainable?

But let me return for a moment to my imagined scenario at the beginning of this chapter. Egyptian records provide us with a few scant pieces of information about those killed at Qadesh, most of them high-ranking officers. Professor Kenneth Kitchen notes that the losses included two of Muwattalli's own brothers, two of his shield-bearers, his secretary, his chief of the bodyguard, four leading charioteers, and six army chiefs of some rank, besides general casualties.[15] We do not know the identities of the Hittite princes killed at Qadesh. Perhaps they were sons of Mursili's second wife Danuhepa and, thus, stepbrothers of Muwattalli and Hattusili. But perhaps the Egyptians simply got this part of their record wrong.

In any case, those who could be identified were just a small part of the horror of the Qadesh encounter, which must have deeply affected even a seasoned warrior like Hattusili. Many among the dead may have been close to him, maybe his long-time comrades-in-arms who had trained with him to become officers, some of them charioteers; others may have been soldiers of lesser rank who had long served him in campaigns in his northern kingdom. Perhaps there were many others, too, but now so badly mutilated by enemy weapons, or by the vast horde of carrion-eaters who feasted upon them, that they were no longer recognizable. Perhaps then and there, as Hattusili surveyed the bloodsoaked, corpse-littered field of Qadesh, he resolved that, whatever his future held in store for him, an enduring peace with Egypt must be one of his primary goals.

9

The Royal Mail

The hazards of travel

You wrote to me, my brother, that you have stopped sending your messengers because the Ahlamu are hostile. What sort of excuse is that? Is your kingdom so weak that you cannot deal with the Ahlamu yourself? Did you expect me to send a thousand chariots to ward off the Ahlamu and meet your messengers in Tuttul?[1] If you then say that the king of Assyria won't allow your messengers to pass through his land, what about your military forces? His infantry and chariotry are surely no match to yours.[2]

These words bring us back to Hattusili's letter to the young Babylonian king Kadashman-Enlil, scornfully dismissing the Babylonian's excuses for failing to maintain written communications with Hattusa. I mentioned this briefly in Chapter 7. Let me now focus on some important practical questions this passage raises. How were letters actually transported between the royal courts? What were the logistics involved? And what were the risks? Answers to these questions, if we can come up with them, will provide some useful background to the letters Hattusili and other members of his family exchanged with their correspondents in Babylon, Egypt and other parts of the Bronze Age world.

Let's begin by considering Kadashman-Enlil's reasons for suspending travel by his messengers to Hattusa. The Ahlamu were predatory tribal groups in Syria and Mesopotamia who often attacked and robbed hapless travellers or travelling bands in the desert regions west of the Euphrates. It made no difference if the travellers were messengers 'On His Majesty's Service', on their way from one royal court to another. A later Assyrian king, Tiglath-pileser I (1114–1076 BC), tells us he crossed the Euphrates no fewer than twenty-eight times in pursuit of the Ahlamu for interfering in his kingdom's affairs. But, even apart from the Ahlamu, many sparsely inhabited regions claimed as subject territory by one Great Kingdom or another were dangerous areas to traverse. So royal messengers needed an adequate armed escort to ensure that their mailbags eventually reached their destination. That is implied in Hattusili's dismissive comments to Kadashman-Enlil. Theoretically, travel to Hattusa via Assyria would have been a quicker and safer option than a route that took messengers partly through desert territory across the Euphrates. But relations between Assyria and Babylon were never very peaceful, and not long after Hattusili's reign they erupted into open war when the Assyrian king Tukulti-Ninurta invaded and occupied his southern neighbour. It was hardly likely Assyria would allow an armed Babylonian force, even a small one, to pass through its territory en route to Hattusa.

The size of a delegation with letters for His Majesty and often other members of his family must have varied considerably. At the high end of the scale, we can place major diplomatic missions, headed by the king's personal representatives who had important business to transact with their sovereign's royal brother. A large array of gifts might accompany such missions, sometimes including sacks or crates of gold bars. We learn a great deal about these missions from the international correspondence of the Amarna letters. Found at the site of Akhetaten (modern el-Amarna) in middle Egypt, they date to the mid-fourteenth-century reigns of Amenhotep III and Amenhotep IV (Akhenaten).[3] Such missions must have been escorted by small armies, for protection against bands of brigands who swooped upon vulnerable travelling groups and sometimes plundered whole towns.[4] Even delegations on a mission from one Great King to another, and bearing His Majesty's royal warrant, had no guarantee of their safety unless they had strong armed protection throughout their journey.

Sometimes, perhaps, even that was not enough. This brings to mind one of the most famous – and infamous – episodes in Hittite history. It has to do with Hattusili's grandfather Suppiluliuma. He'd been persuaded by the widow of a recently deceased pharaoh[5] to send one of his sons to Egypt to marry her. (Egypt's most distinguished diplomat Hani had been sent to Hattusa with a letter from the royal widow reassuring Suppiluliuma of the genuineness of her marriage invitation and rebuking him for his suspicions in thinking otherwise.) No doubt the wedding party that set off from Hattusa, protected by a large bodyguard, took with it an impressive array of fine gifts. But the bridegroom-to-be was killed before he reached Egypt. Suppiluliuma blamed his death on Egyptian treachery and terrible consequences followed.[6] But Egypt's guilt was never proved, and I suspect that the wedding party was ambushed somewhere along the way by a large band of outlaws, who killed the prince after overwhelming his escort and made off with the royal gifts. No doubt there was also a diplomatic pouch with letters for the widow and other members of her inner circle. These were probably cast aside by the robbers and have long since crumbled into dust.

Diplomatic missions

I imagine that Hattusili considered his long and wide-ranging letter to Kadashman-Enlil important enough to have it presented at the Babylonian court by his top diplomat, and no doubt it was accompanied by a rich assortment of gifts for His Majesty. He was, after all, seeking some favours in return – above all, openly expressed recognition from his royal brother as the true Great King of Hatti. There is much we learn from this letter. Not only about the relations between Hatti, Assyria, Babylon and Egypt at the time the letter was written, but also about the diplomatic skills Hattusili was beginning to display in winning acceptance from his peers as the rightful king of Hatti, and in helping maintain a peaceful equilibrium between the great powers of the age.

The business side of these delegations, either before or after a pomp-and-ceremony reception and several days of feasting, probably began with the presentation to the host-king of a letter from his royal brother. It would have been delivered by the visiting chief envoy in the audience chamber of the royal palace. The 'Thus says' and 'Say to' formulaic expressions with which such letters begin indicate that their bearer is merely the conveyor of their own king's words, and let us know, if taken literally, that the letters are read aloud to their recipient.

Letters to Hittite kings from international correspondents were written and spoken in Akkadian, with interpreters on hand to translate them into Hittite. Hittite versions of these letters were inscribed on tablets, to be stored in the royal archives. But, before this, the interpreters would have to testify to an exact correspondence between the written and spoken versions. So, the deliverer of a letter would be expected to learn it by heart, word for word. The so-called 'Tawagalawa letter', written by Hattusili to his Ahhiyawan (Greek) counterpart (see Chapter 12), suggests that, if he altered in any way what his king had actually said, his head would be lopped off.[7] But I very much doubt that this was a serious threat to a kingdom's most distinguished diplomats, even in the unlikely event that they accidentally got a word or two wrong. Of course, deliberate falsification was another matter. And that may be what the passage in the 'Tawagalawa letter' is concerned about.

Travel times

A full-scale diplomatic mission from one royal court to another could take up to three months, or possibly more, depending on weather conditions, road conditions, topographical obstacles, detours to avoid confrontations with bandit groups rumoured to be in the region at the time, the size and nature of the gift consignment, and so on. Thus, such a mission despatched by Ramesses from his capital Pi-Ramesse to Hattusa might have taken two to three months to reach its Hittite destination.[8] So, an enterprise on this scale must have been limited to special events, like the ones we've talked about above. But exchanges of letters, particularly between the Hittite and Egyptian courts leading up to the 'Eternal Treaty', and the royal marriage that followed thirteen years later, must have been much more frequent. In fact, a large number of (generally now fragmentary) letters that passed between the two royal courts, especially those of Hattusili and Ramesses, have been found in the archives of Hattusa. Disappointingly, only one tiny fragment of one letter from this correspondence has survived in Egypt.[9]

Despite the fragmentary nature of much of the correspondence, enough has survived to provide us with important information about Hittite-Egyptian relations. They also give us some flashes of insight into the personal attributes and emotions of their authors – something the great bulk of bureaucratic documents from the official archives cannot do. Of course, because of the constant flow of correspondence between the two royal houses, only the most important letters could have been part of a full-scale diplomatic mission. And that brings us to the lower end of our scale of royal messengers.

The royal postmen

Runners were used as letter-carriers or couriers for short distances, sometimes relays of runners for longer distances. I imagine that two or three runners might have been used for the regular conveyance of bulletins between Hattusili's great-grandfather Tudhaliya III and the king's chief officials in the homeland's administrative centres – like Sapinuwa, which lay sixty kilometres from the capital, and four or more runners to cover the distance between Hattusa and Tapikka, another important administrative centre located almost twice that distance from Hattusa.[10] Alternatively, letter-bearers might have travelled by horse from sender to recipient,[11] which would ensure that the mail reached its destination the same day it was sent.

I think it most unlikely that foot-runners were used for international mail deliveries – from one Great Kingdom to another. More likely, horses were the prime means of transport used by messengers who served as long-distance postmen on royal mail runs. In this case, staging posts would have been established along routes travelled by couriers from the Egyptian to the Hittite royal court and back again. (So, too, for any of the international mail services between other royal courts.) With regular changes of horses and horsemen, the distance from Pi-Ramesse, Ramesses' capital, to Hattusa could probably have been covered within four to five weeks – barring misfortunes or forced detours from regular routes.

But it is inconceivable that these messengers would have travelled on their own – like the pony express riders of other places in later times. Parts of the journey would inevitably have taken them through areas close to bandit lairs, particularly if they travelled by the shortest rather than the safest routes possible. Even the humblest lone traveller foolish enough to venture into bandit territory ran the risk of being attacked, stripped of his clothes and anything else worth taking, and probably left for dead. And a messenger travelling between royal courts would have been a lucrative prize. Apart from the mail, bundled up in wicker or wooden containers, the horse's saddle-packs must have included substantial travel funds, for food and lodging along the way, fodder and stables for the horses, and bribes for rapacious local officials. Sometimes the packs may also have contained small gifts for the royal recipient and members of his family. It would have been almost impossible for a royal messenger to reach his destination if he travelled alone, without an armed escort to deter attacks by outlaws, and to reinforce refusals to pay the excessive 'tolls' demanded by mayors of towns through which they passed. All this must have taken a fair amount of organization by the royal houses or their representatives, and involved no small costs. But a regular mail service between two Great Kingdoms in addition to diplomatic missions was essential to maintaining harmonious, constructive relations between their royal courts. We have noted Hattusili's protest at Kadashman-Enlil's failure to maintain regular mail contact with him, by discontinuing his messenger service, and his scornful dismissal of the Babylonian's excuses for doing so.

Messengers who were no more than letter-bearers were probably relieved of the letters, and any gifts that accompanied them, at a palace's delivery entrance, and then assigned servants' quarters within the palace precincts, until His Majesty gave them leave to return home, with a fresh batch of letters in reply to those he and other members of his family had received. We've noted that the letters exchanged by the royal courts would have been written in Akkadian, requiring the services of interpreters to read them out, translating them into their recipients' own language as they did so. I suspect that Hattusili, and probably Puduhepa as well, were conversant with at least spoken Akkadian, and would thus have no need of interpreters. Probably, too, the royal couple could actually read for themselves the letters addressed to them. But diplomatic protocol, no doubt, still required official interpreters for inter-court communications. I've suggested that Hattusili learned literacy as a child and young adult, while serving as a temple priest for the goddess Ishtar or fulfilling his obligations to her in other ways. Letters he received from his royal brothers in Egypt or Babylon or Assyria could be pondered at his leisure, read and reread by him as he prepared his responses. He may even have written draft replies himself, as a basis for the final versions written up by one of his senior scribes. Perhaps the angry draft of Puduhepa's letter to Ramesses (see Chapter 6) can be explained in the same way.

The personalities behind the diplomatic masks

One of the interesting features of the correspondence passing between the courts of Hattusili and Ramesses is the habit the chief correspondents sometimes have of quoting or referring directly to passages from a letter their royal brother has sent them and responding precisely to what he has said. In other words, 'This is what you said in your letter . . ., and here is my response . . .'. This was a convenient means of highlighting specific issues of concern to the recipient. It ensured that responses to claims made by the writer of the original letter were given appropriate emphasis, often by way of a firm denial of these claims. It also helped ensure that there was no misunderstanding of what the letter's author had actually written. This was an important safeguard against mistranslation when the letter had to be translated from Akkadian into the recipient's own language; and the response written originally in the recipient's language had then to be translated back into Akkadian.

All this is very handy for the modern reader. Think about it for a moment. We have no pairs of letters; that is to say, we don't have both an original letter and the one sent in reply. But the practice of a letter's recipient quoting or referring to a particular passage from the original and reacting with a specific response enables us to create elements of a dialogue between sender and recipient – as if they were actually talking to each other. An example of this is a heated exchange between Ramesses and Hattusili over the whereabouts of Urhi-Teshub. (See below.)

Beyond the letters' formalities, we sometimes get glimpses of their authors' personal attributes and emotions, particularly what stirs them to anger. Just bare glimpses, but more than we learn about them as human beings from most of their other records, either inscribed on tablet or carved on stone. The letters are one-to-one communications, in which formal diplomatic language is sometimes set aside for more personally revealing words. Puduhepa's letter which we talked about in Chapter 6 illustrates the fury of which Puduhepa was capable in her reaction to Ramesses' letter complaining about her delay in sending him a bride. We've also seen in this letter her sneers at Ramesses' alleged lies concerning Urhi-Teshub's whereabouts, and her gibes at the pharaoh's greed in apparently showing more interest in the bride's dowry than in the bride herself. Of course, we should remember that we have only a draft of her letter, and she may have moderated some of what she said before the final version was consigned to the diplomatic pouch.

Hattusili, too, was prone to angry outbursts, as illustrated by his reaction to Ramesses' claim that Urhi-Teshub was not, or was no longer, in Egypt. This we learn from one of the pharaoh's letters, in which he responds to yet another Hittite demand that he track the fugitive down in his own land and extradite him. Once more refusing to accept that Urhi-Teshub is anywhere in Egypt, Ramesses suggests that he is back in Hittite territory – maybe in Aleppo or Qadesh in Syria, maybe in Kizzuwatna in southeastern Anatolia. Maybe the rulers of one of these lands was giving him asylum.[12] Outwardly, he gives the impression he's just trying to be helpful. But his words are no more than thinly veiled sarcasm, intended to humiliate. An infuriated Hattusili flatly denies that the fugitive is *anywhere* in his own lands. If he were, then his subjects would have told him! 'Your subjects are not to be trusted', sniffs the pharaoh in reply.

Ramesses' specific responses to what Hattusili had written to him thus enable us to recreate a small piece of 'verbal' interaction between the pair – as if they were actually talking to each other. But let me once more sound a word of warning. The letters exchanged between the royal families are often fragmentary, and much of the information we derive from them is based on our attempts to fill in the gaps. In our main source for these letters, the monumental two-volume edition of Egyptian-Hittite correspondence published by the German scholar Elmar Edel, the author carefully indicates with square brackets what parts of a letter are purely his restorations. At times these restorations seem soundly based. At other times they are no more than guesses – some of which Itamar Singer describes as 'audacious'. I shall do my best to avoid the 'audacious' ones.

Reading between the lines of their letters, we can reasonably assume that, despite their mutual formulaic expressions of brotherly love, Hattusili and Ramesses did not much like or trust each other, at least up until the time of the peace accord and probably even after that. And from Puduhepa's draft letter to Ramesses, there's no doubt that the Hittite queen shared her husband's feelings. Their accusations that the pharaoh was harbouring Urhi-Teshub, or at least knew where he could be found, may well have had some basis in truth and impeded the peace process, even after the treaty had been concluded. We don't know how long Urhi-Teshub remained at large, or if indeed he was ever taken back into Hittite custody. There is a story that he had eluded his Egyptian pursuers by escaping back into Hittite territory where he was captured by his cousin Nerikkaili; but Nerikkaili had the misfortune to die before he managed to inform his father that Urhi-Teshub was now his prisoner; Urhi-Teshub seized the opportunity to bribe his guards and was soon once more on the loose. This has the makings of an exciting tale of derring-do. Sadly, it's based on a number of 'audacious restorations' by Professor Edel in his translation of a letter from Ramesses to Hattusili.[13]

The pharaonic endorsement

In another example of the continuing Urhi-Teshub saga, Kupanta-Kuruntiya, who ruled the large, Hittite, vassal state Mira in western Anatolia, wrote to the pharaoh after Urhi-Teshub's overthrow apparently asking whether he supported the coup and Hattusili's subsequent treatment of his dethroned predecessor.[14] The letter from Mira has not survived, but we know what it was about from Ramesses' reply. Now, whether or not Kupanta-Kuruntiya thought he was acting in his new sovereign's interests in writing to Ramesses, he was clearly in serious breach of diplomatic protocol. The vassal ruler of a Great King should *never* write directly to another Great King, regardless of what his motives were. And Ramesses cleverly exploited the opportunity this offered for yet again humiliating his royal brother – and being quite disingenuous about it.

In his reply, he expressed his unconditional support for Hattusili as the Great King of Hatti, and for the action he'd taken against Urhi-Teshub, dismissing any rumours about a conspiracy to set him up as ruler in Hatti or anywhere else: *What have I done? Where would I recognize Urhi-Teshub (as ruler)? . . . Have my lips articulated plots? [The word] which men speak to you is worthless. Do not trust it. I am happily in brotherhood and happily [at peace] forever with the Great King* (i.e. Hattusili), *the King of Hatti, my brother*.[15] His letter was addressed to

Kupanta-Kuruntiya, but sent to Hattusa, presumably in the 'diplomatic pouch'. And Hattusa was where it ended up. (It was found in excavations there.)

The pharaoh must have known that Hattusili would read the letter before forwarding it to its addressee. But obviously he had not forwarded it, and Ramesses probably never believed he would. (Alternatively, he *did* forward the letter to make clear to his vassal that Ramesses backed the new regime in Hattusa and doubtless rebuked him for his breach of protocol; he would have had a copy of the letter made for possible future reference.) There was in fact nothing in the letter that was not supportive of Hattusili and his right to the Hittite throne. And nothing whatever that was supportive of Urhi-Teshub. Hattusili's embarrassment lay in the fact that one of his own vassal rulers had communicated with the pharaoh at all, let alone sought his advice on his own overlord's claim to the throne and his treatment of the man he overthrew. That must have rankled more than anything else, certainly in Hattusili's mind, and no doubt also in Puduhepa's.

Whether he liked it or not, Ramesses' endorsement was extremely important to Hattusili – though not through one of his vassals acting as an intermediary. But so long as Urhi-Teshub remained at large, and allegedly in Egypt as Ramesses' *protégé*, Hattusili could not be sure what the pharaoh's ultimate intentions were. He wanted unequivocal recognition from him as the true Great King of Hatti. And Ramesses gave him the assurances he sought. He does so in at least two of the letters he wrote to him, indignantly rejecting his royal brother's complaint that he'd written to him as though he were a mere servant.

Here is my reconstruction of the pharaoh's response to this complaint. It is based on the relevant parts of the remains of two of Ramesses' letters and is not a word-for-word translation of them:

That I would have written to you as to a servant from amongst my servants is simply not true! Have you not received the kingship, and did I not know this? Was it not in my heart? You are a Great King in the Hatti Lands! You are a Hero in all lands! The Sun God and the Storm God have granted that you exercise kingship in the Hatti lands in the place of your grandfather. You must not think that I would have written to you as to a servant. The words you should be writing to me are 'May your heart be full of joy every day', not these empty, baseless words! Thus, I speak to my brother. It is because of the warm relationship we have established between us that I have said these words.[16]

Despite the indignant, mildly patronizing tone of these words, they clearly and unequivocally endorsed Hattusili's official status as Hatti's rightful Great King.

Ramesses might well have been regarded as the *de facto* senior member of the 'Club of Royal Brothers'. If so, his support for Hattusili was all the more important – particularly since, if it was made widely known (as no doubt it was), it must have helped consolidate Hattusili's status among his own subjects. And it would surely provide valuable additional confirmation of this status with his royal peers across the Euphrates.

But a number of jarring issues continued to surface in the correspondence between the Hittite and Egyptian royal courts. Amongst these, Urhi-Teshub's alleged defection to Egypt seems to have been a constant irritant. It had probably begun not long after the dethroned king had fled his place of exile in Syria. Unfortunately, we cannot say how long his escapades both in and out of Egypt lasted, nor do we know much about the escapades themselves. Conflicting claims about the outcome of the Qadesh engagement was another contentious issue. But, while Ramesses emblazoned his 'victory' on the walls of five of his temples, there's just a passing reference in a single surviving Hittite text to a Hittite victory over Egypt, which is given no more significance than the defeat of its subject state Amurru: *Because my brother Muwattalli campaigned against the king of Egypt and the king of Amurru, when he defeated the kings of Egypt and Amurru, he went back to Aba* (i.e. Damascus and its region).[17]

A remarkably understated claim! It really is puzzling that there is not more about the Qadesh engagement and its outcome in Hittite records. (We've already noted, in the previous chapter, the total absence of any direct reference to it in the *Apology*.) Of course, these may have been the subject of texts that no longer exist. Perhaps they were recorded as the climax of Muwattalli's career in a set of royal annals now lost to us. Perhaps Muwattalli never had the opportunity of leaving us an account of his achievements, especially if his death occurred shortly and unexpectedly after Qadesh.

The barren princess

Let's return to the Hattusili-Ramesses correspondence. In Chapter 7, I referred to Muwattalli's and Hattusili's 'borrowing' of two Babylonian physicians, mentioned by Hattusili in his letter to the Babylonian king Kadashman-Enlil. Hittite respect for Babylonian medicine was matched by the long-standing reputation Egypt had for its medical skills and their practitioners. This is what motivated Hattusili in one of his letters to beg a favour of Ramesses. He asked that one of his physicians be sent to Hatti to help his sister Massanauzzi bear children. She'd been married for some time to Masturi, whom Muwattalli had appointed as ruler of the vassal state Seha River Land in western Anatolia; he had then bestowed Massanauzzi upon him as his wife. The fact that he'd wed her to a mere vassal ruler is a clear indication of both his trust in Masturi's personal loyalty to his family line, and the strategic importance of the state which the vassal was expected to rule in Hittite interests. The marriage was no doubt conditional upon the bride being accorded the status of her husband's Chief Wife. That way, a son of the couple, with royal Hittite blood in his veins, would be assured of succeeding to the throne. Which was all very well in theory. The problem was, Massanauzzi hadn't produced any offspring, no doubt after many years of trying, and no doubt despite the efforts of Hattusili's own medical practitioners, ritualists, and scribes well versed in the royal archives' medical records.

As a last resort, Hattusili appealed to Ramesses. This was probably not long after the 'Eternal Treaty' had been finalized, and relations between Hatti and Egypt had become relatively harmonious. Massanauzzi (Ramesses calls her Matanazi), her brother had to admit, was now a lady of mature years, fifty of them to be precise. But Egyptian medical science could work wonders, so it was widely believed. Only recently Ramesses had sent Hattusili ointments to treat an eye disease from which his royal brother suffered, with miraculous results. But to expect that even Egypt's medical miracles could induce pregnancy in a woman of Massanauzzi's years was beyond all reason. Ramesses took great delight in pointing this out to his correspondent, adding that, if anything, Hattusili had underestimated his sister's age. Here is a slightly free translation of the pharaoh's words by the eminent Egyptologist Professor Kenneth Kitchen:

Now see (here), as for Matanazi, my brother's sister, (I) the king your brother know her. Fifty is she? Never! She's sixty for sure! . . . No-one can produce medicine for her to have children. But of course if the Sun-God and the Storm-God should will it . . . But I will send a good magician (incantation-priest) and an able physician, and they can prepare some birth-drugs (anyway).[18]

Ramesses relished the opportunity of humiliating his royal brother – and being thoroughly unchivalrous about it. Was the princess really as old as he claimed? This, I thought, was worth checking. I did so and came to a sad conclusion. Using the available data, I calculated that Massanauzzi, aka Matanazi, must have been at least fifty-eight when Hattusili sent his appeal to the pharaoh, maybe several years older – or more. Unchivalrous Ramesses might have been but, if anything, he was erring on the side of generosity in his claim. (I wrote an article about this and submitted it to the *Journal of Egyptian Archaeology* for possible publication. It was forwarded to Ken Kitchen for assessment. He responded with one word: 'Publish!'[19] This is the shortest and, in its way, the most complimentary review I have ever received.) Information about the ages of the members of the Hittite royal family was very likely provided to Ramesses by Urhi-Teshub. He must have been a valuable source of intelligence on a wide range of matters about the land where he believed he should still be king. We've noted Puduhepa's sneering reference to his role as an informant for Ramesses in her draft letter to the pharaoh.

But one thing, in particular, puzzles me about Hattusili's request. If he was so desperate to ensure that Masturi had a successor with Hittite blood in his veins, in the hope that it would help ward off challenges to the succession after his death (or even before it), how could he have expected his ageing sister to provide this successor? Surely there were still plenty of young princesses in his household well able to fulfil the requirement, either sired by Hattusili or by other princes of his blood. Why could not one of these have been sent to Masturi, as a secondary wife, for child-breeding purposes? There may have been a number of reasons. One possibility is that the marriage between Masturi and his Hittite princess had been a long and devoted one. Maybe a uxorious Masturi refused to accept another wife – but monogamy was probably a luxury only the lower classes could afford.

Other royal letter-writers

We've talked mainly about letters exchanged between Hattusili and Ramesses. But the diplomatic bag (I use this term purely in a figurative sense) also contained letters sent by other members of the royal families to one another. Thus, Ramesses' wife Nefertari (aka Naptera) writes a cordial letter to Puduhepa enquiring about her health and sending her a gift of a gold necklace and fine linen garments.[20] There is no doubt that Nefertari was Ramesses' long-standing Chief Wife. The temple complex at Abu Simbel provides a tangible indication of this. Well, relatively speaking. Just to the north of the main temple, which is fronted by four massive statues of Ramesses (Figure 9.1), Nefertari has a small temple of her own, shared with the goddess Hathor. She is also diminutively represented between the legs of Ramesses' statues in the main temple's façade. If you visit Abu Simbel, virtually or in reality, you'll also find a small carving of Ramesses' marriage ceremony with his Hittite bride. But you'll have to look very carefully to spot it.

Figure 9.1 Ramesses II, Abu Simbel. Author photo.

Letters of goodwill, accompanied by gifts, were also sent to Hattusili by Ramesses' mother, Seti I's wife, Tuya.[21] That brings to mind the biblical story of the Exodus and what leads up to it. As I noted in the Introduction, Ramesses is commonly identified as the second of the two unnamed pharaohs in the Exodus story. (His father Seti would have been the first.) Thus, Ramesses becomes the pharaoh who was forced by divine sanctions, in the form of devastating plagues, to release the Israelites from their bondage in Egypt and allow them to begin their return to their homeland under the leadership of Moses. Then he had second thoughts – with dreadful consequences according to biblical tradition. Professor Kitchen agrees that Ramesses was the pharaoh in question. So does Cecil B. DeMille. And who could forget (if you're old enough) Yul Brynner's performance as Ramesses in the DeMille extravaganza 'The Ten Commandments'? Tuya also makes various appearances in modern films. In the animated movie 'The Prince of Egypt', she becomes the adoptive mother of Moses after finding him in the bulrushes on the banks of the Nile. The great British actor Helen Mirren is her voiceover. Actually, in the original story, it is Seti's daughter, not his wife, who adopts Moses. But let's not quibble.

Most of the correspondence between the royal courts dates to the post-treaty period and includes letters to Hattusili from some of the pharaoh's chief dignitaries, expressing their delight in the peace now established between the two Great Kingdoms. Their letters are accompanied by gifts, especially gold and fine linen cloth. Such gifts also accompany letters of goodwill written by the pharaoh to various Hittite princes. But, apart from his letters to Hattusili, the pharaoh's most frequent correspondence is with Puduhepa. More than mere expressions of goodwill, these cover a range of topics, to do with diplomatic relations between the kingdoms and arrangements for the royal marriage. Despite some acrimony between the pair, it's clear from their correspondence that Ramesses held his 'royal sister' in high regard. That aside, I cannot think of any other case in history where a king or emperor wrote letters, personal or official, to the wife of another king or emperor, or, indeed, even to a woman who alone held the reins of royal power. I have no doubt, too, that Puduhepa was present when all the pharaoh's letters were read out to her husband on their arrival from Egypt, and that she had substantial input into the letters her husband wrote to the pharaoh in reply – in addition to the letters she wrote to him herself.

Ensuring the mail got through

Let me conclude this chapter by asking what to me is an important question, though it cannot be answered with confidence. I've spoken of the hazards of travel within the Near Eastern region in this period (as in almost any other period) by individual travellers, and by groups both large and small, even with armed protection. So how sure can we be that all letters actually reached their final destination? Major diplomatic missions between the courts of Great Kings must have been accompanied by an armed escort sufficiently strong to deter attacks by large bands of desert pirates – to which merchant caravans may often have fallen prey. But what about communications sent from one royal brother's court to another's in between such missions? I believe that individual royal messengers despatched with a bag of letters must often have been the means by which written communications belonging to the Hittite-Egyptian correspondence were transmitted both before and after the treaty was concluded, and before and after the royal wedding. Negotiations over matters of detail of the treaty and the marriage arrangements clearly did not warrant a full-scale diplomatic mission on every occasion, especially given the substantial resources required to mount such missions and the time it would have taken for them to reach their destination. So, as I've already commented, a kind of escort-supported, pony express system, or something like it, must have been organized for more rapid communications.

I've already talked about the logistics which this must have involved. But I wonder whether there was also some sort of 'fail-safe' system in place. Let's suppose that a messenger and his escort are robbed and killed and the letters they carried either lost, stolen or destroyed. This could have been a mere by-product of a plundering expedition in search of more valuable loot. Or the letters may have been the deliberate target of the raid, carried out for an enemy of the correspondents who sought to gain valuable information from the letters (for example, those dealing with peace negotiations) or who simply wanted to prevent them reaching their destination, in an attempt to sabotage relations between the correspondents. As Professor Hoffner comments: 'Since there needed to be a constant monitoring of the health and strength of an international relationship . . . it was vital that the flow of messages and messengers between the two parties be constant.'[22] Hattusili's concern at the Babylonian king Kadashman-Enlil's failure to maintain constant contact with him illustrates this.

Kadashman-Enlil's explanation of why he had not maintained such contact highlights the risks letter-carriers faced on their journeys, even with armed support. So how could a royal court be sure that all its letters actually reached their intended recipients? How would either of them know if they didn't – at least for a long time? This, I believe, partly explains why Ramesses sometimes quotes a passage or passages from a letter he has received from his royal brother in the letter he sends in reply – to make sure that the letter he is responding to is the last one sent to him, and that there is no gap in the flow of correspondence. I wonder, too, whether, as a further precaution, a second messenger or messenger-group was used to convey duplicates of the letters sent from one royal court to another, to help ensure that at least one batch reached its destination. But I have no evidence at all for this and, as far as we're aware, the royal mail system worked pretty well.

10

Managing an Empire

What's in an empire?

I have always felt uneasy about using the term 'empire' to refer to the conglomerate of states, territories and cities over which the Hittites held sway. For many of us, this term conjures images of imperial powers like the Roman and British empires which followed up their acquisitions of far-flung subject lands with direct rule, installing military garrisons to police them and civil administrations to govern them. But the victims of their conquests also benefited from many aspects of their culture and civilization, and many of the material improvements, like roads and freshwater systems, made to their lands. To paraphrase the oft-quoted protest from Monty Python's *Life of Brian*: 'What have the Romans ever done for us apart from the medication, the sanitation, the aqueducts, the roads . . .?' And the list goes on. But substitute 'Hittites' for 'Romans', put this question in a Bronze Age Near Eastern setting ('What have the Hittites ever done for us?') and the answer has to be 'Nothing'. Well, almost nothing, at least in terms of benefits like these.

I'm happier with the term 'Great Kingdom' in referring to the territories subject to Hittite rule. The Hittite king and his three peers, the pharaoh and the rulers of Babylon and Assyria, referred to each other as 'Great Kings', so by extension we can legitimately refer to the lands they ruled as 'Great Kingdoms'. Nonetheless, the term 'Hittite Empire' is commonly used by scholars, and with some justification if one accepts my *Oxford English Dictionary*'s definition of an empire as 'an extensive territory, esp. an aggregate of many states under the ultimate authority of one person (an emperor or empress) or one sovereign state'. In other words, 'empire' has a wide spectrum of meanings ranging from a Roman- or British-type, overarching, administrative and military structure at one end to a Hittite-type, largely *laissez-faire* one close to the other. Throughout this book I have, with some misgivings, used the terms 'Hittite empire' and 'Hittite Great Kingdom' interchangeably.

In its peak period, roughly from the second half of the fourteenth century BC through the first half of the thirteenth, the Hittite empire, or Great Kingdom, extended over much of the Anatolian peninsula as far east as the Euphrates, and south through Syria to the borders of the region of Damascus, where Egyptian subject territory began. Elevated plateaus, rugged, often barely passable mountain ranges, arid deserts, fertile valleys and coastlands, and relatively densely populated urban areas were all part of the imperial topographical blend.

After many fluctuations in its fortunes, including some serious threats to its very existence, the empire reached its height with Suppiluliuma's destruction of the Mittanian empire. It had its size and status consolidated by Suppiluliuma's son Mursili and further secured by Mursili's son Muwattalli as a consequence of the Qadesh engagement. This was the empire eventually inherited by Hattusili, who had made no small contribution to its size and stability, particularly during his brother Muwattalli's reign by his conquests and repopulation of the empire's northern regions.

How did imperial rule by Hatti work?

Let me begin to answer this question by expanding a little on why I place the Hittite Great Kingdom near the lower end of the empire spectrum. Firstly, Hittite rule was most direct within the homeland, that is to say, in the basin of the Marassantiya river and marginal areas, where the king made regular religious pilgrimages and tours of inspection. The homeland's regional centres were administered by Hittite officials and their staff, who were directly responsible to the king and kept in regular contact with him about their regions' activities and problems.[1] Beyond that were two proximate zones known as the Upper and Lower Lands (see Map 1.4), which served to buffer the homeland against enemy attack and were almost certainly garrisoned by troops from the standing army as a first line of defence of the homeland territories. One of Suppiluliuma's lasting legacies was to establish two viceregal posts in Syria, one in the Euphrates city Carchemish, one in Aleppo. This was the first time direct Hittite rule was established outside the core region of the empire.[2] The viceroys were always close relatives of the king, usually his sons. Unfailingly loyal, it seems, they played a major role in maintaining stability in the Syrian vassal states until the empire's end – and, indeed, in the case of Carchemish, beyond it.

But, with these exceptions (and just one other, which we'll come to), Hittite rule of its empire was much less direct. The widespread, heterogeneous collection of Hittite vassal states were largely autonomous. Once conquered or reconquered, and plundered of their treasures, their livestock, and a good many of their people (if they resisted conquest), they were mostly not bothered by their imperial overlord, except for their rulers, who were appointed or reappointed by the Great King. The appointee was bound by a personal treaty, unilaterally imposed upon him by the king, and required to report anti-Hittite movements in his region, provide his overlord with military assistance if called upon and in at least some cases pay an annual tribute;[3] this was presented to His Majesty in person at the Hittite court. In return, the Great King promised to protect his vassal, with military assistance if required, against enemy attack or local insurgency, and ensure the succession of his rightful heirs.

A House of Cards?

This was the state of the empire Urhi-Teshub inherited from his father and a few years later when it was seized by Hattusili. An overall impression was that everything was in pretty good working order. But closer scrutiny reveals the fragility of the imperial structure. Partly, this fragility was chronic. Throughout its history, the empire was held together by what we might consider a network of very fine threads. Its strength and stability depended largely on the loyalty of its vassal rulers, who could turn rebellious, and sometimes did, or else be overthrown by an enemy or insurgents within their state, and sometimes were.

Hittite armies were well trained and could swiftly move to and deal with outbreaks of hostility in regions where their vassal states were located. But, by the time Hattusili ascended the throne, there was a further serious concern. It had always lurked in the kingdom's shadows; it must now have come to the fore as a matter of increasing urgency. There were two complementary aspects to it: an ever-worsening shortage of human resources, that is to say, enough able-bodied men of fighting age to protect the kingdom; and, at the same time, enough other people physically able to defend the core regions of the kingdom and ensure their food needs were met while the warriors were on campaign. This concern is rarely made explicit in our texts but can, I believe, be inferred from a number of them.

The *Apology* provides us with one small specific example. When Hattusili was assigned by his brother the task of ruling the kingdom's upper regions, he had particular responsibility for defending these regions against attacks by Kaska tribes. Yet only limited resources could be spared for him to do this: *My brother*

Muwattalli sent me but gave me troops and chariots (only) in small numbers.[4] And later, when confronted with an enemy force of eight hundred teams of horses and countless troops, *My brother ... gave me (only) 120 teams of horses, but not even a single military man was with me.*[5] Muwattalli's main concern was to muster as large an army as possible for his forthcoming conflict with Ramesses. This meant leaving the rest of his kingdom with only meagre resources to defend it. Even allowing for some exaggeration, the statements made by Hattusili gives us an indication of how thinly stretched the empire's military resources were at this time.

Let me place this in the context of a broader question.

How many people lived in Hattusa?

In a recently published paper, Jürgen Seeher, a former director of the German excavations at Hattusa, has come up with an astonishing calculation of the size of the Hittite capital's population.[6] Astonishing because of Hattusa's size (at 181 hectares it was one of the largest cities of the Bronze Age Near Eastern world) and importance as the supreme city of the Hittite empire. Its pre-eminence is also reflected in its monumental architecture, particularly its six kilometres of massive external walls, its vast sprawling Temple of the Storm God, the largest temple in the Hittite world, and its great palace, secure within its own ring of fortifications. Then there are the city's other features, not the least of which are its thirty additional temples, built at various times during its history.

So how many people actually lived in Hattusa? Of course, the numbers must have fluctuated over the city's five centuries of occupation. Earlier estimates by archaeologists put the population at somewhere between 9,000 and 15,000 inhabitants. Surprisingly small, it might seem, for the capital of one of the Great Kingdoms of the age. But Dr Seeher has concluded that the population was smaller still – no more than 4,600 inhabitants at its maximum and as low as 2,300 at its minimum. These figures are based on the city's excavated residential areas. Finding it difficult to believe that the population could be so small, I have had a number of email exchanges with Dr Seeher, plying him with questions. Might there be other residential areas yet to be discovered? Could there have been dwellings built of less durable materials, which have left no detectable remains, dwellings perhaps for temporary residents, like casual labourers summoned on a seasonal basis for building and maintenance works? Might there have been large peripheral settlements outside the walls, which have similarly left little or no trace in the archaeological record?

Dr Seeher has held firm to his conclusion that all the city's residential areas have now been uncovered, and that even the flimsiest of dwellings would have left some traces of their existence. He says there may have been something like such structures for short-term accommodation of labourers for building projects, transported people or the like:

> But to survive in the harsh climate in Central Anatolia for years and decades (and actually centuries) you have to build proper houses. Mudbrick walls perish, but as far as we know all buildings – Bronze Age, Hittite, Iron Age – had foundations of stone, in order to avoid dampness and water affecting the mudbrick superstructure. And these foundations survive and can be detected, either by excavation or by remote sensing methods.

There is also, he notes, a small amount of evidence for settlement outside the city walls – principally to the north, but otherwise indications of peripheral extramural settlements are sparse. He concedes that at its peak Hattusili's population could have been a little higher, perhaps five thousand at the most. But the hard facts of archaeological remains must provide an overriding consideration in any attempts to estimate how many people lived in Hattusa.[7]

The size of Hattusa's population, according to Seeher's estimate, is what I was referring to in Chapter 1 when I said that from a bird's-eye perspective there is something odd about Hattusa. From above, this city must have appeared almost empty of inhabitants for much of its existence, with many if not most of its inhabitants out of sight on temple duties or penned within the secluded, heavily guarded palace complex. There are no large market places, no manufacturing industries, like bronze foundries. The capital was otherwise defined. With its large array of temples and sacred places, it had all the hallmarks of a sacred and ceremonial city, as befitting the spiritual centre of the Hittite world.[8]

Were there more populous cities in the kingdom? The homeland was occupied by a number of important cities, some quite large in area, like Sapinuwa (modern Ortaköy), sixty kilometres northeast of Hattusa. Several of these cities appear to have contained 'palaces' where the king took up residence on his visits there, during his religious pilgrimages and probably for other reasons. Seeher suggests that the king's court was often itinerant, like some courts in medieval Europe. Presumably, on such occasions His Majesty had a large entourage accompanying him. This would have reduced the size of the capital's population at particular times of the year. Unfortunately, no Hittite cities apart from Hattusa have left sufficient remains for us to determine how many people inhabited them, or exactly how extensive they were.

How many people lived in the whole empire?

That leads us on to another question more comprehensive in scope. How large was the population of the entire Hittite empire at its peak, encompassing all territories subject to it from western Anatolia to Syria? The Hungarian scholar Zsolt Simon has come up with a figure of 140,000 or 150,000 inhabitants,[9] which, despite the thorough research that underpins his conclusions, seems too small to me to sustain the empire as a credible major international military and political power, on a par especially with the Great Kingdom of Ramesside Egypt.

So how big was Hatti's population, particularly at the time Hattusili was Great King? Let's do some lateral thinking by considering the statistics of the battle of Qadesh – as provided by Ramesses' inscriptions. In these inscriptions, Ramesses claimed that the Hittite army was 47,500 strong, including 2,500 three-man chariot-crews. Of course, we need to set aside the nonsensical claims made by Ramesses in these inscriptions, that he 'won' the battle singlehandedly and accepted the craven submission of his 'defeated' opponent, 'the Wretched Fallen One of Hatti'. Besides, in recording his military exploits a king may often exaggerate the numbers of his enemy, either to enhance the magnitude of his success if he is victorious, or to provide a plausible excuse if he is defeated. But, despite the absurdities of much of his narrative, Ramesses' statement of the size of the Hittite army may well be close to the truth. Pharaohs employed officials who were diligent in their collection of battlefield statistics, and Ramesses very likely included in his inscriptions enemy numbers they provided for him. (We might compare the Israelite alliance of 40,000 infantry, 3,000 chariotry and close to 2,000 cavalry – and one thousand camels – mustered against the ninth-century Assyrian king Shalmaneser III, as recorded by the king's scribes.[10])

Almost certainly, many, if not all, of Hatti's vassal states contributed levies for the conflict, and Ramesses may well be right in his claim that there was a substantial mercenary contingent in Muwattalli's army as well. These mercenaries could have been largely stateless nomads, like those referred to by Simon,[11] from Luwian areas in the south (predominantly soldiers of fortune from the Lukka regions?) and Kaska regions in the north. Let us suppose a notional figure of 7,500 mercenaries, leaving about 40,000 troops drawn from various regions which were subject to Hittite rule. Muwattalli could well have drained his kingdom, both the homeland and the subject states beyond, of much of the military resources available to him for the conflict. But sufficient defence forces must have been left in place to guard the kingdom's most important regions, including the capital, and the essential food-producing areas.

All in all, it would seem to me that the Hittite kingdom at its peak could call on up to 100,000 men to engage on various military enterprises, this number inclusive of forces required to defend homeland and subject territories while regular forces were on campaigns often far from their homeland base. Many were probably reservists, some normally employed as labourers on the estates of landowners who were obliged to provide contingents of troops whenever they were requisitioned by the king. But there was also a standing army, which was on all-year-round duties and could engage in policing activities or contribute to road-building and wall-maintenance projects when not on active military service. It seems that members of the standing army were stationed both in Hattusa and in various parts of the empire.[12] Purely as an estimate, I suggest that the standing army, essentially the Hittite empire's professional troops, consisted of about 10,000 infantry and chariot-troops. Perhaps the buildings found in Hattusa that have tentatively been identified as barracks (for elite officers?) of the standing force and horse-stables[13] provide some archaeological confirmation of this – or at least of the provision of accommodation for troops and horses within the city. Further to these figures, Beal concludes from documentary evidence that the size of a Hittite field army on a major expedition could have been well in excess of ten thousand.[14] Occasionally, though very exceptionally as in the case of the Qadesh engagement, the number appears to have been almost five times greater.

Considering all these figures, I suggest that the population of the kingdom as a whole numbered well upwards of 200,000 at the time of the Qadesh engagement. This estimate takes into account the proportion of the population that could have taken no part in military activities, including women and children, and men incapable of bearing arms due, for example, to the infirmities of old age. And note that the overall figure I've arrived at is largely extrapolated from Ramesses' calculation of Hittite battle numbers at Qadesh. So, it cannot be used in any precise way when calculating the size of Hatti's population. We should also be conscious of the number of transplantees Mursili II claims to have brought back to Hattusa in the wake of his frequent military campaigns. These amounted to not just hundreds but sometimes thousands of prisoners of war – booty-people – acquired from rebellious vassal states and enemy regions. Of course, many of them or their offspring may have been recruited for the Qadesh killing fields, and never left them.

Even so, Hatti's total population must have been dwarfed by the size of Egypt's population. On its own, Ramesses' capital Pi-Ramesse, from which the pharaoh's Qadesh campaign was launched, had by one reckoning some 300,000 inhabitants, with an estimated three million for his kingdom's total population. I have suggested in several of my earlier publications that the Qadesh conflict brought the kingdoms of both sides close to exhaustion, to the point where neither had the resources to engage in another conflict on this scale. Hence an eventual peace treaty. I've been giving some further thought to this. Ramesses probably had the resources to fight a Qadesh campaign many times over. (Why he didn't is something I've briefly considered in Chapter 8.) But the cost to the Hittite kingdom was huge in both blood and treasure. It could no longer fight a battle on anything like the scale of Qadesh. This despite winning the disputed territories over which the battle was fought.

Managing the empire's population losses

Several other factors must have made the impact of Hittite losses at Qadesh on the empire's future military capacity all the more severe. Amongst these was one of the legacies left by Suppiluliuma to his successors: the plague, which allegedly ravaged the Hittite land for twenty years and decimated its population. Details are provided by his son and second successor Mursili in a series of 'Plague Prayers'.[15] Admittedly, prayers are not a record of historical fact, and, while we can hardly doubt that there *was* such a plague, we might have reservations about how long it lasted and how severe its impact really was. As we've noted, the plague had been brought to the Hittite heartland by prisoners taken by Suppiluliuma after his attack on Egyptian subject territory in the Syro-Palestinian region. A consequence of this was a considerable ratcheting up of tensions between the two Great Kingdoms, culminating eventually in the two engagements at Qadesh[16] and the heavy casualties from these conflicts. So, in more ways than one, Suppiluliuma, often hailed as the greatest Hittite king of them all, had much to answer for in the substantial losses of his subjects' lives his actions had caused.

Add to that the dangerously unstable condition in which he had left the western half of his kingdom by concentrating his attention almost entirely on its eastern half – above all, on the destruction of the Mittanian empire. His son Mursili had through regular campaigns in the west succeeded in reasserting Hittite sovereignty over the rebellious vassal states in the region. And the thousands of 'booty-people' he brought back to the homeland in the wake of his campaigns must initially have given a substantial boost to the homeland's population. The benefits of his population transfers continued into his son Muwattalli's reign, when no doubt many of the transplantees were used to repopulate the kingdom's northern regions. This was a task assigned to the king's brother, the future Great King Hattusili. But, after Mursili's reign, the supply of booty-people to the homeland almost completely dried up, since the very small number of attested campaigns resulted in few or no compulsory immigrants to the homeland, with Qadesh, the one major campaign – almost certainly resulting in a substantial reduction in the number of its able-bodied males.[17] The relatively small size of the empire's population must have imposed severe strains on its stability and the maintenance of its defence capabilities. This, I believe, gives important context to the reign of Hattusili the usurper and plays a major role in the policies and strategies he adopted, and the successes he could claim. Most notable among the latter was of course the landmark event of his career, the 'Eternal Peace', concluded with his former enemy and future son-in-law Ramesses.

Hattusili's reign was a long one, lasting perhaps thirty years by my reckoning. During his time on the throne, we know of just two major campaigns he personally undertook, both to the west. One we learn of from the fragmentary remains of his *Annals*,[18] which deal with a major uprising in the region called the Lukka Lands; these were located in the southwestern part of the Anatolian peninsula. The Lukka people were nominally subjects of Hatti, but were a fractious, often rebellious lot, divided among themselves and difficult to control. From what we can glean from the *Annals*, it seems that an uprising in their region, with presumably the potential to spread more widely through the western lands, was sufficiently serious for Hattusili to mount a large-scale expedition against them.

The 'second' expedition concerns a notorious insurrectionist who made constant inroads into the Hittites' western vassal states, with the backing of the Greek kingdom Ahhiyawa, prompting Hattusili to take action against him. Chapter 12 has the details. If, as some scholars believe, the events referred to here belong to the campaign recorded in the *Annals*, that would mean there was only *one* known major military campaign conducted by Hattusili, or by any of his subordinates, during his entire reign and, as we shall see, that enterprise appears to have achieved very little, if anything.

Was there a *pax Hethitica* during Hattusili's reign?

Of course, there may have been other military campaigns whose records are lost to us. Even so, I believe there's a striking difference between the extensive campaigning conducted by Hattusili's grandfather Suppiluliuma throughout his reign, the almost yearly campaigns conducted by his father Mursili throughout his, and the apparently minimal military operations in which Hittite forces were engaged during Hattusili's reign. Certainly nothing on the scale of the encounter between his brother and the pharaoh Ramesses at Qadesh. Towards the end of the *Apology* Hattusili refers to his military conquests and the annexations of conquered territories. These claims may be genuine enough, but must refer to victories he had won and repopulation programmes he had carried out in the northern parts of the kingdom, and the regions beyond, while his brother Muwattalli was still Great King. Hattusili is merely recalling in these final sections some of the achievements he's already reported in the first part of the document.

Generally speaking, then, a *pax Hethitica* seems to have prevailed in most of the Hittite lands for most of Hattusili's reign, albeit at times an uneasy and fragile one. For this much credit is due to Suppiluliuma for destroying the Mittanian empire and imposing Hittite sovereignty over most of the Syrian vassal states, Mursili for his comprehensive campaigns of conquest and subjugation of the Anatolian vassal states, which largely compensated for Suppiluliuma's lack of attention to these states, and Muwattalli for his victory, in terms of its ultimate outcome, at Qadesh. And Hattusili himself before his accession had done much to re-establish Hittite control over most of the homeland's northern regions through his military campaigns and repopulation programmes there.

Within this overall context, then, the future looked propitious for a period of relative calm and stability throughout the empire. And Hattusili sought to maintain these conditions for as long as he occupied the throne. The apex and defining feature of his reign was his conclusion of the 'Eternal Peace' treaty with Ramesses. The problems, both internal and external, his kingdom faced he sought to resolve by diplomacy rather than brute force, and by astute appointments to important positions within the kingdom. He might thus be regarded as Hittite history's greatest peacemaker and diplomat.

In the reigns of his predecessors, almost constant warfare had drawn heavily on, and expended, a large proportion of the kingdom's human resources. To some extent, the losses were made good by repopulation programmes resulting from the transplantation to the homeland of 'booty-people', the spoils of successful military campaigns. But the supply of these forced immigrants had now almost dried up. Critically lacking in the human tools essential to maintain, let alone, expand, his empire, Hattusili had to resort to other means to ensure it remained a major power among the Bronze Age Near Eastern kingdoms. Within this context, appointees to strategically important posts in the empire, who were often granted special powers or concessions, must have played a major role in helping secure the stability and cohesion of the imperial structure as a whole.

The Assyrian Menace

Let's now look at the main components of this structure, especially during Hattusili's reign. We'll start with the empire's eastern states, particularly the Syrian ones.

As we've noted, the viceroys stationed in the Syrian cities of Carchemish and Aleppo, almost always sons of the reigning king or one of his predecessors, had proved consistently loyal and competent deputies ever since the first pair were appointed by Suppiluliuma. Throughout the Syrian subject territories they exercised all the powers of their overlord, on his behalf. Carchemish, whose current viceroy was Hattusili's son Ini-Teshub, was of vital strategic importance to the empire. It lay on the right bank of the Euphrates in the northeasternmost part of the Syrian region, just a river's breadth away from territory annexed by the Assyrians from Hanigalbat, the last remnant of the now extinct Mittanian empire. Already in Mursili's reign the Assyrians had crossed the Euphrates and won control of Carchemish and its surrounding region until they were repelled by a military force under Mursili's personal command.

Even so, Assyria remained a serious menace to Hatti's Syrian territories, and Carchemish a likely launch-point for a more comprehensive invasion of them. Yet the Assyrian king Adad-nirari had made a gesture of peace to the current Hittite king, almost certainly Urhi-Teshub, by requesting acknowledgement as a royal brother. This gesture had been brusquely rejected by Urhi-Teshub, probably despite protests from his uncle Hattusili who had to live with the consequences when *he* became Great King. Aware that he simply didn't have the resources to defend his Syrian territories by military action against a large-scale Assyrian invasion, Hattusili had no option other than to try using his diplomatic skills to avoid a military confrontation.

This might prove no easy task. The aggressive Adad-nirari had swiftly conquered all states east of the Euphrates that were formerly part of the Mittanian empire and, more recently, puppets of the Hittite empire. Buoyed by these easy successes, the Assyrian surely had his sights now set on Hittite territories across the Euphrates. Relations with the Hittite regime had for some time been at a low ebb, no doubt due partly to Urhi-Teshub's rejection of the Assyrian's request for 'brotherhood', and also to the alleged mistreatment of Assyrian envoys at the Hittite court during Urhi-Teshub's reign: *The messengers whom you regularly sent here in the time of King Urhi-Teshshup often experienced [. . .] aggravation.*[19] So much we learn from the letter Hattusili sent to Adad-nirari complaining, amongst other things, of the Assyrian's failure to acknowledge his accession with appropriate gifts. (I've already referred to this letter in Chapter 7.) But he distanced himself from his predecessor's treatment of the Assyrian envoys and promised to fulfil Adad-nirari's request for 'good iron' as soon as its manufacture was complete.

His letter must have been written in response to one by Adad-nirari, who now recognized Hattusili as Hatti's legitimate ruler and may even have initiated peaceful relations with him. Hattusili replied positively to his letter, though in a guarded way. A more effusive response could be construed as weakness. But peace between Assyria and Hatti seems to have been maintained (with only one known exception; see below) throughout Hattusili's reign, which still had some twenty-five years to run. Adad-nirari died just a few years after Hattusili seized Hatti's throne. He was succeeded by his son Shalmaneser I, who received a very amicable letter from Hattusili, probably not long after his accession, congratulating him on becoming Assyria's new Great King.[20]

What to do about Hanigalbat?

But there was an ongoing problem, of some embarrassment to Hattusili, with the potential to derail his efforts at firming up good relations with Assyria. The problem was yet another resistance movement by rebels from the former kingdom of Hanigalbat attempting to break their country free of Assyrian rule. It was the third such attempt. This courageous but quixotic rebellion was led by a man called Shattuara. Already uprisings by his grandfather, also called Shattuara, and his father (or uncle?) Wasashatta had been ruthlessly put down by Adad-nirari, who punished the rebels by imposing direct rule over their formerly semi-independent kingdom. By so doing, he had extended the territories fully under his control all the way to the left bank of the Euphrates. But Shattuara no. 2 was determined to prise his people free from the iron fist of Assyrian dominance and appealed to Hattusili for assistance.[21] Here is a possible scenario:

Shattuara has sent a delegation with armed escort to Hattusa with an urgent appeal to the Great King. The city seems almost empty on their arrival, for

the king and his retinue are away on one of his regular piligrimages through the homeland. He is expected back within the next few days, and the delegation has no option but to await his return, despite the urgency of their mission. To try to intercept him while his pilgrimage is still underway would be unthinkable, so the delegation is advised.

But the officials Hattusili has left to manage the palace's affairs during his absence are sympathetic to the mission's cause, and inform the king as soon as the pilgrimage party returns that it urgently seeks an audience with him. This is promptly granted, though reluctantly, as His Majesty has no doubt what the purpose of the mission is. With some understanding of the rebels' plight, and without waiting for a reader or translator, the king takes personal delivery of the letter the delegation has brought with it, breaks open the clay envelope that contains it and reads it himself. It is written in Akkadian, but the king had learnt the language during his scribal training and has no need of a translator.

The contents of the letter are what he expected. He summons Puduhepa and discusses the appeal with her. She too can read the letter for herself. Both feel deeply for the rebels' cause and the courage they are showing against insuperable odds. For purely practical, political and logistical reasons, there should be only one response to their request. Hattusili simply cannot afford to provoke conflict with the increasingly powerful Assyrian king, even if his resources were up to the task. He should maintain peace with his royal brother by adopting a policy of strict neutrality. The delegation should be sent away empty-handed. But the royal couple are moved by the plight of the supplicants and their fellow countrymen. With the greatest reluctance Hattusil orders his captains to mobilize a small figthing force to go to the defence of the land of Hanigalbat against its Assyrian oppressor.

The Hanigalbatean delegation to Hattusa is entirely my invention. However, in an inscription of Adad-nirari, Shalmaneser's father, we are informed that Wasashatta, Shattuara's father (or uncle) had earlier travelled to Hatti seeking Hittite assistance for his rebellion, and allegedly offered bribes, which the Hittites kept, to help him secure it[22] (though the so-called bribes may have been funds offered to pay for Hittite weapons). The appeal was unsuccessful. But the rebel's son/nephew Shattuara no. 2, taking on Adad-nirari's formidable successor, Shalmaneser, also sought Hittite assistance for his own rebellion. He must have realised he had little chance of success, but thought it worth a try. I've suggested that, instead of risking a personal trip to the Hittite capital with little chance of success, and a lengthy absence from the rebellion he was leading, he sent a small delegation with a letter for Hattusili, in which he made his case for Hittite support as persuasively as he could.

With some success. A Hittite expeditionary force was sent to the war zone. How did it fare? The only information we have comes from one of the invading king Shalmaneser's inscriptions.[23] To judge from this, the Hanigalbateans, supported by the troops from Hatti and by local tribesmen called the Ahlamu (we've already met them), had some initial successes against the invaders. But, inevitably, the tide turned as the Assyrians struck back with overwhelming force, and according to Shalmaneser, carried out mass slaughter of their enemies. The Assyrian claimed 14,400 casualties. This is almost certainly an exaggeration. But the defeat of the Hittite force and the losses it sustained, however great or small they were, dissuaded Hattusili from any further ventures against the powerful foe east of the Euphrates – even if he could now call, in theory at least, on Egyptian support.

As a footnote to this episode, Shattuara and his rebel army held out against the Assyrians for some considerable time, even without Hittite assistance. It was probably only after Hattusili's death that the rebels finally succumbed. And Hattusili maintained peaceful relations with Assyria for the rest of his reign, though he could never be sure that the Assyrians would always stick to their side of the river.

Elsewhere in the east

Aleppo, the second viceregal kingdom in Syria, was located in northern Syria to the southwest of Carchemish. It had formerly been the capital of Yamhad, once the most powerful kingdom in Syria until its capital was destroyed by the Hittite king Mursili I, about 1595 BC. Aleppo was rebuilt and subsequently became a vassal state of the Mittanian empire. After Suppiluliuma destroyed this empire, Aleppo was placed under the direct rule of his son Telipinu and, like Carchemish, remained a viceregal kingdom until the empire's end. During Hattusili's reign, it was governed by Talmi-Sharrumma, one of the king's cousins.

By and large, the Syrian vassal states stayed relatively calm, stable and loyal to their Hittite overlords as long as the Hittite empire existed. This was no doubt due largely to effective oversight by the succession of viceroys appointed to Carchemish and Aleppo. Treaties were drawn up by the king with his viceroys just as they were with his vassal rulers. A number of these treaties have survived, including one between Talmi-Sharrumma and Muwattalli, actually the replacement of a treaty which had gone missing in the reign of Muwattalli's father Mursili.[24] Further to the southeast, extending inland from the coast to the Orontes river, lay the large, strategically important, vassal kingdom Amurru. It had a long history of switching sides between Egypt and Hatti, but became permanently attached to Hatti after the battle of Qadesh. Before then, it had been forced by Ramesses's father Seti to change its allegiance back to Egypt, shortly before the earlier Qadesh conflict which Seti claims to have won.

Let me expand a little on what I said about this in Chapter 5. Muwattalli was furious at the kingdom's defection. In fact, the question of who controlled Amurru had helped ignite the main Qadesh conflict some years later. Its vassal ruler Benteshina was held personally responsible for his kingdom's 'treachery' and, as soon as Muwattalli regained control of Amurru, the hapless vassal was deposed, taken prisoner and deported to Hatti. Of course he could hardly be blamed for declaring his loyalty to Egypt, with an Egyptian army right on his border poised to attack if he failed to do so. Hattusili felt some sympathy for him. He prevailed upon his brother to grant him custody of the prisoner and resettled him comfortably in Hakpis, Hattusili's northern capital, in a fully staffed home of his own. Looking to the future, he clearly thought him worth cultivating. Benteshina might one day prove a useful ally.

Subsequently, Benteshina was reinstated on the throne of Amurru, probably already in Urhi-Teshub's reign, and, if so, almost certainly at Hattusili's instigation. If not until Hattusili's own reign, then Benteshina must have been one of his first vassal appointees. In either case, Muwattalli's choice for the Amurrite throne, a man called Shapili, was unceremoniously dumped to make way for its former incumbent. The appointment was of no small importance, for Egypt might make another claim upon Amurru, after the Qadesh conflict and in the years before the peace settlement between the two Great Kingdoms. To reduce the risk of this happening, Hattusili no doubt trusted that the dethroned ruler he had so warmly embraced and cared for during his exile would remain steadfastly loyal to him once he had got his throne back. A treaty (still surviving) which he drew up with him helped ensure this.[25]

In fact it was Benteshina who requested the treaty, partly to guarantee that his lineal descendants would never be dispossessed of the vassal throne. Hattusili set at rest any such concerns by consolidating the links between Great King and vassal ruler with a double wedding. He married one of his daughters to Benteshina – and his son Nerikkaili to one of Benteshina's daughters. Whether or not he felt aggrieved at being thrust aside from the succession to the throne, if he'd been Crown Prince, Nerikkaili continued to play an important role in the

Hittite administration, and did so even after being married off to a mere vassal ruler's daughter. To be fair, Benteshina was considered a very important vassal, as well as being a close friend of Hattusili. But, at least to outward appearances, Nerikkaili's progression from likely successor to the Hittite throne, to the son-in-law of a Syrian liegeman seems to have been a precipitous fall in status.

Hattusili apparently had an inexhaustible supply of daughters for marriages with foreign peers or important vassal rulers. And new ones probably kept being produced.[26] Such marriages were a common way of cementing alliances between two Great Kings, or a Great King and an important vassal. Thus, Hattusili married one of his daughters to the vassal ruler of Isuwa, a strategically important kingdom in the north located between Hatti and the lands over which Assyria was increasingly extending its sway. And he married another daughter to the Great King of Babylon. Apart from its strategic value, the Babylonian marriage provided Hattusili with additional international prestige. But apparently Ramesses did not think so. According to Puduhepa's draft letter, the pharaoh had reacted with scorn to the assumption that the ruler of Babylon was a Great King, and Babylonia a Great Kingdom. This drew an angry response from Puduhepa: *If you should say 'The King of Babylonia is not a Great King,' then my brother* [i.e. Ramesses] *does not know the rank of Babylonia*.[27] Indeed, Puduhepa implies in her letter that both a son *and* a daughter of the Hittite Great King and Queen had married offspring of the Babylonian king, just as there had been a double marriage between Hattusili's and Benteshina's families.

The kingdom of Tarhuntassa[28]

Let's turn our attention slightly further westwards now, to the south-central or southeastern part of the Anatolian peninsula where a kingdom greatly exceeding Amurru in importance was created. This was the kingdom of Tarhuntassa, built largely from scratch by Muwattalli when he moved his capital there. After Urhi-Teshub shifted the capital back to Hattusa, the question of what was to become of Tarhuntassa was soon resolved. When Hattusili became Great King, he promptly installed Urhi-Teshub's (step-?) brother Kuruntiya as ruler of the evolving kingdom: *When my father deposed Urhi-Teshub from the kingship, my father took Kuruntiya and installed him in kingship in the land of Tarhuntassa.*[29]

By the time he became king of Tarhuntassa, Kuruntiya was probably in his early to mid twenties (about the same age as his grandfather Mursili when he became Great King of Hatti). Before then, he may have spent much of his time in the northern regions gaining battle experience in the ongoing conflicts fought by or on behalf of his uncle, to win and maintain control over these regions. But once Hattusili had seized the Hittite throne, he probably moved with great haste to transfer Kuruntiya to the kingship of Tarhuntassa. This prestigious appointment effectively conferred viceregal status upon Kuruntiya. It would serve as sufficient compensation for the young man, his uncle must have hoped, for being forever excluded from the Hittite throne – which his father no doubt intended for him in the event of his elder brother Urhi-Teshub's death, and as Hattusili may have promised.

It was a gamble. Kuruntiya had closely bonded with Hattusili and his immediate family ever since he'd been entrusted by Muwattalli to his brother's safekeeping as a child. He'd developed a warm friendship with Hattusili's son Tudhaliya, and apparently had little, if anything, to do with his brother Urhi-Teshub. We don't know whether he played any part in the coup that unseated his brother. But Hattusili must have been concerned that the supporters of the exiled former king might now switch their allegiance to his brother in a further bid to return the throne, as they had every right to do, to another of Muwattalli's descendants.

The risk Hattusili took in appointing Kuruntiya king of Tarhuntassa was that it gave Muwattalli's younger son a base from which he could build strong support for either restoring Urhi-Teshub to Hatti's throne, or taking it himself. Kuruntiya's long-standing close bonds with Hattusili's family, especially Tudhaliya, might help maintain his loyalty to the illegal regime. But, as Hattusili must have feared, they couldn't guarantee it. So he made the kingship of Tarhuntassa as attractive an appointment as possible to ginger up his appointee's loyalty. This southern kingdom became a valuable part of Hattusili's empire, particularly if it extended to the Mediterranean Sea, giving the Hittites a coastline for the first time in their history. As we've noted, its strategic location within a relatively short distance, now by both land and sea, of Hatti's Syrian territories, and its potential as a base for military operations to the west, particularly the southwest, if needed, were but two of its many assets. Though no longer the imperial capital, it was no mere vassal state. It was now in effect a viceregal kingdom, and Kuruntiya was its first viceroy – a status ranking him alongside the rulers of Carchemish and Aleppo.

Further concessions were granted in a treaty Hattusili drew up with him.[30] It's called the Ulmi-Teshub treaty, because that's the name given to the king of Tarhuntassa. How do we explain this name? Who was this person? Most scholars agree that he was none other than Kuruntiya. Ulmi-Teshub was in fact the prince's *original* (Hurrian) name, so the argument goes; it was changed to the

Luwian name Kuruntiya when the prince was appointed king of Tarhuntassa, which lay in a Luwian area; that is to say, the primary motive for the name-change was a political one.

One of the concessions granted to the kingdom concerned the 'divine obligations' imposed on the land, in this case the military levies demanded by Hattusa in the form of infantry and chariotry. Hattusili abolished the chariotry obligation and reduced to two hundred the number of infantry requisitioned for Hittite military campaigns. That was a major concession, since levies from subject states made up a large part of Hittite expeditionary forces. And, if my initial hypothesis is right, Hattusili became Great King at a time when shortages in able-bodied males in the kingdom became increasingly critical. The concession was probably intended in part to consolidate further Kuruntiya's loyalty to his overlord. It must also have done much to win the goodwill of the people of Tarhuntassa, who may still have had strong reservations about the legitimacy of the new regime to which they were subject.

There was perhaps also another reason for the concession. Despite having served for a short time as the empire's capital, Tarhuntassa was still a kingdom in the process of being built. Even its boundaries had yet to be properly defined. That's why so much space is devoted in the treaty to naming districts, regions and cities in the border regions and specifying whether they belonged to Tarhuntassa's territories, and, if not, to which lands they did belong.[31] Within Tarhuntassa itself, the reduction in the number of able-bodied men required for Hittite military service was an important concession. It would mean that this essential human resource for the protection of the new kingdom and the maintenance of its food production and other population-sustaining activities was now only marginally affected.

The western subject states

Using various means, including treaties with both vassals and foreign kings, and judicious appointments to the vassal states, Hattusili seems to have kept the eastern half of his empire pretty well under control. But he had serious concerns about his western states, particularly members of a group called the Arzawa lands. These were a conglomerate of territories which were probably once a single kingdom, but later fractured into independent states.[32] During Suppiluliuma's and Mursili's reigns, they became bound to Hatti by vassal treaties. Yet, despite its control of much of western Anatolia, Hatti's interests were more focused on the southeast and south, its vassal states there and the foreign kingdoms that lay beyond. And its western territories, while once a valuable source of transplantees and livestock captured from rebellious states, were likely to prove a serious drain on its resources if rebellions broke out once more there.

But Hattusili could not risk allowing the western states to regain their independence. Bitter experience from the reign of his great-grandfather Tudhaliya III had shown that, if left to their own devices, the Arzawan states could seriously threaten the empire's southern territories and ultimately pose a threat to the homeland itself. In the historical preamble to one of his decrees, Hattusili describes an attack made by enemy forces on the homeland from many directions, now commonly referred to as the 'Concentric Invasions'.[33] Combined Arzawan forces seem to have played a prominent role in these invasions to the extent that the pharaoh Amenhotep III wrote a letter to an Arzawan king called Tarhundaradu seeking one of his daughters in marriage as the basis for an alliance between the two kingdoms. The pharaoh declared that the kingdom of Hatti was finished, and clearly believed that Arzawa would become the next great Anatolian power.[34]

He proved wrong, of course. Tudhaliya and his son (?) Suppiluliuma regained their kingdom, repulsed their enemies, and the Arzawan lands were reduced to Hittite vassal status. Their subjection to Hittite rule was consolidated by Suppiluliuma's son Mursili early in his reign when he conducted campaigns of conquest against those who rose in rebellion against him. Hittite sovereignty over the western states seems to have been relatively well maintained by Mursili's successors Muwattalli and Hattusili, who had no doubts that control of a large slice of the western Anatolian region was essential to the empire's cohesion and security. Yet at least one Greek (Ahhiyawan/Mycenaean) kingdom was making increasing inroads, politically, territorially and perhaps militarily, into Hittite subject states located there. Greek expansion into western Anatolian regions, with the way for this paved by a notorious anti-Hittite activist (see Chapter 12), was a threat to Hittite control of these regions that could not be ignored.

Even so, Hattusili was extremely reluctant to use military force to maintain peace in the west, especially with what I believe to be the much reduced military resources available to him. Campaigns against the states in this region were expensive undertakings, both in terms of the infantry and chariotry required to put down a rebellion, and the time taken to conduct such campaigns – and thus the time able-bodied men were kept from more productive activities, like food production. In a paper delivered at the Tenth International Congress of Hittitology held in the Oriental Institute of the University of Chicago in 2017, I calculated that a Hittite army would need approximately seventy days to march from the Hittite capital to the western coast of Anatolia.[35] At least double that number for the round trip, and add extra days for the battles themselves, the sacking of conquered cities, and the conveyance of livestock, transplantees and other plunder back to the homeland. Overall, a campaign to Hatti's westernmost territories would have occupied an entire campaigning season – at least.

Once more diplomacy, expressed mainly through treaties and marriage alliances, was the preferred way of keeping the peace. Hatti's relationship with the kingdom of Seha River Land, a large Arzawan state extending inland from the Aegean coast, illustrates this. With the island of Lesbos as an important dependency, Seha River Land was highly vulnerable to exploitation, by insurrectionists both within and outside it and by predatory Greeks. What's more, Hittite overlordship was probably never popular in the vassal state after it had been forced into submission by Mursili.[36] It became even less so when his successor Muwattalli sacked and banished its long-reigning king Manapa-Tarhunda, replacing him as vassal ruler with Masturi, probably the old king's son.[37] Increasing incompetence due to old age may have been the reason for Manapa-Tarhunda's removal from his throne. But, if the king was well liked by his subjects, as I suspect he was, his banishment on top of his removal from the vassal throne may well have stoked up simmering unrest among his subjects. Urhi-Teshub had the sense, perhaps on his uncle's advice, to bring the exiled old man back home, while retaining Masturi as vassal ruler. It was a wise diplomatic move that may have proved effective, for a while.

What did it really mean to be a member of the Hittite empire?

Before leaving the west, let's briefly consider what membership of the Hittite empire actually meant to an ordinary man or woman living in one of the vassal states there. The answer is probably very little, if anything. As we've noted earlier, the main link between a vassal state and the empire to which it belonged was a personal pact between the Great King and the vassal state's ruler, concerned mainly with guaranteeing military support for each other should the need arise. There was the added obligation of the vassal supplying the king with early warning of any uprisings in his region. Otherwise, with few exceptions, the vassal ruler had complete autonomy in the ways he managed his kingdom's affairs, free of the oversight of Hittite administrative establishments.

So, unless a Hittite-approved or -appointed vassal were overthrown, or local insurrectionists threatened the stability of the whole region, the Hittites had little to do with the western states they claimed as part of their empire. Particularly during Hattusili's reign. As we've further noted, in contrast to his father Mursili, Hattusili conducted just two *known* western campaigns – at most – during his thirty-or-so-year reign. Nor did he, in Hadrianic style, undertake regular tours of inspection throughout his empire, to make himself personally known to his subjects and to build up their goodwill towards him. For most, if not all, of their lives, many of the king's subjects, in the west at least, would not have known who their sovereign ruler was or, indeed, have much sense of being part of a great empire.

The empire's homeland subjects

The situation must have been different in the king's homeland territories. Here, there were a number of (now partially excavated) administrative centres, like Sapinuwa, Sarissa and Tapikka, managed by officials appointed by the king.[38] Sapinuwa (modern Ortaköy), sixty kilometres northeast of Hattusa, is often mentioned in the texts, and played an important role within the kingdom as an administrative centre, a cultic centre and a military base. Among the buildings so far excavated in the city one has been identified as a palace, no doubt one of His Majesty's homes away from home. More than three thousand texts were found in the city's own archives. While most of them are written in Hittite, about a quarter are in the Hurrian language; mainly ritual texts, they indicate the increasingly important role of Hurrian elements in Hittite culture.[39] The Hittite texts are mainly letters. They consist almost entirely of correspondence between the Hittite king, queen and the king's officials from all parts of the Hittite world. The letters date about a century before Hattusili, probably to the reign of his great-grandfather Tudhaliya III. But, no doubt, Sapinuwa continued to play an important role in the homeland's administrative and religious activities down at least to Hattusili's reign. It was perhaps the empire's second city, and the palace there may often have served as the king's residence. Unfortunately, not enough of the city has been excavated to enable us to make any assessment of its size or the size of its population.

A large building identified as a palace has also been unearthed in the city of Tapikka (modern Maşat), 116 kilometres northeast of Hattusa and almost certainly another of the homeland's administrative centres. Here, too, a tablet archive has been discovered, probably again dating to Hattusili's great-grandfather's reign. It consists of 116 texts, ninety-six of which are letters exchanged between the king and his locally-based officials, and between these officials and their colleagues in other parts of the empire. Cultic texts were also found in the archive. The city was destroyed during the so-called 'Concentric Invasions' but subsequently rebuilt, probably by Suppiluliuma, and no doubt provided, or continued to provide, the homeland with an important administrative and cultic centre during Hattusili's reign. The same applied to the city of Sarissa (modern Kuşaklı), just south of the Marassantiya River and probably another important cultic centre of the homeland, to judge from its material remains and cultic tablet-finds.[40]

All three of the above cities and very likely other homeland centres would have been important points on the routes of Hattusili's tours of inspection. These often took the form of religious pilgrimages. The Hittite calendar was filled with religious festivals, celebrated both in the capital and in many other urban and rural locations in the homeland. As the gods' deputy on earth, His Majesty was obliged to participate in person in many of these festivals, particularly the most important ones.[41] They were held at critical periods in the agricultural year, like the beginning of spring or autumn. As his entourage progressed from one cultic site to another, the local populace had many opportunities to catch sight of their king, though a large bodyguard would have kept him a safe distance from them. Religious festivals were far from solemn affairs. Texts tell us of the feasting and entertainment and sports competitions which accompanied them, no doubt enjoyed by the common folk as well as their superiors.

Hattusili must have welcomed these pilgrimages and accompanying celebrations as a means of winning and maintaining the goodwill of his subjects, particularly the homeland ones, and their acceptance of him as their legitimate king. He had illegally seized the throne, but he had done so, he claimed, with the backing of the gods. Their physical presence at the festival celebrations, in statue form, was a guarantee of this. The political value of the king's pilgrimages must have been considerable. Jürgen Seeher suggests (in an email to me) a comparison with Franconian kings of the Middle Ages: 'Their rule by constantly changing between various residences is a possible parallel for the Hittite system where the king is often on the road for the various festivals in various towns.' A former student of mine, Dr Rosemary Gill, later to become an expert on medieval history, comments: 'Medieval royalty was often peripatetic, not least because it was deemed politic for the king to be seen, and for him to be assured of the loyalty of his more distant subjects.' No doubt Hattusili also conducted pilgrimages to important cult centres outside the homeland, like Puduhepa's home town, Lawazantiya, whenever he considered it appropriate and circumstances permitted. Hittite travelling courts, like those of the Middle Ages, meant that the king was absent from his capital for much of his reign – as many kings were for the military campaigns they led. Perhaps this helps explain Hattusa's surprisingly small population, according to Seeher's calculations, even during Hattusili's reign; though probably few of his absences from the capital were devoted to military enterprises.

A tangible expression of the empire's might

This brings me to my final point in this chapter. A Great King's royal capital was the physical embodiment of the power and military might of the empire over which it held sway. To outward appearances, Hattusa with its towering external walls extending 6.6 kilometres over rough terrain – fortifications far exceeding the defensive needs of the city – admirably served this purpose. Let us for a moment imagine ourselves there in Hattusili's reign. The vast empire which he ruled, relatively small though the population of many of its regions may have been, was still largely intact. And, as diplomats from another kingdom and other visitors approached the capital, the massive enclosure wall with its main entrance guarded by two fierce sculpted lions roaring a challenge to all who sought entry was an impressive introduction to the royal seat of the Great King of Hatti.

Think then of Seeher's estimated size of the city's population – between 2,300 and 4,600, or five thousand at most. The immense rugged area inside the walls must have appeared sparsely inhabited, leaving aside the enclosed Lower City where the palace and Great Temple were located. Indeed, without industrial workshops or a large market place, the capital must have seemed almost deserted, especially when many of those who lived there were busily occupied within the confines of the city's temples, or absent from the city on religious piligrimages or for other reasons. So, to one entering Hattusa via the Lion Gate, did the external impressiveness of the walls give way to anti-climax when the city inside them first came into view?

I cannot imagine this was the case. Hattusa was what we might call a cultic centre on a grand scale. I suggest that many of the areas we see today as empty, rock-strewn wasteland were filled with gardens, sacred groves, and ceremonial places giving the city a special character no longer apparent to us. This, I believe, is what made Hattusa a truly impressive city for those who visited it. Also, when the city was to host important foreign delegations from one of His Majesty's royal brothers, special colourful pavilions may have been erected in the city to house them and their retinues. I am reminded of the pavilions erected outside the ancient city of Persepolis by Iran's last Shah in October 1971; these were to house his international guests who had come to celebrate the 2,500th anniversary of the birth of Cyrus the Great, founder of the first Persian empire.

Like Persepolis, Hattusa was, in a limited way, a multi-functional capital. But, like Cyrus, and perhaps more than any of his own predecessors, Hattusili was eager to maintain his royal capital's image as an important spiritual symbol, to all who beheld it, of the might of the empire over which he held sway, an empire which boasted a pantheon of a thousand gods. To be sure, archaeological evidence indicates that there were already signs of decline in parts of the city during Hattusili's reign. But temporary cosmetic makeovers can work wonders in preparation for visits by foreign dignitaries, or for any events of international importance that took place there – without leaving any trace in the archaeological record.

Postscript

There is a group of questions I haven't answered in this chapter about the management of the empire. What were the empire's sources of income? What form did this income take? Who paid it? How was it collected? On what was it spent? These questions are relevant to Hattusili's career, but not specific to it. So, I've decided to deal with them separately from the main text, in Appendix 2, 'The Economy'. Could I suggest that you read this Appendix now that you've come to the end of this chapter?

11

'Beware of Greeks Bearing Gifts'[1]

The Classical tradition

The title of this chapter is one of the best-known quotations (not quite correctly translated) from the great works of literature, on a par with those memorable pithy statements from Shakespeare and the Bible embedded in our language today. It comes from the epic poem *The Aeneid*, composed by the Roman poet Virgil towards the end of the first century BC. More correctly translated, it reads: 'I fear the Danaans, even (when they come) bearing gifts.'[2] These words were spoken by the Trojan priest Laocoön. They were a warning to Priam, king of Troy, that the enormous wooden horse the Greeks had left as a gift-offering, before they abandoned (so it seemed) their ten-year-long siege of Troy, was a trap. After the Trojans dragged the horse into the city and ended their celebrations in wine-sodden sleep, the Greeks hidden inside the horse opened the hatch in its belly, crept out, and then flung wide the city gates, letting in their Greek companions who had concealed themselves close by. They set about massacring Troy's inebriated, slumbering citizenry, and then looted the city before burning it to the ground.

Virgil tells the story through the lips of the Trojan prince Aeneas, who, after escaping his burning city by sea with a band of refugees, is blown by a storm onto the coast of Africa, on his mission to establish a New Troy, which happens to be Rome, in Hesperia, 'the Land of the Evening Star' – that is to say, Italy. While repairing his small fleet in Africa, he and his followers are hosted by the Carthaginian queen Dido, to whom he tells his terrible tale.

Troy in its historical context

Almost everyone now agrees that Troy was a real place, and that the citadel of Troy, which is the setting for much of the eighth- (or seventh-) century BC poet Homer's epic, *The Iliad*, occupies a mound called Hisarlık in Turkish today, on

Figure 11.1 Sign at entrance to Troy. Author photo.

the northwestern edge of the Anatolian peninsula. In Homeric epic, Ilios (originally Wilios) alternated with Troia (Troy) as the name of the stronghold of the Trojans. The Hittite version of this name is Wilusa. Today, at the entrance to the site of Hisarlık, now a thriving tourist attraction, visitors are greeted by a laconic endorsement of the once much disputed equation. It is a stone sign engraved with just two words: ILIOS and underneath WILUSA. That surely puts an end to all scholarly debate about the matter!

On how much historical fact the legend is based is still greatly debated. But there's now fairly common agreement that, if there *were* a Trojan War, even one on a much smaller scale than Classical tradition would have us believe, it belongs somewhere in the first decades of the thirteenth century. This would place it within the period of the youth and early manhood of our Hittite prince and future king.

The Hittite dimension

The *Iliad* provides us with lists of all the allied Greek states who according to Homeric tradition banded together under the leadership of Agamemnon, king of Mycenae, for the siege of Troy. Correspondingly, we are provided with a list of states who allied themselves with Troy.³ Now, we know from Hittite texts that many western Anatolian countries, extending to the Aegean Sea and including the northwestern region where Troy was located, were actually vassal states of the Hittite empire – at least from time to time. So, the Hittites should certainly have been involved in any major conflicts with the Greeks in western Anatolia. But, surprisingly, there is not one single reference to them anywhere in Homer. Just a short time after the collapse of their empire, it seems that the Bronze Age Hittites had entirely vanished, at least from our written sources.

Do the Hittites themselves throw any light on contacts, and possible conflicts, with their western neighbours? In the 1920s, the Swiss scholar Emil Forrer claimed to have found Greeks in the Hittite tablets. The Greeks, he said, appeared in a small number of texts which referred to a place called Ahhiyawa,⁴ and several times to a king of Ahhiyawa. He noted that Homer in his epics, didn't call the Greeks Greeks (that was a much later name for them), or even Hellenes (their Classical name), but Argives, Danaans and Achaians, seemingly interchangeably.

From the last of these, the place-name 'Achaia' was postulated. Ahhiyawa, Forrer concluded, was the Hittite name for Achaia. He then went on to equate the names of legendary heroes in the Trojan War with the names of persons who appear in historical Hittite texts. This was a step too far for many scholars. There was much acrimonious debate over Forrer's conclusions, especially his name equations, which ended up with the baby being thrown out with the bathwater, and Forrer being banned from any advancement in his academic career.

Now, however, the pendulum has swung back in Forrer's favour. (Forgive my mix of metaphors.) Though we don't have actual hard proof, the equation between Bronze Age (commonly called Mycenaean) Greece and Hittite-named Ahhiyawa is now almost universally accepted. This means that, in addition to some archaeological material, we have, in the Hittite texts which mention Ahhiyawa, *historical* evidence, not just legendary traditions, of the Bronze Age Greek world's dealings with Anatolia. To be sure, the 'Mycenaean' Greeks had a rudimentary script that we call Linear B. But the surviving tablets on which this script was written deal very largely with inventories of weapons and tools, land allocations, list of slaves, temple goods and the like. They provide us with almost no historical information. For this we have to rely on the admittedly sparse and often fragmentary Hittite tablets referring to Ahhiyawa.⁵ These date from the fifteenth to the thirteenth centuries BC. They tell us not what we learn from archaeology about Greek trading contacts along Anatolia's western and southern coasts, but about Greek involvement with and interference in the political and military affairs of the western Anatolian states. And most of these were vassal kingdoms of the Hittites.

What precisely was the Greek kingdom called Ahhiyawa?[6]

Before we go any further, we have an important question to answer. What did the Hittites, or, more precisely, their kings and their advisers, think the name Ahhiyawa actually meant? Our small number of surviving 'Ahhiyawa texts' (only about twenty-nine of them) sometimes use the term in what I think is a broad sense referring to the Bronze Age Greek world in general – in particular, the large landmass lying across the Aegean Sea, with some islands in the Aegean and eastern Mediterranean seas probably thrown in for good measure. But other texts refer to a king of Ahhiyawa. So there must have been at least one specific kingdom of Ahhiyawa. What *was* this kingdom?

There has been a lot of toing and froing on this topic. When I was a young student, a common view was that in the last part of the Late Bronze Age (Late Helladic III in archaeological terms) a 'Mycenaean empire' developed, which

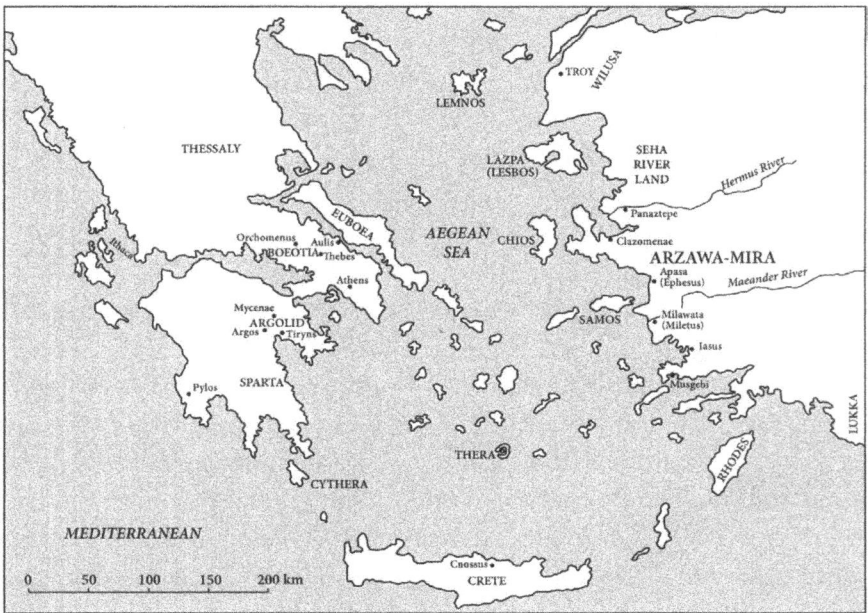

Map 11.1 Bronze Age Greece and western Anatolia. Author map.

controlled the Greek mainland palace centres and a number of islands including Crete, and that Mycenae itself was the head of this empire. We've noted that in legendary tradition Mycenae was ruled by King Agamemnon, leader of the Greek coalition assembled to fight against Troy.

Subsequently, a number of Mycenaean scholars took the view that, while there was much cultural homogeneity among the Bronze Age polities, and perhaps even collaboration between them on military and trading enterprises, the palace centres like Mycenae, Thebes, Argos and Pylos were politically independent of one another. Currently, some scholars have once more adopted the view that the Greek world (or at least a large part of it) was politically united, presumably under the rule of a man the Hittites called 'the King of Ahhiyawa'.[7] Professor Jeremy Rutter envisages a 'powerful western Aegean state that developed gradually over as long as two centuries prior to emerging in the later 15th century BC as a "Great Kingdom" to merit comparison with such longer-established and far better textually documented Near Eastern states as Hatti, Egypt, Assyria, and Babylon'.[8] However, Nicholas Blackwell concludes that, while 'the Hittites understood Ahhiyawa as a unified territory rather than as a group of small, competing polities, ... the Hittite portrayal of a unified Ahhiyawa is an inaccurate assessment of the 13th-century Aegean political landscape'.[9]

A very important consideration is that the kingdom called Ahhiyawa in Hittite texts clearly controlled at its height part of Anatolia's western coast. This must indicate that it had at its disposal a sufficiently large maritime force not only to maintain trading contacts along this coast, but also to establish possession of islands in the Aegean Sea. Most likely these included the large islands Samos, Chios and Lesbos which lay close to the Anatolian mainland. But that would seem to rule out inland Mycenae and Thebes as candidates for the kingdom of Ahhiyawa. Unless their kingdoms extended to the Greek coast and included subject territories, with seaports and other coastal facilities, which could supply them with significant maritime resources, powerful enough to extend their control to Anatolian territory across the Aegean Sea.

Unfortunately, we have no hard evidence that prominent kingdoms like Mycenae and Thebes had such capabilities, and therefore no proof that either of them was the kingdom of Ahhiyawa referred to in Hittite texts. This is why I wrote a somewhat counterintuitive article suggesting that Pylos might have been the kingdom in question. It controlled a large slice of the western Peloponnese (southern mainland Greece) with ample coastal facilities, and it obviously had sizeable fleets whose trading activities extended to the Anatolian coast and its offshore islands. These fleets could very likely be used for political and military purposes in the Anatolian region.[10] Also, for what it's worth, the remains of a large marine fresco was recently discovered in one of the halls of the palace at Pylos[11] – in contrast to other palace centres which have almost no depictions of marine motifs in their surviving artworks, either on their walls or as decorations on pottery vessels and other artifacts.

I submitted my article to Anna Lucia D'Agata, editor of the Italian journal, *Studi Micenei ed Egeo-Anatolici* (*SMEA*), for possible publication. She accepted the article and then went on to say: 'Considering the high level of interest that surrounds the Ahhiyawa question, I wonder whether you agree to publish it as a forum article in the next issue of *SMEA*. A few, mostly Aegean, scholars might be invited to discuss your hypothesis. What do you think? Would you agree with such a project?' I happily did so, and five scholars, three Mycenaean, and two Anatolian, responded to my article. As I expected, none of them agreed with me, though one did not completely rule out Pylos as a candidate for the kingdom of Ahhiyawa. But the whole enterprise proved a most useful one. In sending me the responses, Dr D'Agata commented:

> Even if none of the colleagues seems to accept your proposal of Pylos as the centre of Ahhiyawa, most of them consider your opinion an option to think about. The final result is a very good re-considering of the much-discussed question of Ahhiyawa. It is remarkable that, as responses to your text, this vexata quaestio of the Eastern Mediterranean archaeology is considered from different points of views that have never been accounted for together.

Once again, I was reminded of Professor van den Hout's comment: 'Daring to be wrong is what often makes scholarship progress more than just daring to be right.'

One of the problems with Pylos was its location on the western side of Greece, the 'wrong side' for my proposal in logistical terms. Professor Robert Schon, one of the respondents to my proposal, neatly summed up the logistical problems in these words:

> Distance is a concern. Pylos lies roughly three hundred nautical miles from Miletos, to use one example from the Hittite texts.... It would take weeks travelling at optimal cruising speed to reach the western coast of Anatolia from Pylos. Completing a return trip, with the captive women Bryce cites in the Linear B texts would be that much more difficult. A similar trip from the Argolid, Boeotia, or Attica ought to be far easier to accomplish. Add to this the fact that such a journey would also require multiple stops at friendly ports – something easier to attain from the eastern Peloponnese given prevalent currents and the

configuration of the Aegean islands which promote island hopping – other candidates for a naval threat seem just as, if not more, likely.[12]

That brings us back to the question: what specifically *was* the kingdom ruled by the man called the King of Ahhiyawa. (There are actually at least two such kings, of different periods, referred to in Hittite texts.) In fact, we are really back to square one. Almost all bets are on Mycenae as the kingdom with the Hittite-attested 'King of Ahhiyawa' as its ruler. Support for this is based on the fact that Mycenae, with its relatively well-preserved palace fortifications and the tholos tomb commonly and mistakenly called the Treasury of Atreus, was the first major Bronze Age site investigated by Heinrich Schliemann and is the most visually impressive 'Mycenaean' site; hence the name applied to all sites of the period. Of course, there is also the fact that in legendary tradition Agamemnon, king of Mycenae, was the supreme leader of the Greek forces in the Trojan War.

But we cannot rule out other possibilities. Thebes in the northern half of Greece has sometimes been touted as a candidate for the kingdom of Ahhiyawa. And thereby hangs an interesting modern tale. On 9 and 11 August 2003, the distinguished Anatolian scholar Professor Frank Starke held press conferences at Troy for German and Turkish journalists, respectively. He spoke of a very fragmentary Ahhiyawan letter that had long been known to scholars, but had allegedly been misinterpreted. It was a letter exchanged between a king of Ahhiyawa and a king of Hatti.[13] But the beginning of the document had largely broken away, and the names of the writer of the letter and his addressee, which must have appeared there, are now lost. The letter, which probably dates to the reign of Muwattalli (our Hattusili's brother), deals with a generations-long dispute between Ahhiyawa and Hatti over the ownership of some islands which lay between them, maybe large islands off the Anatolian coast.

Starke made the exciting claim that he had identified in the letter the name of the Ahhiyawan king with whom the dispute had begun; it was Kadmos, well known in Greek legend as a king of Thebes. Starke's claim was of major importance: firstly, because it seemed to provide historical evidence that Kadmos was an actual historical Greek king, not just the stuff of legend; secondly, because it apparently proved that Thebes not Mycenae was the centre of the kingdom of Ahhiyawa. And there was an important third reason. Starke claimed that, despite the lack of an identification in the letter, the document *originated* from the Ahhiyawan king. That is to say, he was the author. What we have would thus be a Hittite translation of the letter preserved in Hattusa's archives. And, if Starke were correct in his identification, the letter would be the first known document in the history of writing in the west.

A couple of years later, when Starke had not yet published his theories, Professor Annette Teffeteller of Concordia University, Montreal, organized a symposium (January 2006) with the title 'Mycenaeans and Anatolians in the Late Bronze Age', and invited a number of Mycenaean and Anatolian specialists, including myself, to take part. The symposium was designed to focus on the claims made about the letter by Professor Starke who agreed to be the symposium's keynote speaker. He had 'dared to be wrong' and, alas, 'being wrong' was in this case the verdict of the Symposium's other participants. They did, however, concede that he was right in assigning authorship of the original letter to an Ahhiyawan king. As far as I'm aware, Starke has never published his claims and, without publication, his views cannot be seriously entertained, although they were enthusiastically endorsed by the Swiss scholar Joachim Latacz.[14] Even the claim that the Ahhiyawan king was the author of the letter has now been disputed.[15]

So, we are still left with the conundrum: *what* was the kingdom of Ahhiyawa? Mycenaean Greece presents us with a broad range of possibilities – from a conglomerate of independent principalities of varying size, to a supranational kingdom which controlled much of the Greek mainland and probably a number of Aegean islands. The latter is the view now taken by a number of distinguished scholars. Then there is a middle ground between these two extremes: there were many small principalities in Mycenaean Greece, but most of these were absorbed into a small number of larger kingdoms, like Mycenae, Thebes and Pylos, which between them held sway over much of mainland Greece. A similar political and administrative structure may have applied to the larger Greek islands, like Rhodes and Crete. But there is no written evidence to support any views about what shape the political structure of the Mycenaean world took. And there are likely to be many more swings in scholarly opinion on the matter.

A major seagoing power

For the time being, I think we must come back to identifying the kingdom of Ahhiyawa with Mycenae and whatever territories were subject to it. But there is a strict condition in doing so. In Hittite texts the kingdom has a substantial seagoing capacity which, besides providing it with extensive trading contacts along the Anatolian coast, enables it to control a number of islands off the coast and, most importantly, to establish a major land-base on the coast, Milawanda (Classical Miletos) – on what was shortly before Hittite subject territory. It also becomes powerful enough in western Anatolia to give major support to the activities of an insurrectionist determined to destabilize regions which are subject states of the Hittite kingdom, and perhaps establish his own control over them, probably as a proxy of the Ahhiyawan king. Inevitably, the Ahhiyawan/Mycenaean presence in Anatolia was of great concern to the Hittites. Military conflict between the two kingdoms was becoming increasingly likely.

In sum, the kingdom of Ahhiyawa's potential to control or at least influence the course of history in Anatolia's western coastal regions could not have been realised unless it had access to significant naval resources, capable of transporting to Anatolia a substantial military force, establishing at least one major base on the Anatolian mainland, with civilian settlers and traders as well as military personnel, and providing a regular and reliable line of support from the Mycenaean mainland. All this would have been beyond the capacity of an apparently landlocked kingdom like Mycenae – *unless* Mycenae had control of petty kingdoms, population centres and other territories all the way to mainland Greece's eastern coast; that is to say, if all these became part of the kingdom of Mycenae.

This is what Jorrit Kelder concludes when he says:

> there is plenty of evidence that indicates that Mycenae and Thebes stood out amongst the palaces of the Late Bronze Age world. A salient feature is that both centres were situated in close proximity to various other major palaces and fortified settlements. Mycenae is a stone's throw away from Tiryns and Midea, whereas nearby Nauplion – which boasts one of the largest Mycenaean cemeteries known to date – and Argos must have been major centres, too. In view of their proximity to Mycenae, it is almost inconceivable that these centres – and as a result, their manpower and resources – did not fall under its control.[16]

In light of the currently available evidence, Mycenae is in his view the most likely candidate as the capital of Ahhiyawa. And, in this scenario, control over Nauplion, with its substantial seaport facilities, could well have given it the status of a major seagoing power.

I concur with Kelder's conclusion, about Mycenae, in particular, while allowing that there may have been other major palace centres in Mycenaean Greece, with extensive subject territories, not only Pylos or Thebes, but others as well, including some on the large offshore islands like Rhodes and Crete. Unfortunately, explicit written evidence for any of this, is not found in the surviving Mycenaean texts. The small number of remaining Linear B tablets are of no help in this regard. Kelder raises the possibility that much of the Mycenaean administration was likely conducted on media other than clay, such as papyrus, wood or even parchment.[17] But, if these highly perishable materials were ever used by the Mycenaeans as writing materials, they would long since have rotted away, if not already destroyed in the conflagrations that reduced to rubble the palace centres where they were stored.

Relations between Hatti and Ahhiyawa

There is one important point to add. While it is clear from the Hittite Ahhiyawa texts that relations between the Hittites and a specific Ahhiyawan/Mycenaean kingdom were often fraught, the texts also indicate that they sometimes maintained relatively close diplomatic relations. This is evident from the Hittite king's references to his Ahhiyawan counterpart as a 'Great King' and his addressing him as 'my brother', terms which in the Near Eastern world are reserved for only the greatest of the rulers of this world – the pharaoh of Egypt and the kings of Hatti, Babylon and Assyria.[18] There is just an occasional reference to gift-giving in the Ahhiyawa texts,[19] and *if* gifts were regularly exchanged between the Hittite and Ahhiyawan kings, they may have helped strengthen the ties between their kingdoms. This is what Bronze Age gift exchanges were supposed to do. But no doubt the Trojan priest Laocoön wasn't alone in his mistrust of the Greeks. Hittite kings, too, feared, or at least remained wary, of the Greeks, even if they did occasionally come bearing gifts.

If the Trojan War has any basis in historical fact, it belongs to the era when Anatolia was dominated by the kingdom of the Hittites. And, as we've noted, the possible historical time frame for the war can be narrowed down to the thirteenth century BC, according to many scholars and archaeologists, probably (as we've also noted) to the early decades of the century. Troy, called Wilusa in Hittite texts, was one of the empire's vassal states and, during its period of vassalhood, its overlords sought, by both force and diplomacy, to maintain their sovereignty over it and to protect it from its enemies.

So, if there *were* a major conflict between Greeks and Trojans, the Hittite king at the time, perhaps Muwattalli, would have been involved. His brother Hattusili, then a young prince, may have played a role as well. There is no mention at all of the Hittites in any of our Classical sources, from the *Iliad* onwards. But, despite this, our Hittite texts provide links, both diplomatic and conflictual, between

Bronze Age Greece and Hittite Anatolia. They may thus contribute to the evolution of the tradition of a Trojan War. Events during the reign of Hattusili may have been part of this contribution, particularly those we'll be dealing with in the next chapter.

12

'Bleating in Cuneiform Across the Wine-Dark Sea'

Shortly before my first visit to Oxford, in 1974, I'd been reading again the lively and entertaining book, *History and the Homeric Iliad*, by the late Denys Page, one of the most eminent Classical scholars of his age.[1] In this book, Professor Page entered into the then robust debate about whether the word 'Ahhiyawa' in Hittite texts was the Hittite way of referring to the contemporary Bronze Age Greeks. Strongly disagreeing with those scholars who maintained a Greek mainland location for Ahhiyawa, he believed, and argued eloquently, that Ahhiyawa was the island of Rhodes. To me, it seemed typical of Professor Page that, when his arguments had little or no evidential support, his prose became all the purpler, and he would sometimes dismiss opposing views simply with a disarmingly witty turn of phrase. Brushing aside arguments in support of a mainland Ahhiyawa across the Aegean Sea, he referred to 'a letter of complaint', written by a Hittite king to his Ahhiyawan counterpart. Can you really imagine, he asked his readers, a Hittite king 'bleating in cuneiform across the wine-dark sea?' This rhetorical question has always stuck in my mind; and Professor Page did present more substantial arguments in support of his thesis.

Who and what is this document all about? Was Hattusili its author?

Here is a translation of the first *preserved* lines of the 'letter' to which Page refers: [. . .] went and destroyed the town of Attarimma. He burned it down together with the fortified royal compound. [Then] when the people of Lukka appealed to Tawagalawa, he went down to those lands. They likewise appealed to me, so that I came down to those lands.[2]

Thus 'begins' one of the best-known documents commonly attributed to the reign of Hattusili.[3] But, before we talk about it, there are several important negatives we should bear in mind. First, the document is obviously incomplete. It begins part way through a narrative passage of which the first lines are missing. In fact, the 'letter', so called, extended over three tablets. Only the third of these has survived. We know this from the colophon, which is a statement at the end of a document indicating such things as the number of tablets on which it is written. It tells us that the tablet we have is the third and final one of the composition.

Unfortunately, neither the name of the Hittite king who composed it nor that of the Ahhiyawan king to whom it's addressed has been preserved. Presumably, both would have appeared at the beginning of the first tablet. So we could not until recently be confident that Hattusili was the document's author. My longtime friend and mentor, Oliver Gurney revived an earlier view that it was Muwattalli, Hattusili's brother and antepenultimate predecessor on the throne. But a new, thorough, comprehensive edition of the text, edited by Susanne Heinhold-Krahmer and Elisabeth Rieken, with contributions by a number of other scholars, has virtually settled the matter. On the basis of their comprehensive studies of the text – philological, palaeographical, epigraphic, historical, graphological – these scholars have argued convincingly, to my mind conclusively, that Hattusili, not Muwattalli, was the document's author.[4]

Another thing is that, despite the name we now give it, the main subject of the 'letter' is not Tawagalawa at all. We're told that Tawagalawa, brother of the Ahhiyawan king,[5] had come to western Anatolia specifically to visit Millawanda;[6] this was apparently in response to an appeal from refugees who were seeking some sort of assistance, perhaps asylum in Ahhiyawa. But it's unclear in what capacity he made his visit. As the current Ahhiyawan king's *representative* or as his *predecessor* on Ahhiyawa's throne? In §5 of the letter we find the statement: *When Tawagalawa himself, (as the representative of?) the Great King, crossed over to Millawanda,* ... Thus Gary Beckman translates these words. But, if you remove the speculative parenthesis, the conclusion seems to be that Tawagalawa was also a Great King, presumably preceding his brother, the document's addressee. And, if you look again at the last two sentences of our document's opening lines, it's possible that the appeals from the people of Lukka to both Tawagalawa and the Hittite King were made at different times, the earlier one to Tawagalawa when he was the Ahhiyawan Great King, the later one to Hattusili.[7] Well, that remains open to question. But what is *not* open to question is whom this document is mainly about. As we've noted, it's not Tawagalawa. In fact it's a renegade called Piyamaradu, a perennial thorn in the Hittites' side. So, if we feel that our incomplete document needs some sort of tag, we might more appropriately call it the 'Piyamaradu affair' – leaving open the possibility, indeed even the probability, that the document isn't a letter at all. We'll come back to that.

The document has been discussed many times in many articles and books, so let me let me just briefly here explain what it's about. Trouble had flared in southwestern Anatolia, involving people from the land called Lukka (whose inhabitants I referred to in Chapter 10 as a fractious, often rebellious lot, divided among themselves and difficult to control), serious enough to warrant an expedition to the west led by the Great King Hattusili himself. A notorious troublemaker called Piyamaradu, who already in Muwattalli's reign had engaged in disruptive activities in the western vassal states, was once more active in the region. Tantalizingly, the remaining portion of our document begins part way through what Hattusili is telling us about the Lukka people. If, by chance, the first part of the missing passage came to light (it must have appeared at the bottom of the second tablet), we'd no doubt have a clearer picture of the nature of the Lukka appeal to the Hittite king, and what Piyamaradu had to do with it. Anyhow, it's clear that Piyamaradu had stepped up his campaign of destabilization in the west, knowing he had at least the tacit support of the Ahhiyawan king, and trusting that he could avoid a major confrontation with the Hittites. My guess is that he aimed to carve a kingdom of his own in the west out of existing Hittite subject territory, in alliance with the king of Ahhiyawa, or at least as his western proxy.

But, to judge from a passage which follows the document's opening words, he tried to do a deal with Hattusili when the Hittite king had already embarked on a campaign to the west to flush him out of his strongholds and put an end to his nefarious activities. Let's look at this attempted deal from two opposite perspectives.

First perspective

You are King Hattusili. You've become increasingly concerned about what's going on in your western provinces. Some of the vassal rulers there had expressed support for Urhi-Teshub, your ousted predecessor, in the conflict that put you on his throne. You have doubts about their loyalty to you now. You're also increasingly worried about your Ahhiyawan counterpart's intentions in the region. Will he be content to confine himself and his subjects to peaceful trading activities? Or do his ambitions go further? But, above all, there is the Piyamaradu problem. He continues to destabilize the western states, and may even have invaded and occupied one of them for a time. So long as he remains at large, your hold on your western subjects remains precarious.

Yet military campaigns in the west are very costly operations, particularly in terms of the human resources required, and the likely shortage of manpower these will entail for other purposes – like the kingdom's food production and the defence of its core territory while the campaign force is away. You summon a meeting of your top military officers for consultation on the likely benefits, costs and risks of a western campaign. Your mentor and most trusted adviser, the Chief Scribe Mittanamuwa, is also present. He has consulted records of past campaigns in the region and provides advice on the logistical requirements of a new campaign there. Do the hoped-for benefits outweigh the likely costs? Have you really any choice in what you must do?

You decide you haven't. You will lead a western campaign in person, and to add to the significance of the campaign, you will take with you the second highest officer in the land, your son, the crown prince.[8] Your army may be smaller than is usual for a major military campaign. But your presence at the head of this army is an emphatic statement of the importance you attach to reasserting your authority in the west, and the message this will send to your vassal rulers, to Piyamaradu, and not least to your royal brother, the King of Ahhiyawa.

Your expedition is now well underway but, when you arrive in the town of Sallapa, where your army pauses for rest, refreshment and replenishing its supplies, a surprise is in store for you. A horseman is seen galloping towards your camp at high speed. Your guards quickly seize the man and bring him before you. He says he has been sent to you by Piyamaradu, with a message and a proposition. Apparently intimidated by the approach of your army under your personal command, Piyamaradu humbly offers his submission and begs to be appointed one of your vassal rulers. There is one condition. He asks that the crown prince go to his camp, to provide him with a personal escort back to your royal presence; thereupon, you can formally endorse his status as a vassal ruler and decide with him which vassal state he will be appointed to: perhaps an existing one, perhaps one newly created. His offer is tempting. Maybe it's too good to be true. There is a risk that, if you send him the crown prince, as he asks, your successor will become his hostage. Nevertheless, you decide to take the risk and despatch the prince to the enemy's lair – providing him with a strong bodyguard, just in case.

But Piyamaradu reneges on the deal. He treats the crown prince with contempt and ups the stakes by demanding an appointment 'on the spot' – presumably as ruler of the land where he is now. If you refuse, the deal is off. He sends you a messenger with the ultimatum. You are furious! The man is obviously resorting to delaying tactics. Even though your army is on the march towards him, he believes that by buying more time, through bogus negotiations, he can successfully defy you – especially if he has some assurance of support from Ahhiyawa. In spite of this, you still hope that the Piyamaradu crisis can be resolved diplomatically – as your army draws ever closer to his strongholds.

Second perspective

You are Piyamaradu. How should we understand from your perspective the episode we've just learned about from Hattusili's?

We, the modern readers, do not know what your original status was: a renegade from Hittite authority of noble birth, a freelance Ahhiyawan, an agent of the Ahhiyawan king, or a former disgraced ruler of a western vassal state? Or someone quite different?[9] Anyhow, you appear to have been a stateless person for some years, dating back to Muwattalli's reign when you attempted to seize the Hittite vassal kingdom Wilusa. You may even have gained control of Wilusa for a while, and to do this you must have had a strong body of support, with enough military muscle to stage a takeover. Quite likely, you had assistance from a large part of Wilusa's population as well.

Your attempted takeover failed when you and your forces were driven from the vassal state by a Hittite expeditionary force sent by Muwattalli. But you escaped capture, and won the backing of the Ahhiyawan king in continuing your disruptive activities in the region. Now, under some pressure from an approaching Hittite army determined to finish you off, you want a deal: a vassal kingdom of your own in return for acknowledging the Hittite king as your overlord.

Negotiations have started off well, it seems. Hattusili has agreed to your request that he send you the crown prince to escort you back to him, for the formal conferral of vassal rulership upon you. But then things go pear-shaped. According to Hattusili, you make a specious complaint about the king failing to follow correct protocol and you demand a kingdom 'here on the spot!' as a strict condition before you will return with the crown prince. Are you simply playing games, engaging in delaying tactics and humiliating His Majesty, as the Great King believes? Or are you sincere in your willingness to submit to the king if your request for a local vassal kingdom is granted?

Has something happened in your meeting with the crown prince that Hattusili has kept from us? Maybe Hattusili's son has brought with him new terms and conditions that you find unacceptable. Very likely you suspect from the prince's words and demeanour that if you return with him to his father, you will be walking into a trap. That must be a serious risk. You'll simply be arrested and taken back to Hattusa as part of Hattusili's war booty. You might even be assassinated. So, you prefer to take your chances – that the Great King will call off his campaign or that if he doesn't, your own forces, with Ahhiyawan backing, will be sufficient to protect you. You send the crown prince away with a flea in his ear.

A tough, elusive enemy[10]

Which, if either, of these two scenarios do you think more likely? Whichever it is, the die is now cast. What Hattusili sees as a gross insult to His Majesty, and indeed to the Hittite kingdom in general, cannot go unpunished. Piyamaradu retreats with the army he has mustered to the mountainous terrain around a place called Iyalanda near the Aegean coast. Though his forces must be substantially smaller than those of his enemy, he is well aware that the Hittites prefer to do battle on open ground, and no doubt his men are well trained in fighting their enemy in thickly forested, mountain country.[11]

Hattusili has no choice but to fight Piyamaradu in a place of his opponent's choosing. As his army draws ever closer to its prey, Hattusili sends a final message to Piyamaradu. He still leaves open the possibility of a peaceful settlement, but Piyamaradu's troops must first abandon their mountain stronghold. Piyamaradu does not even bother to reply. Hattusili continues his march to where the enemy forces are ready to meet him. He knows his chariots and bows and arrows and long spears will be of limited use in rugged, densely forested terrain. And he knows that Piyamaradu will never send his forces from their well protected mountain retreats to engage the Hittite army on open ground. So, with great reluctance, he orders his men into the mountains, to flush out and destroy the enemy.

Three times the Hittite forces are ambushed, no doubt with significant losses. But, finally, their sheer weight of numbers prevails and Piyamaradu's forces are overwhelmed and defeated. Retribution inevitably follows. Except for one fortress, the entire land of Iyalanda, which had been home to Piyamaradu whether it liked it or not, is ravaged, its crops and settlements destroyed. But Piyamaradu escapes capture and takes final refuge in the city of Millawanda (aka Milawata) on the coast. It is a major Bronze Age city and is later to become the important Classical city Miletos. Piyamaradu is now trapped – or so it seems.

Hattusili appeals to the Ahhiyawan king for an extradition order to hand Piyamaradu over to him. The request is granted. An order is despatched by the Ahhiyawan to his agent in Millawanda, a man called Atpa, who also happens to be Piyamaradu's son-in-law. 'Comply with the Hittite request', he is told. A messenger is sent to Hattusili to inform him of the Ahhiyawan's decision. It is hardly a warm response to his royal brother. The messenger brings with him no gifts, no personal words of greeting from the Ahhiyawan court, Hattusili complains. Both could have been expected as part of normal diplomatic relations between royal brothers.

But at least Hattusili has finally got his man. Or has he? He has cleared all diplomatic hurdles for entering the territory of his brother-king. But, when he arrives in Millawanda to take delivery of Piyamaradu, his quarry is no longer there! He has escaped by ship, no doubt an Ahhiyawan vessel, and found refuge out of his adversary's reach, probably on an offshore island like Samos which is very likely under Ahhiyawan control. That leaves him free to continue his disruptive activities in the Hittites' western states, just as soon as Hattusili and his troops have left the region.

Hattusili's 'letter' in the aftermath of these events seeks his royal brother's cooperation in ending the renegade's activities, either by settling him somewhere in Ahhiyawa and keeping him on a tight leash, or forcing him to seek refuge in another land outside Hittite control. Or better still, by handing him over, finally, to Hittite authorities. More generally, the document attempts to win Ahhiyawan cooperation in stabilizing the west, especially by not interfering in Hittite subject territory, or encouraging the likes of Piyamaradu not to do so.

This at least is what I believe we can infer from the badly broken text from which I've tried to piece together the relevant information.

An enigmatic reference to Wilusa

But in this context let me refer to an oft quoted and much debated couple of lines in the 'letter'. Gary Beckman translates them thus: *The King of Hatti has persuaded me about the matter of the land of Wilusa concerning which he and I were hostile to one another and we have made peace.*[12] The Hittite verb *kururešuen*, translated here as 'were hostile to', has a range of possible interpretations – from outright military conflict to a mere disagreement, diplomatic or otherwise.[13]

So what relevance does Wilusa have to other matters discussed in our 'letter'? We've noted that Wilusa was the Hittite way of referring to what the Greeks called

Ilios (later Ilion) or Troy. Bronze Age, or Ahhiyawan, Greeks may well have sought control over Wilusa, which was a Hittite vassal kingdom for much of its existence. And Piyamaradu is associated in our Hittite texts with attacks on the kingdom, and perhaps temporary occupation of it, maybe acting as the Ahhiyawan king's proxy.[14] Possibly this is what the statement about hostility between the Ahhiyawan king and Hattusili in some past time is all about. In any case, Piyamaradu continued to escape Hittite justice on this and later occasions, with or without Ahhiyawan support, and carried out his insurrectionist activities for some years to come.

What is the actual nature and purpose of our document?

That brings us to two important questions. What is the *actual nature* of the so-called 'Tawagalawa letter'? And what primarily is its purpose? Remember that only the last third of it has survived. And, while that third deals primarily with the anti-Hittite exploits of Piyamaradu, and Hattusili's attempts to persuade his royal brother to put an end to them, we shouldn't assume that the *whole* document is about Piyamaradu. Our thinking about it may be skewed because we know nothing of the contents of the first two tablets.

So let's start with the first question. What exactly *is* the 'Tawagalawa letter'? (From this point on, I shall refer to the document simply as TL.) The basic answer is straightforward enough. It's a communication prepared by, or on behalf of, one Great King for the reception of another, and delivered to the recipient perhaps as part of a diplomatic mission. Many of the letters we have dealt with could be described in similar terms. But a number of scholars have taken the view that this document should not be called a letter. Professor Heinhold-Krahmer suggests that it is a briefing document for the envoy(s) who will go to the court of the Ahhiyawan king and present the Hittite king's case.[15] More precisely, I see it as a scripted piece of oratory whose final version is to be delivered orally to the Ahhiyawan king and his court by his royal brother's carefully chosen representative.

As I mentioned in Chapter 2, Michael Wood delivers part of TL as an oration in the Roman theatre at Miletus (Greek Miletos, Hittite Millawanda/Milawata). Anachronistic though its setting is, Wood ably demonstrates how effective TL might have been as a display of Hittite rhetoric. It is a powerfully charged speech, certainly not an abject admission of failure by a Hittite commander-in-chief who has slunk back to Hattusa in defeat. In fact, Nicholas Blackwell notes that, although the tablet came to light in the Hattusa archives, the source of its clay is the area of

Ephesos and Miletos; this suggests that the writer 'composed the text while (still) on campaign, perhaps in the vicinity of Millawanda'.[16] Let me go further and suggest that Hattusili composed it during his actual occupation of Millawanda. His presence there would give him important leverage – which he uses in a nuanced way. He is confident, assertive, at times angry and menacing, while at other times conciliatory and almost supplicatory, seeking cooperation not conflict with his Ahhiyawan royal brother over a matter that has seriously strained relations between them. His sentiments must be powerfully conveyed, by one of his best orators. 'Bleating in cuneiform across the wine-dark sea' may be a witty modern turn of phrase but it does scant justice to the speech's full dramatic range.

TL is addressed to a Greek/Ahhiyawan King – let's call him Agamemnon as many writers do – and must have been translated into Greek when presented to the Ahhiyawan king and his court. Now, native Hittite speakers who were also fluent in Greek were probably very hard to come by. I think it more likely that the orator was a native Luwian speaker, fluent in Greek as well as in Hittite, a trusted member of one of Hatti's westernmost subject territories which had close commercial contacts with Greeks. Through such contacts, many Luwian inhabitants of these territories, particularly Millawanda, must have developed at least some knowledge of the Greek language. And communications with the relevant local vassal rulers would have identified a person thoroughly loyal to his Hittite overlord and fluent in three languages – Luwian, Hittite and Greek – who could serve as the king's messenger at the court of the Ahhiyawan king. I've no doubt the man chosen was well rehearsed by Hattusili in his presentation before he set out on his mission. And, if the text was actually written when Hattusili was in Millawanda, this was probably the homeland of the man selected as his representative at the Ahhiyawan court.

The document was too important, I believe, to entrust its translation to a native Greek interpreter, who might unintentionally, or deliberately, misconstrue the original speaker's words (such an offence, if committed by the king's representative, was punishable by beheading[17]), and would almost certainly fail to convey any of the original speech's rhetorical impact. Hattusili couldn't allow the speech to be interpreted by a native Greek, even if there *were* one able to speak Hittite, especially if the speech was presented to his royal brother's entire court, including his kingdom's military commanders. It was a speech composed for an audience of many, not simply the man to whom it was specifically addressed. We can assume that a written version of it as well, also in Greek, was prepared for the Ahhiyawan king, for consideration at his leisure, in council with his chief advisers.

Of course, all this is purely speculative. But let's continue for a while down my speculative path. Hattusili had entered Millawanda, now Ahhiyawan territory, in a last failed attempt to run Piyamaradu to ground. But, after the fugitive had eluded him, he remained in the city, with an armed force, to ensure his control of it while he sought a final settlement of the Piyamaradu affair with the renegade's chief supporter, the Ahhiyawan king. While the main purpose of the speech, if we can so judge from the remaining third of it, is to establish a more cooperative relationship with its prime recipient, or to consolidate a pact or treaty with him, despite his many alleged breaches of diplomatic protocol, it none the less emphasizes Hattusili's resolve to maintain his control over his western states, with a hint that he is prepared to go to war to ensure this.

To be sure, he was incapable of fighting a war on Ahhiyawa's home territory, wherever on the Greek mainland that may have been. But he *was* capable of depriving Ahhiyawa of its Anatolian possessions, of which the most prized was Millawanda. While he stresses his entry into Millawanda in pursuit of Piyamaradu was not intended as a breach of Ahhiyawa's sovereignty over it, he had demonstrated that Millawanda could easily be subdued by him and might permanently be reclaimed as Hittite territory. The orator Hattusili chose to deliver the speech (a man of western Luwian origin, I suggest) might also have been tasked with presenting written copies of it, perhaps even an oral version, in Luwian, at the courts of Hattusili's western vassal rulers. It would have provided them with some hope that, despite their overlord's setbacks in the west, Piyamaradu would cease menacing their territories, and that the Great King would continue to attach considerable importance to maintaining peace and stability in the territories they ruled.

Let me add one final piece of speculation. It's possible that the western campaign, recorded in the fragmentary remains of Hattusili's *Annals*, took place subsequent to the events recorded in TL; perhaps, after a complete breakdown of diplomatic relations with Ahhiyawa, this campaign resulted in Hattusili's reconquest of Millawanda and a firm reassertion of his authority over his western subjects, or at least the curbing of Ahhiyawan expansion within their region. We'll have more to say about this in the next chapter.

Were there treaties between Hittite and Ahhiyawan kings?

Before attempting to answer this question, let me provide a bit more detail about the significance of Millawanda in all we've been discussing. The city, and presumably its surrounding territory, had long been a major western Hittite possession, though it had leanings towards Ahhiyawa. In fact, early in the reign of Hattusili's father Mursili, it had allied itself with the Greek kingdom, and Mursili had to send a large expeditionary force under two of his most experienced generals to wrest it back.[18] But, at some time in the period between Mursili's early regnal years and Hattusili's accession, it had fallen firmly under Ahhiyawan control, as Hattusili clearly implies in TL. That's also borne out by archaeological evidence, which has shown conclusively that Millawanda was now a Mycenaean settlement.[19]

When and how did this happen? My guess is that it occurred peacefully during Muwattalli's reign as he prepared for his conflict with Ramesses. As part of his arrangements for ensuring stability in the western part of his empire while making ready for war in the eastern part, he had drawn up a (still surviving) treaty with his vassal ruler Alaksandu, king of Wilusa (Troy).[20] (He may have concluded treaties, now lost, with his other western rulers as well.) He also reached, I suggest, some sort of accord with the king of Ahhiyawa, conceding to him the land of Millawanda. It would have been a major concession, after Mursili had been so determined to keep the Greeks out of it. But the handover must have been subject to the Ahhiyawan king's agreement to certain conditions in return. Most important among these, if my speculations are correct, was an agreement to a non-aggression pact, stipulating that Ahhiyawa would not seek to encroach on any other Hittite territory in the west, either directly or through proxies.

Was there an actual peace accord, a pact or treaty, drawn up which specified the terms of this agreement? There is absolutely no evidence for a treaty either in the Hittite archives or in the extremely limited written material, the Linear B tablets, surviving from Mycenae or any other part of the Greek Bronze Age world. But let's keep an open mind about whether such an accord once existed.

On the Hittite side, we know of a number of treaties from the discovery of the treaties themselves, or fragments of them, inscribed on clay, and the one inscribed on a bronze tablet found by chance just outside the walls of the Hittite capital in 1986. But we seldom find references to these treaties, or to any others that have long since perished, elsewhere in our surviving texts. Even the famous 'Eternal Treaty' drawn up between Hattusili and Ramesses is known to us only from its two existing versions (one in the Hittite archives, the other on the walls of two temples in Egypt), not from any external references to it.

On the Greek side, Professor Kelder makes the point that '(not only) numerous clay tablets are likely to have been lost to the sands of time (at Mycenae, for instance, it is likely that the palace archive slid into the adjacent ravine when the palace collapsed), but also because much of the Mycenaean administration was likely conducted on media other than clay, such as papyrus, wood, or even parchment'.[21] Kelder goes on to say, 'More frustratingly, we lack all documentation regarding diplomatic affairs: no letters, no treaties – nothing comparable to the Hittite texts.' We cannot, then, rule out the possibility that diplomatic communications passed between the Hittite and Ahhiyawan courts, culminating in a treaty, but that all traces of them – or any treaty arising from them – are now lost.

Such a treaty might have provided the context for a number of matters discussed in TL, as well as in other diplomatic communications between the royal courts, both before and after a formal agreement was drawn up. (I should say here that my arguments about a possible Hittite-Ahhiyawan accord complement the case persuasively presented by Nicholas Blackwell in his article 'Ahhiyawa, Hatti, and Diplomacy'. Blackwell argues that 'Hattusili III's actions in the Tawagalawa letter indicate his adherence to an existing pact with Ahhiyawa, the parameters of which recall a more or less contemporary Hittite agreement with Egypt'.[22] I have preferred the term 'treaty' to 'pact', though the terms are generally considered synonymous.[23]) The emphasis TL's author gives to his strict observance of protocol, his justification for his breach of Ahhiyawan sovereignty by entering Millawandan territory, and the cooperation he expects in terminating Piyamaradu's activities in Hittite territory might all reflect conditions stated in a treaty between the two kings. Perhaps this treaty was referred to in the two missing tablets of the document.

Now if there *were* such a treaty, the prevention of military conflict between the two powers may have been its principal aim. Ahhiyawan kings were clearly interested in extending their territorial claims to the Anatolian coastal lands, and hostilities may have flared up from time to time with their Hittite counterparts, who were determined to ensure the security of their western vassal states. Perhaps we can see a remote connection between these supposed hostilities and the Greek legend of the Trojan War. Perhaps this was what the 'hostility' referred to in TL was all about.

Of course, neither Hattusili nor any other Hittite king, for that matter, had anywhere near the resources needed to launch an invasion against a mainland Greek kingdom, even if he had at his disposal a fleet drawn from vassal states which bordered upon the Aegean Sea. On the other hand, the Ahhiyawan king very likely did have the means of transporting sufficient numbers of his military forces, both infantry and chariotry, across the Aegean, probably using one or more of the (presumably) Ahhiyawan-controlled islands off the Anatolian coast, like Lesbos, Samos or Chios, as launching bases for his troops if he sought to invade the Hittites' western subject states.

He would also have been aided and abetted by the disruptive military activities in the region of at least one local warlord, Piyamaradu. Indeed, the threat of direct aggressive action by Ahhiyawa against the Hittites' western states may have grown ever greater as the Hittites' hold on these states grew ever weaker. An apparent decline in Hittite authority in the region may already have become evident in Muwattalli's reign, with the redirection of the bulk of Hatti's military resources to the southeast as a military confrontation with Egypt became inevitable. And now, in Hattusili's reign, several factors may have combined to reduce to a critically low level the able-bodied male population on which the king could call for military operations against a foreign enemy.

There was the lingering aftermath of the plague which probably peaked early in Mursili's reign and may have significantly diminished if not decimated Hatti's population. Mursili had been able to restock the homeland, at least partly, with his numerous campaigns of conquest, resulting in the transplantation of thousands of captives which helped replenish its population. But Muwattalli's war with Ramesses had almost certainly resulted in high casualties, both among the lower ranks and the king's experienced officer class. Their losses could not so easily be made up. And, even if Hattusili's brief civil war with his nephew did not result in a large casualty list, it must have further weakened Hittite royal authority, especially in the west where Urhi-Teshub probably retained a significant degree of support.

Apart from this, Hattusili very likely found himself in a catch-22 situation: the able-bodied manpower of his kingdom had now fallen to such a low level that any major campaign far from the homeland came close to imposing unacceptable costs upon the kingdom, particularly because of the consequent reduction of his homeland defences and essential food-producing, labour force. On the other hand, campaigns of conquest, now almost ceased, had been the chief means of restocking the kingdom's declining population.

From the very fragmentary remains of Hattusili's *Annals*, too fragmentary to be of much use for any historical information they provide, it seems that the king did conduct at least one western campaign, as we have noted. The events recorded in TL may have been part of this campaign. But, even if it had some success in restoring Hittite authority in the west, and we can by no means be sure that it did, its tangible results in terms of plunder from conquered cities and new transplantees to the homeland were likely to be minimal. All in all, a treaty with the Ahhiyawan king offered Hattusili the best prospects of stability in the western parts of his empire with the least demands on his military establishment.

For the king of Ahhiyawa, a treaty would probably confirm his status as a Great King – a status conferred upon him by his treaty partner. But the title may have been meaningless in the rest of the Near Eastern world; none of the other Great Kings – of Egypt, Assyria and Babylon – so much as acknowledges the existence of Ahhiyawa, or a ruler of it, let alone a Great King. Even so, the importance to Hattusili of forming and maintaining a peaceful relationship with his western neighbour might well have been sufficient reason to accord him, unilaterally, Great King status, and to address him as 'my brother', as he does in TL.

Further, if a treaty *were* concluded between the kings of Hatti and Ahhiyawa, it would very likely have given the latter an even firmer foothold on the Anatolian mainland, after Millawanda had already been conceded to him or his predecessor just a few years after Mursili had sent an expeditionary force to the west to fight to maintain it. There is no indication that the Ahhiyawan intended to use Millawanda as a military base, an advance post for further incursions into Anatolia's western regions. Archaeological evidence indicates that during Muwattalli's reign and in subsequent years it was a purely domestic and probably commercial settlement (though the core city was heavily defended by walls) intended to expand Ahhiyawa's trading interests in the region. While we should note the very limited evidence that exists for commercial interactions between Mycenaean Greece and any part of Late Bronze Age Anatolia,[24] Ahhiyawa may well have sought from Anatolia trade items that leave no trace in the archaeological record – gold and other minerals, and personnel for palace workforces. Perhaps it also imported horses from Anatolia.

So in summing up our hypothetical treaty, let's review some of the likely issues with which it might have dealt. On the Greek side, trade concessions of the kind just mentioned might well have been sought and agreed upon, along with confirmation of Greek sovereignty over Millawanda and perhaps other Anatolian territories. On the Hittite side, guarantees might have been demanded of the Greek king, and agreed to by him: that he would no longer support the activities of insurrectionists like Piyamaradu, or seek to expand his own kingdom into Hittite subject territory, and that he would cooperate in ensuring peace and stability within the region as far as it lay within his power to do so. This, I believe, may be hinted at in TL. But the Piyamaradu affair may have been only one of the matters dealt with by TL. The whole document perhaps covered a range of issues considered and resolved by both parties before an actual treaty had been drawn up, and then constantly reviewed by both parties to ensure that each was adhering to the treaty's terms once agreement on all matters had been reached.

But Piyamaradu remained a fly in the ointment in the peace negotiations, both before and after our hypothetical treaty had been concluded. Unfettered and apparently continuously supported as he was in his activities by his Ahhiyawan sponsor, the freedom he enjoyed in undermining Hittite authority in the west remained a major obstacle to any lasting peace between the two kingdoms. Hattusili's insistence that he had given the renegade every opportunity to submit to Hittite authority, and had followed diplomatic protocol to the letter in doing so, was conceivably a response to a complaint of some kind made to him by the Ahhiyawan king about his handling of the Piyamaradu matter. Seen in this light, TL was perhaps one of a series of communications between the Hittite and Ahhiyawan kings, some preparing the grounds for, others reviewing the results of, what was supposed to be an abiding peace treaty, the first ever between an Asian and a European royal power.

If I am right in what I have written above (and, again, I may well be wrong), the supposed peace accord between the Hittite and Ahhiyawan kings proved very short-lived. The Ahhiyawan seems to have given little or no heed to any promises he may have made to his royal brother. In any case, his kingdom would soon become a total irrelevance in the Near Eastern world. We shall see why in the next chapter.

13

A Poisoned Chalice

A smooth transition

It was almost like being handed a poisoned chalice. Though it all started well enough. Or seemed to. On Hattusili's death, around 1237 BC, the succession passed, as the old king planned, to his son Tudhaliya. Preparations for the transmission of power appear to have gone smoothly. Whoever had been the earlier heir presumptive – most likely Nerikkaili in my opinion – had apparently accepted without protest his replacement by Tudhaliya. By the time of his accession, the new king had already established his military credentials with extensive campaigns in the Kaska region, Urhi-Teshub no longer seems to have been a threat (perhaps he had died by then), and Muwattalli's second son Kuruntiya seems to have maintained his loyalty to Hattusili's family, being content with his kingship in Tarhuntassa. Already before his accession, Tudhaliya apparently sought to make his peace with the descendants of Muwattalli. He even considered providing some compensations, in the form of land grants, to Urhi-Teshub's sons.[1] All this might be seen in the context of reconciling Muwattalli's family to the continuation of the royal succession in Hattusili's family line.

Importantly, Hattusili ends his *Apology* by announcing that Tudhaliya will follow in his footsteps, with lifelong service to Ishtar.[2] This, I've suggested (in Chapter 7), served as a forerunner to a formal (unpreserved) announcement by Hattusili that Tudhaliya would succeed him as Great King of Hatti. Just as he had claimed the goddess's endorsement of his own occupation of the throne, the reward for his service to her from his early years, Hattusili was now passing on to his son the obligation of continuing this service, no doubt with the principal aim of ensuring Ishtar's endorsement of his succession. Indeed, Tudhaliya may have become his father's co-regent in the last years of Hattusili's reign; his career followed a rapid trajectory very similar to his father's, including his appointment as Chief of the Royal Bodyguard, his military campaigns and successes against enemy and rebel forces in the north, and his appointment as Chief Priest, virtually ruler, of the cities Nerik and Hakpis.³ To most outward appearances, Hattusili had left the empire in good hands, and in reasonably good shape.

Long did she (co-)reign!

Puduhepa continued to play an important role in Hittite affairs during her son's reign, at both micro- and macro-levels. In accordance with Hittite tradition, she retained the powers of reigning Hittite queen after her husband's death and would do so as long as she lived – provided she didn't overreach these powers like at least two of her notorious predecessors. From the early stages of her son's reign, she seems to have maintained her interest and involvement in matters affecting the management of the kingdom, if we can so judge from a letter her son wrote to her about a rebellion in one of the vassal states (see below) and a decree issued in both their names concerning apportionments of the estate of one of the viceroys.⁴

But, almost inevitably, the continuing assertion of her dominant role within palace circles and her prominent role in state affairs rekindled the animosities of branches of the royal family opposed to her. We get a hint of this in an oracle text which indicates factions involving the women of the court who had divided themselves into two groups – supporters and opponents of the Great Queen.⁵ The leader of the anti-Puduhepa faction was very likely Tudhaliya's Babylonian wife,⁶ who bore the title Great Princess.⁷ If we are right about a new royal wrangle, Puduhepa may initially have got the worst of it and was expelled from the palace.⁸ But, if so, she was soon reinstated and her position actually strengthened. No doubt this was her son's doing. From then on, she probably remained a powerful force for the rest of her life in both the domestic and foreign affairs of the kingdom. Living probably to the ripe old age of ninety, she died around 1190 BC,⁹ outliving by some years her son Tudhaliya and equalling the longevity of her royal brother Ramesses, who reached his ninetieth birthday a few years later. Hittite Great Queen and Egyptian Great King may well have continued their correspondence after Hattusili's death. If so, all records of such correspondence are sadly lost to us.

A foiled assassination attempt

But let's go back to our starting point in this chapter. Early in the new king's reign, the metaphorical poisoned chalice almost became reality. Plots, intrigues and conspiracies had plagued the court circles of many Hittite kings. And we've seen specific examples of the toxity of the palace environment during the reigns of Hattusili and his two predecessors. Hattusili himself was no small contributor to these. Indeed, his elevation to Great Kingship was due at least as much to his manipulation and exploitation of divisions within the royal household as to any blessings bestowed upon him by his patron deity.

This helped set the scene for an almost fatal reckoning, some years later, for his successor Tudhaliya. Probably soon after his accession, the royal intelligence service (or its Hittite equivalent) uncovered a plot against the king's life by a group of high-ranking dignitaries led by one of his brothers, or half-brothers, called Heshni.[10] Tudhaliya was touring his northern regions at the time and was thus more vulnerable to an assassination attempt. In case this first attempt failed, a second was planned in which the assassin's dagger would be replaced by a poisoned chalice. All this came to light when the conspiracy was uncovered and the conspirators brought to justice. The ordeal left the king badly shaken. He summoned those of his dignitaries and high officials who'd been cleared of any part in the conspiracy and demanded their unconditional loyalty.[11] Further treachery by members of his own extended family was his greatest concern, as revealed in a set of instructions to them. Professor van den Hout speaks of 'the psychological cost of the pervasive-sounding paranoia in the several loyalty oaths known from his reign'.[12] For example:

My Sun (i.e. the Great King) has many brothers and there are many sons of his father. The Land of Hatti is full of the royal line: in Hatti the descendants of Suppiluliuma, the descendants of Mursili, the descendants of Muwattalli, the descendants of Hattusili are numerous. With regard to kingship, you must acknowledge no other person (but me, Tudhaliya), and protect only the son and grandson and great grandson and descendants of Tudhaliya. And if at any time (?) evil is done to My Sun – (for) My Sun has many brothers – and someone approaches another person and speaks thus: 'Whomever we select for ourselves need not even be a son of our lord!' – these words must not be (permitted)! With regard to kingship, you must protect only My Sun and the descendants of My Sun. You must approach no other person.[13]

Van den Hout comments that when the fifteenth-century king Telipinu laid down rules for the royal succession, he 'intended or hoped to put an end to the internecine murders that plagued the generations before him. What he did not foresee was how the overpopulation of the royal family and the resulting bloated elite in the thirteenth century BC introduced a virulent nepotism that ultimately was to be the bane of the Hittite kingdom.'[14] It's a classic example of what the complexity scientist Peter Turchin calls 'elite overproduction'. In this case, too many royals were bred without enough jobs for them to do. The result was an unending series of intrafamilial disputes, plots and conspiracies as individual royals or competing factions within the ever-expanding royal family attempted to struggle upwards through the hierarchy, with Great Kingship as the ultimate prize. That had already often been the case in the Hittite kingdom, as indeed in many other kingdoms. And with the passage of time it only got worse, particularly as the kingdom neared its end.

The beginning of the empire's disintegration

Beyond the homeland, Tudhaliya had grave concerns that the empire was breaking up. Already early in his reign, the people of Lalanda in the Lower Land, the homeland's southern buffer region, had rebelled against Hittite rule. The king wrote to his mother Puduhepa about it, expressing fears their uprising might spread further throughout the Lower Land. Other vassal states too may have seized the opportunity provided by the old king's death to sever their ties with Hattusa.[15] But the western states were one of Tudhaliya's chief concerns. His father's campaign or campaigns in the region left him with unfinished business there. The west's chief troublemaker, Piyaramadu, was still at large, having already lived through the reigns of three Hittite kings and defied them all. And Tudhaliya inherited the legacy of his father's failed attempts to persuade Ahhiyawa to help stabilize the western Anatolian regions, particularly by keeping Piyamaradu out of them or by handing him over to Hittite custody.

It was somewhat reminiscent of the crisis confronting Tudhaliya's grandfather Mursili on his accession, with rebel vassal states and enemy lands threatening the kingdom's very existence. Yet, with exemplary speed and and effective leadership, Mursili had re-established control over the wayward vassals, inflicted heavy defeats on the enemy lands, and brought back to the homeland large numbers of prisoners of war and livestock as part of the rich spoils that came from his conquests. It seems, too, that Mursili had the good fortune of not being distracted by family squabbles and conspiracies as he rebuilt his empire, which frequently meant military campaigns far from his homeland – once he had banished his second Chief Wife, Tawananna, the most disruptive troublemaker of his household. The outbreaks of hostility against Tudhaliya may have been more gradual and less widespread than those experienced by Mursili. And Tudhaliya was far better prepared for kingship, thanks largely to his father, than his grandfather was. But critical shortages of manpower, I believe, seriously curtailed his ability to restore control over rebel states by brute force. At the same time, his kingship was at constant risk from a pack of baying royals and their supporters at home.

But then there was good, faithful Kuruntiya, son of Muwattalli and brother of Urhi-Teshub, who'd been brought up by Hattusili, and remained loyal to him throughout his reign. He'd been rewarded by Hattusili with appointment to the kingship of the increasingly important, subject state Tarhuntassa, briefly in his father's reign the capital of the empire. His appointment was renewed by Tudhaliya, his cousin and close friend; and his loyalty was assured, as we learn from his treaty with Tudhaliya engraved on the bronze tablet, by concessions further to those already granted by Hattusili in earlier treaties with him. Kuruntiya was given additional territories not included in previous agreements; he was granted freedom of choice in the matter of his successor in Tarhuntassa; the taxes and *corvées* imposed upon his kingdom were further reduced; and, most importantly, Tudhaliya formally acknowledged his status as a king equivalent to the Syrian viceroys and second only to the Great King in Hattusa. All this helped keep him on side with the new regime – or so it appeared – at least in the early part of Tudhaliya's reign. But let's not go into that before we tie up a loose end, and then look at what appears to have been a major new development in the empire's closing decades.

What happened to Ahhiyawa?

To judge from the continuing disruptive activities of Ahhiyawa's *protégé* Piyamaradu in the west, any agreement, pact or treaty Hattusili may have concluded with his Ahhiyawan royal brother seems to have had little or no effect in curbing Ahhiyawa's threat to expand into Hittite territory in the region. Indeed, this threat increased when the important, western state Seha River Land fell into the hands of a usurper, Tarhunaradu, who rebelled against his Hittite overlord, apparently with Ahhiyawa's backing.[16] The rebellion was shortlived. It was crushed by Tudhaliya's forces, and Tarhunaradu and his family were transported, probably to the Hittite homeland. That is the last we hear of Ahhiyawa. Well, almost.

In the surviving draft of a treaty Tudhaliya drew up with one of his Syrian vassals, all his fellow Great Kings are listed as potential enemies (or friends), including the King of Ahhiyawa. But his name was put there inadvertently, it seems, while the tablet inscribed with the draft was still damp and soft, and subsequently crossed out. To summarize what I've said elsewhere, this suggests to me that Ahhiyawa had recently ceased to have any relevance to Hittite affairs, and that it no longer constituted a threat to Hittite sovereignty in the west. Probably by then Tudhaliya had reasserted Hittite control over Millawanda and any other Ahhiyawan-controlled regions in Anatolia.[17] If so, this was a substantial achievement by Tudhaliya.

And there was, apparently, an even more substantial one.

Tudhaliya claims the conquest of Alasiya (Cyprus)

We've noted that Tarhuntassa's territory very likely extended to the peninsula's southern coast, giving the central Hittite kingdom, for the first time in its history, a coastline with the potential for building seaports, in addition to any already there. And one or more of these seaports may have provided Tudhaliya with what appears to have been a major achievement of his reign: his alleged conquest of the island Alasiya. The Hittites had claimed possession of Alasiya at least as far back as the reign of the early fourteenth-century king, Tudhaliya. But, without a seacoast and a navy to connect it to the island, Hatti's assumed sovereignty over it could hardly have been more than tokenistic. Now, probably by building a naval and marine force, perhaps using ships and troops from already seagoing subject states like Ugarit, Tudhaliya was well placed to mount an attack on Alasiya, launched either from seaports on Anatolia's southeastern coast or from one or more ports along the shores of the Syrian coastal states, or from all of these.

For Tudhaliya, the Alasiyan enterprise was an important feather in his regnal cap. He had a record of it inscribed on a statue of himself, probably constructed to commemorate the victory he claimed. The inscription was carved in the Luwian hieroglyphic script, now regularly used on statues, cliff-face monuments, and built stone structures. Luwian was the language of the majority of the empire's population. Inscriptions written in hieroglyphs in this language were much more likely to be read and understood by His Majesty's subjects than Hittite-language inscriptions carved in the cuneiform script. As you might expect, the statue itself no longer exists, but a cuneiform copy of its text has survived as the first of two inscriptions on a tablet from the reign of Tudhaliya's son Suppiluliuma II.[18] We'll say more about the second inscription later, but here is a translation of part of Tudhaliya's: *I seized the king of Alasiya with his wives, his children, [and his   ]. All the goods, including silver and gold, and all the captured people I removed and brought home to Hattusa. I enslaved the country of Alasiya, and made it tributary on the spot.*[19] A list of the tribute imposed, including the silver and gold, then follows, and subsequently a list of the deities, beginning with the Sun Goddess of Arinna, upon whom this largesse will be bestowed. Presumably the king also took a share of the spoils and paid off his troops and ships' captains out of them. Perhaps most important of all, the campaign provided Tudhaliya with a much-needed supply of new transplantees.

To outward appearances, Tudhaliya's achievement was an impressive one. But what actually *did* he achieve? The campaign's success no doubt enhanced his credentials as a warrior-king in the traditional Hittite mould and gave at least a temporary boost to the empire's sagging fortunes. The king's reported conquest, looting and 'enslavement' of a kingdom across the sea was clear proof, it seemed, that his military forces could still pack a powerful punch. Indeed, Tudhaliya's victorious overseas campaign was unprecedented in the annals of Hittite history.

But beyond that, royal rhetoric, I believe, outstrips reality. Here are my thoughts on the matter. To begin with, the apparently unprovoked attack on the island ran counter to Hattusili's policy of maintaining peace throughout his empire and in his relations with the lands beyond. And the old king's long reign and the *gravitas* which it earned him seemed sufficient to ensure the peace as long as he lived. But the empire's fragility soon became evident after his death, as subject states began to assert their independence. Perhaps just a few for a start, but others would soon follow. Tudhaliya's position was further weakened by the resurgence of factional disputes within his own extended family, provoked particularly by those who sought to return the throne to Muwattalli's direct line.

The empire no longer had the resources to fight major campaigns against rebel vassals, nor could Tudhaliya afford, for political reasons, to be away from the seat of his power for the lengthy absences such campaigns often entailed. Instead, the king sought to demonstrate that the empire now had a significant seagoing capacity; and his alleged conquest of the island kingdom of Alasiya served not only to demonstrate that Hatti was still a formidable military power, but also as a clear warning to all its subjects of the heavy price they would pay for defiance of the Great King's sovereignty.

Let's take a closer look at all this. Firstly, it's likely that the Alasiyan capital lay on or close to the sea and had a large seaport, like a number of Hatti's subject states in western Anatolia and western Syria. (Think Wilusa/Troy in the former, and Ugarit, Sidon and Tyre in the latter; Tyre lay actually *in* the sea.) In contrast to the thousands of troops often required for land campaigns against rebellious vassal states, a city on or near the sea could be seized by a well-equipped force of marines in no more than a dozen ships and conquered quickly. It took just seven enemy ships to invade and inflict great damage on the prosperous kingdom of Ugarit in the reign of Suppiluliuma II, the last Hittite king.[20] No doubt Tudhaliya's marine force plundered much of Alasiya's inland territory as well before its departure with its spoils.

But I see the Alasiyan enterprise as no more than a one-off raid, primarily for the reasons I've suggested. I don't doubt the truth of the raid, the seizure of the Alasiyan king and his family, and their removal along with the rest of the raid's plunder, back to Hattusa. But then reality gives way to rhetorical fiction. Permanent subjection of the island's people (called 'enslavement' here) was a far cry from the usual provisions Hittite kings made for conquered states by putting new loyal vassal rulers in charge, or contrite former rulers back in charge, and allowing them virtual autonomy in governing their own people. There is no suggestion that this was what Tudhaliya did in the aftermath of the Hittite raid. Nor did the king have sufficient available manpower to impose anything like direct rule over the island and its population, or enforce regular tribute payment. This is smoke and mirrors stuff. Besides, when we look ahead a few years, we find Hatti at war with 'enemies from Alasiya'. This we learn from the second text on the tablet from Suppiluliuma II's reign (referred to above). Copied in cuneiform like the first which recorded Tudhaliya's raid on Alasiya, probably from an original hieroglyphic inscription, it reported three naval engagements by Suppiluliuma and a subsequent land engagement against these enemies:[21] *The ships of Alasiya met me in the sea three times for battle, and I smote them; and I seized the ships and set fire to them in the sea. But when I arrived on dry land (?), the enemies from Alasiya came in multitude against me for battle.*[22]

So, if Tudhaliya actually did secure control over the whole island, it was very short-lived. While we're on the subject, we should admit the possibility that Tudhaliya's attack on Alasiya was not the king's initiative but actually provoked by Alasiya. Sea trade across the eastern Mediterranean, including from Egypt to Hatti in its broadest sense, and from Hatti's maritime Syrian states to its southern Anatolian territories, and thence to the homeland, was at constant risk from pirate attacks, some of which may have been launched from Alasiya. If so, Tudhaliya's Alasiyan enterprise could likely be seen as a response to such attacks, with an attempt to ensure they did not recur in the future. And, if that's the case, his attempt failed, to judge from the attacks launched from Alasiya in Suppiluliuma's reign.

What became of Kuruntiya?[23]

But perhaps these attacks belong within a broader context, which I'll talk about soon. For the moment, let's return to our baying pack of royals. It's the wild card in this pack that I'm particularly interested in. We've already met him several times: Kuruntiya, son of Muwattalli, ward and nephew of Hattusili, cousin and close friend of Hattusili's son and successor Tudhaliya, ruler of the prestigious appanage kingdom Tarhuntassa – and after his brother Urhi-Teshub, the rightful heir to the Hittite throne. As we've seen, Uncle Hattusili had won his loyalty and, after Tudhaliya's accession, he apparently remained content with being king of Tarhuntassa instead of seeking to claim his genuine birthright as ruler of Hatti – if his brother was no longer able to do so. Let me stress the words 'apparently remained content'.[24]

In these last few decades of Hittite history, our records become increasingly sparse, eventually petering out altogether. So, it becomes very tempting to clutch at the small snippets of information we do find, and sometimes draw from them conclusions which subsequently prove untenable. In daring to be wrong, we often are. In my previous book, *Warriors of Anatolia*, and elsewhere, I referred to hieroglyphic inscriptions found at three sites in south-central Anatolia which name a 'Great King' called Hartapu who identifies himself as the son of a 'Great King' called Mursili. Along with a number of other scholars, I identified this Mursili with Urhi-Teshub.[25] Remember that Urhi-Teshub adopted the prestigious name Mursili as his throne-name, though his uncle continued to call him Urhi-Teshub.

Just after my book appeared, an important new hieroglyphic inscription was published naming a Great King Hartapu, son of Mursili, in the same region as the other Hartapu-Mursili inscriptions. The scholars who have studied the inscription have dated it to the mid-eighth century BC, in the so-called (Iron Age) Neo-Hittite period.[26] There is no doubt about a post-Bronze Age dating. That's a blow to us who thought we had new information about the last years of the Hittite empire. The coincidence that there were two Hartapus (a name not otherwise attested in the royal dynasty), both sons of a Mursili, one dating to the Bronze Age, the other to the Iron Age, is just too great to be plausible. Unfortunately, this rules out what may have been evidence for a possible resurgence of Urhi-Teshub and at least one of his successors reclaiming the title 'Great King' – and thus reasserting their right to the throne of Hatti, as the Bronze Age kingdom entered its final years.

But what about Urhi-Teshub's younger brother, our wild card Kuruntiya? Peter Neve's excavations at Hattusa uncovered three seal impressions inscribed with the words 'Kuruntiya, Great King, Labarna, My Sun'.[27] Further to this, a rock-cut hieroglyphic inscription dating to the thirteenth century, accompanied by the relief of a striding, armed god, has Kuruntiya as its subject, identifies him as the son of Muwattalli and calls him a 'Great King'.[28] Since there could be no more than one 'Great King' of Hatti at a time, what are we to make of Kuruntiya's assumption of this title? Did he finally decide to make a bid for the throne in Hattusa? And was his bid successful? A good time to have made it was when Tudhaliya was on campaign in northern Mesopotamia, suffering an apparently disastrous defeat there when he attacked the army of the Assyrian king Tukulti-Ninurta in the region called Nairi (Nihriya).[29] Perhaps Kuruntiya actually occupied the Hittite throne. But, if so, he must barely have had time to warm its seat; for what remaining records we have indicate that Tudhaliya saw out a relatively long reign, even if it *was* briefly interrupted, and was succeeded by two of his sons, Arnuwanda III and then Suppiluliuma II, the last kings of the Hittite empire.

Without more context, we can't be sure what the circumstances of Kuruntiya's 'Great King' titles were or what eventually happened to Kuruntiya. One of my theories is that Tudhaliya established a kind of diarchy with him, in like manner to the Roman emperor Diocletian's appointment more than two millennia later of a fellow military officer Maximian as his junior co-emperor; Diocletian ruled the eastern half of the Roman empire and Maximian the western half. In the Hittite scenario, Kuruntiya was given formal control of the empire's southern Anatolian regions, ruling from his capital Tarhuntassa and awarded the title 'Great King', while Tudhaliya remained ruler of the northern regions, from his capital Hattusa, as the senior 'Great King'. Such an arrangement would not have greatly differed from Muwattalli's with his brother Hattusili. But in reverse. Hattusili was given control of the kingdom's northern regions, probably including Hattusa, though only with the title 'King', while Muwattalli ruled in the south from his new capital Tarhuntassa.

What about the rest of the empire, including its Syrian and western parts? Almost certainly they remained under Tudhaliya's control, though it's possible that greater autonomy and more extensive control were allowed to one of the Syrian viceroys in the east and to a powerful local ruler in the west. That would mean the Hittite empire in its last years was ruled by a kind of tetrarchy, just as Diocletian's empire was in the second half of his reign. But that still leaves us with the question of how three of Kuruntiya's seal impressions, emblazoned with the 'Great King' title, ended up in Hattusa. They are, of course, portable objects and any number of theories might be offered to explain their discovery there.

But let's move on. In the northern part of Hattusa, just south of the royal acropolis, a two-chamber domed structure was discovered in 1988 with a hieroglyphic inscription in one of the chambers.[30] The author of the inscription was a king called Suppiluliuma and until recently it's been assumed that this was the second Hittite king of that name, last ruler of the empire. The inscription records at least one southern campaign, in which the king allegedly conquered a number of lands which *may* have included Tarhuntassa. Unfortunately, it is quite uncertain how the passage referring to it is to be interpreted.[31] And a number of scholars have argued that the inscription belongs not to the second but to the first Suppiluliuma, 150 years earlier.[32] Despite this, there is now an increasing swing back to the second Suppiluliuma. While such uncertainty prevails, I think it best to leave this controversial inscription out of our ponderings on the Hittite empire's final decades.

The old order changeth

All this illustrates just how fascinating but frustrating research can be. We are ever hopeful of finding new evidence about what happened in the Hittite empire's last years and, indeed, its last days. We clutch at straws, only to see them drift away from us, one by one. We wish for new information, miraculously find some, only to see it contradict what we thought we already knew and leaving us knowing less. How true the adage 'Be careful what you wish for'!

There is no shortage of theories about how and why the Bronze Age came to an end across Greece and the Near East, some of them plausible, others implausible, and none necessarily mutually exclusive of the others. Reflecting the modern zeitgeist, a 'global' economic collapse is sometimes given an airing, with the argument that the fall of trading centres in one region had a flow-on effect to others, causing catastrophic disruptions to supply chains linking the kingdoms of Egypt, Greece and the Near East. Climate change, too, gets an occasional look-in, though I have yet to find anyone suggesting that this was due to anthropogenic activity.

Anyhow, I'm increasingly drawn to the view that the Bronze Age 'ended' in a far less dramatic fashion than is sometimes supposed – in a long, slow petering out rather than a sudden big bang. Maybe it's misleading to speak of an 'ending' at all – except when applied to the kingdom of the Hittites and some other smaller states. Rather, what occurred was a gradual progression and, generally, a smooth transition from old to new, from Bronze to Iron Age. Certainly, there were some cataclysmic events during this transition which saw the destruction of cities and kingdoms that would never rise again, like Ugarit in Syria and the palace-centre at Pylos in mainland Greece.³³ And very likely there were major population shifts as peoples displaced from their homelands by war or famine or the collapse of the kingdoms that protected them sought new, safer places to make their homes.

There is some archaeological evidence for settlements destroyed by enemy forces or bands of predators during this period, but no evidence of widespread waves of destruction,³⁴ which in other periods of history marked a transition from one phase of civilization to the next. In many parts of the Near Eastern world, a Bronze Age to Iron Age transition would have been barely recognizable – except that rule by the Great Kingdoms over vassal states in Anatolia and Syria was now replaced by the rise of independent cities, city-states and small kingdoms, like the clusters of Neo-Hittite states.³⁵ For several centuries, Egypt ceased to have any significant influence in the Near Eastern word and the former Great Kingdom of Hatti ceased to exist at all. Hattusa was abandoned by at least its elite elements, including the royal family, who took with them all their most important possessions.³⁶ Hattusa sank slowly into ruin, the likely prey of enemy forces and wandering bands of looters. Where did the last king Suppiluliuma and his retinue go when they left the capital? Tarhuntassa is my best guess. Maybe for a very brief time Tarhuntassa became once more the capital and focus of the 'Land of Hatti', the capital of an empire whose disintegration was probably almost complete before Suppiluliuma left Hattusa.

'Gods Carved in Stone'

Let me finish this chapter on a positive note, by returning to Tudhaliya. Though in a traditional sense, he may not have been an achiever of great deeds, like his namesake, the first Tudhaliya, he has left for us the most important sculptured monument of the Hittite empire. I am referring to the figures carved into the rocky outcrop located a kilometre to the northeast of the Hittite capital and now known as Yazılıkaya. This is a Turkish word meaning 'Inscribed Rock'. The outcrop's principal natural features are two open-air chambers, one large, one small and narrow.

For centuries, perhaps millennia, Yazılıkaya may have been revered as an important sacred site. Then, during his reign, Hattusili confirmed its sacred character by having a gatehouse and temple complex built across the front of the site. But it was his son and successor, Tudhaliya, who gave Yazılıkaya its distinctive character by embellishing its walls with carvings of the gods of the Hittite pantheon. The chief feature of the main chamber is a procession of these gods or, more precisely, their Hurrian equivalents with their names inscribed in Luwian hieroglyphs next to them. They are arranged in two files of deities, one almost entirely male, the other almost entirely female, approaching each other. One is headed by the pantheon's chief male god Teshub (the Hittite Storm God). His wife Hepat (the Hittite Sun Goddess) leads the other. They have convened at this place for a special ceremony, maybe to participate in the New Year spring festival.

We enter the smaller chamber through a narrow passage guarded by a pair of winged, lion-headed demons with human bodies. For me, this second chamber has always had a mystical, rather eerie feel about it. On one wall, a column of twelve figures, armed with sickle-shaped swords and identified by these and by their conical headgear as warrior-gods, march purposefully towards an unknown destination. They are commonly identified as underworld deities. On the opposite wall is another god, the so-called dagger-god. His upper torso has a human head with the foreparts of two lions hanging underneath; the blade of a dagger or sword apparently plunged into the ground forms his lower torso. He, too, is believed to be an underworld god.[37]

But the dominant sculpture in this chamber depicts the god Sharrumma, son of Teshub and Hepat and Tudhaliya's patron deity, with his arm around a smaller figure. This is Tudhaliya himself, skull-capped and in the garb of a priest. Both figures are identified by their names in hieroglyphs next to them. Is Sharrumma merely holding his *protégé* in a protective embrace? Or is the king now deceased and the embrace a welcoming gesture as his divine patron escorts him into the next world where he will take his place in the pantheon of gods? For when a king dies, he assumes divine status. That is what is meant, I've already explained, when a son who succeeds to the throne says of his paternal predecessor: *When my father became a god*. There is a further point of interest in this small chamber. At the northern end of it is a large stone block which may once have served as a base for a monumental statue of Tudhaliya. Maybe this chamber of death was a mortuary chapel for the king. Maybe it was Tudhaliya's burial place. If so, Yazılıkaya is the empire's only known royal tomb.

That said, the sanctuary is surely as much about new life as it is about death, especially if the New Year festival was celebrated here. But, whatever purpose or purposes Yazılıkaya served in the past, it is a place which still inspires feelings of awe and reverence amongst visitors who spend time there. To experience fully these feelings, you should visit the place on your own, or with a partner, when there is no one else around (if that is at all possible today). While I was in Hattusa during the making of Tolga Örnek's film, *The Hittites*, I had the opportunity of spending some hours at Yazılıkaya, just by myself. As the late afternoon sunlight

Figure 13.1 Tudhaliya and Sharrumma. Author photo.

rippled across the contours of the rock surface before melting slowly into twilight shadows, I felt very close to these gods worshipped by five centuries of Hittite kings. Here, too, I could sense the presence of the Great King Tudhaliya, to whom Yazılıkaya, perhaps the most important cult-centre in the Hittite world, would become an everlasting memorial.

14

Hattusili's Reign in Review

Pivotal events in Hittite history

If I were asked to name three pivotal events in the 500-year span of Hittite history, I'd begin with the first Hattusili's campaigns across the Taurus ranges into Syria and his conquest of many of the local states allied with or subject to the greatest power in the region, the kingdom of Aleppo. These 'international' military enterprises, in the mid-seventeenth century BC, paved the way for the establishment of the Great Kingdom of Hatti, one of the most formidable political and military powers of the Late Bronze Age.

For my second pick we need to fast forward to the third quarter of the fourteenth century, to the Great King Suppiluliuma I's defeat and destruction of the Mittanian empire, ending with the capture of the last Mittanian stronghold Carchemish around 1326 BC. This terminated centuries of warfare between the Hittites and peoples of mainly Hurrian origin. From their homeland in northern Mesopotamia the Hurrians had spread ever further westwards, posing a continuing existential threat to the kingdom of Hatti, especially when they coalesced into the kingdom of Mittani in the late fifteenth century. Suppiluliuma had now eliminated one of the Great Kingdoms of the first half of the Late Bronze Age.

My third pick brings us to the peace accord between Hattusili and Ramesses concluded in the year 1259 BC and establishing a permanent peace between the two great rivals for dominance of the Syrian states lying between them. The threat of warfare, ever present during the reigns of many of their predecessors, had ended in the bloodbath at Qadesh. The 'Eternal Peace' treaty that followed some fifteen years later was to last forever – and it did, at least until the end of the Bronze Age.

Which of these events do I regard as the most significant? In my summary of the first event, 'paved the way for' are key words. Hattusili I's vision of what his kingdom could become was a limited one. To change my metaphor slightly, he had blazed a trail for his successors to follow, demonstrating that a well-trained, well-armed military force even of a young kingdom like Hatti could campaign successfully in lands far from the homeland, leaving a path of destruction in its wake, and bringing back much plunder from the cities it had looted and destroyed. But Hattusili's military operations were little more than smash-and-grab raids with no attempt, indeed no capacity, to establish permanent control over the lands and cities that fell victim to them. And the chief kingdom in their Syrian killing fields, Aleppo, remained intact, despite Hattusili's apparently repeated attempts to capture it. Hattusili demonstrated to his successors what they could achieve militarily but, as far as we can tell, he had no idea of the political and administrative potential of his conquests, whose realization was essential to the achievement of imperial, or Great Kingdom, status.

To judge from his son Mursili's biography, Suppiluliuma had brought the Hittite kingdom from the brink of annihilation to domination of much of the Bronze Age Near Eastern world by his destruction of the Mittanian empire. But, with the wisdom of hindsight, Suppiluliuma's grandson Hattusili III may have seen his achievements in a rather different light, once he took account of the unintended consequences of these achievements. The destruction of Mittani had left a power vacuum east of the Euphrates which an aggressive Assyria, unleashed from its vassal status to Mittani, was filling, gobbling up in the process remnant Mittanian states that had become puppets of the Hittite administration. Further, with his focus on Syrian affairs, Suppiluliuma appears to have given only limited attention to the increasingly restive vassal states in the west, and elsewhere in the peninsula. It was left to his son Mursili to restore order when he was suddenly and unexpectedly thrust into kingship of the Hittite world after the deaths of his two predecessors, his father and then his elder brother. Both died of the plague that, according to Mursili, ravaged the Hittite homeland for twenty years. Many of the vassal states had seized the opportunity to cast aside their Hittite allegiance, and the enemies of Hatti began moving in for the kill. As we've noted, the plague was brought to Hatti by Egyptian prisoners of war in the wake of Suppiluliuma's blunder in attacking Egypt's Syro-Palestinian states. This put Hatti and Egypt on a continuous war footing – until, some sixty-five years later, his grandson Hattusili made a permanent peace with the pharaoh Ramesses.

Hittite history's most significant event

This, my third pick, is the one I place at the top of my list. The peace treaty with Egypt was, in my opinion, Hittite history's most significant event, and almost certainly Hattusili was its instigator. Rivalries between the two Great Kings, inherited from their predecessors, had now been replaced by a genuine partnership, later cemented by a marriage alliance. I believe that the threat of Assyrian invasions and conquests of the lands west of the Euphrates was one of the main incentives for the treaty. The guaranteed military support one treaty partner would provide for the other in the event of an enemy attack on either of them may well have deterred the current Assyrian king Shalmaneser I and his successors from crossing the river. Instead, they turned hostile eyes on their southern neighbour Babylon. But that was not the only beneficial outcome of the treaty. Peace between Egypt and Hatti helped ensure a high level of stability throughout the Syrian and Syro-Palestinian regions, providing a basis for flourishing trade there, general affluence, and the growth of networks of international trading centres throughout them. As we know from letters exchanged by merchants, all this lasted as long as the peace itself, quite literally, until the very last days of the Bronze Age kingdoms.[1]

Of course, my pick of the most important event in Hittite history reflects the perspective of a modern observer. Ironically, in the records of its own time the peace achieved by Hattusili and Ramesses barely rates a mention.[2] Even in the *Apology*, the 'Eternal Treaty' is not mentioned. On the other hand, no one today – except for scholars and students specializing in Bronze Age Near Eastern history, and a gratifying number of amateur enthusiasts – will have heard of the first Hattusili or Suppiluliuma, let alone their once widely acclaimed military achievements. Yet, the Great Kings Ramesses and *our* Hattusili, whose names will forever be on world display, will now be remembered in perpetuity as the world's first international peacemakers. Such is the fickleness of history.

Hattusili's early years

I originally intended to write a chapter with the title 'A King Who Reigned Too Long?' But I now think it best to incorporate this question into a general review of Hattusili's reign. According to my chronology, Hattusili, the youngest of Mursili's children by his first wife, was born no later than 1310 BC, the year before his mother died, and probably no earlier than 1315 BC. The end of his reign and his death I have dated to about 1237 BC. Some scholars suggest a slightly earlier date, about 1240 BC. In any case, he lived until his seventies, probably longer than any other Hittite king. This was in itself a remarkable achievement, especially given the illnesses which seem to have dogged him all his life

I have no doubt that he was a highly intelligent man, perhaps a literate one as well. I've suggested he learned to read and write during his childhood while training as a priest in the service of the goddess Ishtar. In his early adult years, he must also have undergone some military training, including active service perhaps against the enemy from the Kaska lands. This is not mentioned anywhere in our texts but his brother King Muwattalli clearly recognized his leadership potential, both on and off the battlefield, and he was given strategically important responsibilities for Hatti's northernmost regions, including kingship of the city Hakpis. In effect, he became ruler of the northern half of the kingdom. Though we have only his own word for it (in the *Apology*), Hattusili seems to have carried out his responsibilities in the north, both administrative and military, with distinction. His permanent resettlement and restoration of the holy city of Nerik was the highlight of his achievements there.

Puduhepa's likely 'role behind the scenes'

Subsequently, Hattusili fought alongside his brother at Qadesh, in 1274 BC, again probably with distinction as a high-ranking officer in the Hittite army, and almost certainly as second-in-command. He was in his late thirties or early forties at the time. On his way home from Qadesh, he married a fifteen-year-old (or thereabouts) girl called Puduhepa, daughter of a Hurrian priest. Puduhepa was accorded the status of his Chief Wife. She was to become one of the most powerful and influential figures in the kingdom for at least the rest of her husband's reign.

She must have spent the early years of her marriage with her husband in his northern capital Hakpis, while the Hittite throne was occupied by Urhi-Teshub. But neither she nor Hattusili had any intention of remaining there, even if Urhi-Teshub had not precipitated a crisis by stripping his uncle of his most important powers. Hattusili makes no mention of Puduhepa in his growing disputes with his nephew. Nor would he have done so, even if she became closely involved in the plans to overthrow the king. That would have been most impolitic!

Our sources are silent about what Puduhepa was up to at this time. But she very likely played a major role, in support of her husband, in the intrigues and plots that festered beneath the surface of palace life during Urhi-Teshub's reign – especially as tensions between uncle and nephew approached flashpoint. The political atmosphere in the royal court in Urhi-Teshub's last years as Great King must have become highly toxic, with adherents and family members of Hattusili's long-term enemy Arma-Tarhunda still seeking revenge, and Urhi-Teshub and his supporters growing ever more fearful of his uncle's ambitions and what he would do to achieve them.

And, while a crisis was building in the capital, I cannot imagine that Puduhepa sat idly by in Hakpis or even in Hattusa if her husband was there at the time, minding children and confining herself to domestic chores. Apparently, if we are to believe the *Apology*, relations between Hattusili and his nephew were initially cordial and constructive, with the uncle acting as the young man's mentor. Was Puduhepa in any way responsible for the souring of their relationship? Later to exercise considerable, widespread power in the kingdom, she already had, I believe, ambitions that extended well beyond her current status in the royal household, and helped her husband realise these by persuading him, or reinforcing his already held conviction, that Urhi-Teshub's tenure of power lacked essential legal and divine backing.

Within this context, as Hattusili's own ambitions became increasingly evident and Urhi-Teshub grew ever more suspicious of his uncle's ultimate intentions, the young king began stripping the man who sought to dethrone him of the means of launching a successful coup. More specifically, Urhi-Teshub took away from Hattusili all the northern countries which at Muwattalli's command he had successfully resettled, and finally demanded that he relinquish control of two of the north's most important cities, Nerik and Hakpis.[3] We know that Hattusili was in the north at the time, probably in his capital Hakpis, when the demand came, for Hattusili tells us in his *Apology* that he wrote back to his nephew defying his order and in effect declaring war upon him. This is the import of his words: *So come. Ishtar of Samuha and the Storm God of Nerik will judge us.*[4] The war is thus presented as a legal dispute to be decided by the gods. It's not unlikely that Puduhepa had a hand in this. After all, Ishtar had already assured her in a dream that she would lead her husband's forces in battle. And with such backing, who could doubt the outcome of this 'legal dispute'?

The overthrow of the rightful king

We cannot assess how good a ruler Urhi-Teshub was, or could have been, because his successor didn't allow him a long enough reign to display qualities appropriate to Great Kingship. Short though his reign was, however, it may not have been totally free of achievements, even aside from his restoration of Hattusa as the imperial capital. But Hattusili saw to it that no record was left of them. Even

Urhi-Teshub's royal title Mursili III was denied him. He was henceforth referred to only by his birth-name, by Hattusili and Ramesses alike. It was as if his reign never had legitimacy, thus boosting Hattusili's own claim to be the rightful occupant of the throne. Yet his deposed predecessor never gave up his attempts to regain it. Following his overthrow, he proved a persistently wily fugitive, defying all Hattusili's efforts to recapture him and, as long as he was at large, he and his supporters remained a threat to the regime that replaced him.

Of one thing we can be sure. Hattusili blatantly lies in the *Apology* about the circumstances in which he became king and the validity of his kingship. His claim that he himself appointed, not simply installed, Urhi-Teshub as his father's successor to the throne cannot be true. There is no way Muwattalli would have failed to appoint a Crown Prince before his death, especially given the perilous circumstances in which he knew he would soon find himself at Qadesh. From all we know of Muwattalli, he seems to have been a meticulous planner, the most conspicuous example of which was his resiting of the royal capital at Tarhuntassa, and he would hardly have failed to name an heir to his throne at the earliest opportunity.[5] He may well have entrusted his brother with the responsibility of ensuring that his wishes were put into effect in the event of his death. A distorted, incomplete version of that appears in the *Apology*: though Hattusili merely installs his brother's successor on the throne, he claims that he himself (on his own initiative) takes up Urhi-Teshub and makes him the next Great King. We must wonder, then, what else he is lying about, what other facts he is distorting, and what else he is conveniently omitting from his *Apology* to justify his accession.

The pathway to supreme power

Thus, we can briefly summarize the career of a prince whose early years were spent as a priest in Ishtar's service, who suffered from a chronically weak constitution, who nonetheless probably served with distinction in the Hittite army, who effectively administered the northern half of the kingdom while his brother Muwattalli was Great King and Tarhuntassa the royal capital, and who seated his brother's chosen successor upon the Hittite throne, only to seize it from him, on quite spurious grounds, a few years later.

His abilities were a spur to his ambitions, which knew no check. From reading his *Apology*, sometimes between its lines, I believe we can piece together a picture, incomplete as it may be, of this multi-talented, cunning, ruthless and manipulative youngest, sickly child of Mursili in his progression from princedom to supreme ruler of the Hittite world. I also believe that Puduhepa, despite her still tender years, played no small part in the achievement of her husband's ambitions, displaying political skills and a ruthless disposition which perfectly complemented those same qualities in her husband. Let me hasten to say that much of what I've just said is part of one of those three intertwining strands I mentioned in the Introduction – in this case the speculative strand.

Assessing Hattusili's reign

Hattusili was in his early to mid forties at the time of his accession, and thus a man in the prime of his life, given that Hittite medical skills probably ensured that life expectancy, at least for the upper classes, was relatively high. The new king's apparent bouts of illness do not appear to have had a serious or continuing impact on his health, for his reign lasted some thirty years. Theoretically at least, this allows plenty of scope for asking the big questions. What were the distinctive features of his reign, features that differentiated it from the reigns of his predecessors or successors? In what ways did the Hittite world change during the three decades of his rule? Did he leave it in better or worse shape than he found it?

Overall, I suppose we could say that he left it in no worse a shape than he found it. This seems like damning with faint praise. And, despite Hattusili's claims towards the end of his *Apology*, it's most unlikely there was any significant expansion of Hittite territory during his reign. But much credit may be due to him for maintaining, at least to outward appearances, the empire's stability for three decades or more in a world of increasing political and military instability. His seizure of the throne by force could have led to far greater divisiveness within the empire than it actually did. That applied to both the upper echelons of Hittite society and the wider Hittite world of vassal states, whose rulers pledged their loyalty as a matter of course to the king who actually sat upon the throne in the treaties he drew up with them. In his *Proclamation* where he laid down the rules of royal succession, the Old Kingdom ruler Telipinu recalled the earlier days of the kingdom's slide towards anarchy and almost total collapse when a pretender's dagger or a poisoned chalice despatched one king after another. Now, the overthrow of Urhi-Teshub, the conflict that followed, even if a brief and limited one, the escape of the ex-king from his place of banishment, and his unrelenting efforts to regain his throne all had the potential to destroy the monarchy completely, and thus bring about the disintegration of the loose network of vassal states which were one of the empire's defining features.

To his credit, Hattusili managed a successful transition of power from his nephew to himself at apparently little cost in terms of human casualties, and little political cost, with his eventual acceptance as Hatti's new Great King seemingly at all levels of Hittite society (with the obvious exceptions of Urhi-Teshub and his supporters and the surviving members of Arma-Tarhunda's family). Of course, I should qualify this by emphasizing that I am basing much of what I say on what Hattusili himself tells us. Records presenting a more negative view of his accession and the events which accompanied and followed it have not survived, due either to accidental destruction or deliberate obliteration by the new Great King's scribes. Or they never existed at all. And I have no doubt that Hattusili pursued his ambitions in as ruthless a way as he believed necessary, with scant respect for his brother's wishes and his nephew's unquestionable right to the throne.

Acceptance by his subjects and royal peers

Winning credibility amongst his royal peers, as well as his own subjects, was one of the major challenges confronting Hattusili in the early years of his long reign. The Assyrian king Adad-nirari had pointedly snubbed him by failing to send representatives to his coronation. Hattusili did, however, succeed in establishing close relations, and an alliance against Egypt, with the aged Babylonian king Kadashman-Turgu. But Kadashman-Turgu died just a short time later. His son and successor Kadashman-Enlil re-established his kingdom's ties with Egypt and, allegedly at the promptings of his 'evil' vizier, he had initially been hostile to the Hattusili regime. Hattusili's long letter to him, discussed in Chapters 7 and 9, indicates the Hittite's success in renewing ties with Babylon and seeking to improve them.

But, most important of all, was acknowledgment by the pharaoh Ramesses of Hattusili as Hatti's rightful king. His confirmation of this is illustrated both in a letter he wrote to Hattusili, and in his declaration of support for the new regime in a letter he wrote in reply to a query from the Hittite vassal ruler in Mira. Though the letter was sent via Hattusa and may never have been forwarded to its addressee, Hattusili no doubt made sure that the endorsement he'd received from the pharaoh was made widely known among his own subjects as well as his foreign peers.

The turbulent former king

Yet a number of factors put his reign at constant risk of destabilization. Prominent among these were the activities of Urhi-Teshub, who should more correctly be referred to by his throne-name Mursili III. Once he fled his allotted place of exile in Syria, Hattusili never succeeded in recapturing him, nor did the fugitive ever give up his attempts to win the support of both foreign rulers and his own former subjects in his attempts to regain his throne. In the process, he had seriously compromised relations between Hatti and Egypt, because of Hattusili's accusations that Ramesses had provided him with asylum, which enabled him to acquire a following amongst the pharaoh's own subjects.

The latter is evident from the Hittite-Egyptian correspondence. The 'Eternal Peace' treaty may have put to rest Hattusili's fears of any future pharaonic complicity in Urhi-Teshub's campaigns for reinstatement. But Hattusili must have been concerned about the ex-king's activities in Hittite territory, including the Syrian principalities, and the possibility of his building a strong support base for himself in one or more of these regions. Ramesses' suggestion in one of his letters that Urhi-Teshub might be found in Aleppo or Qadesh or Kizzuwatna may not have been without substance.

The wild card in the royal pack

Urhi-Teshub's brother Kuruntiya may well have been a further cause for concern. Ever since Muwattalli entrusted him from childhood to his brother's care, he had become an integral part of Hattusili's immediate family, an 'older brother' and close friend of Hattusili's and Puduhepa's (?) son Tudhaliya. Hattusili made him ruler of the kingdom of Tarhuntassa and drew up a treaty with him granting him and his kingdom special privileges. Tarhuntassa, whose chief city had been for a short time capital of the Hittite empire, now ranked in importance with the viceregal kingdoms of Carchemish and Aleppo. Further favours would be bestowed upon Kuruntiya and his kingdom by Tudhaliya when he succeeded his father to the throne. Treaties which Hattusili and subsequently Tudhaliya drew up with Kuruntiya gave assurance of this.

But was all this sufficient to deter Kuruntiya from seeking the main prize, to which his birthright entitled him? Possibly not, as we noted in the previous chapter. The dilemma for Hattusili was that the greater the powers and privileges he bestowed upon his favoured nephew, the greater the incentive there was for this nephew to use these powers to make a bid for the top job. It's not unlikely that he built up a strong following amongst the subjects of his 'viceregal' kingdom, which may have acted as a magnet for other disaffected members of his immediate family and those of Hattusili's arch-enemy Arma-Tarhunda. And did Tarhuntassa become the final place of refuge for Kuruntiya's brother Urhi-Teshub? In his later years, Urhi-Teshub may have abandoned his attempts to regain his throne, but not his ambitions to restore the throne to his own family, passing the baton for Great Kingship to Kuruntiya.

This is, of course, speculative. But it surely reflects some of Hattusili's fears, perhaps not for his own kingship, but for the succession of his son. He may well have seen Kuruntiya as a significant threat to this. The rights of Kuruntiya's own family and the allure of Great Kingship could well have outweighed the loyalties instilled in him over many years by his adoptive family. I have suggested that the *Apology* was essentially a widely circulated piece of propaganda designed to pave the way for the 'divinely sanctioned' succession of Tudhaliya. Its composition is probably to be dated late in the king's reign, with one of its main purposes being to justify retention of the kingship in Hattusili's direct family line instead of shifting it back to Muwattalli's where it rightfully belonged.

Maintaining authority in the west

Hattusili's western campaign, part of which is perhaps recorded in the misnamed 'Tawagalawa letter', emphasizes the importance the king attached to maintaining his control in the west, which he demonstrated to his subjects there by leading the campaign himself. The part of the campaign perhaps preserved for us in the 'letter' did not end well, since its apparent chief object, the capture of the renegade Piyamaradu, was not achieved. But the western mission provided Hattusili with an opportunity of seeking, or re-seeking, the support of the king of Ahhiyawa in maintaining peace and stability in the western lands, which included his cooperation in ending Piyamaradu's subversive activities there. Perhaps some sort of pact, if not an actual treaty, had already been concluded, and Hattusili was tacitly referring to it in stating his own scrupulous conduct, during his western military operations, in avoiding violation of any terms of agreement he had reached with his Ahhiyawan royal brother.

In Chapter 10, I suggested that the king's western operations were essentially pragmatic or strategic in their objectives – to prevent any repetition of invasions of Hittite homeland territories from the west. But Hattusili's decision to go west was possibly prompted by ideological and political considerations as well. In Hittite ideology, Hittite kings were warlords whose credibility amongst their subjects and foreign peers required demonstrations of their prowess in the field of battle. By divine right and with divine assistance, they had conquered and made subject many lands which had all become part of their empire. They were the supreme lords of 'the land of a thousand gods' – the multitude of gods they absorbed into the Hittite pantheon from the many lands they conquered.

But Hattusili was not a typical Hittite warlord. He sought to maintain the stability of his kingdom and control over it primarily by the exercise of diplomacy rather than brute force, both internationally and within his own kingdom. As several of his predecessors had shown, there were times when the stylus or engraving chisel could be mightier than the sword. In Hattusili's case, this was most famously demonstrated in his treaty with Ramesses, after a long history of hostility between the two kingdoms culminating in the bloody conflict at Qadesh. No doubt, too, the general lack of restiveness amongst Hatti's subject states during Hattusili's long reign was further testimony, at least in part, to the king's diplomatic rather than his warrior skills.

But the western vassal states remained problematic. They could not simply be cut adrift, for ideological *or* strategic reasons. For Hattusili, political considerations required him to demonstrate that despite his preference for diplomacy over brute force, he could resort to the latter and was willing to do so, when all softer options had been closed off. Failure to take forceful military action in this case not only risked for Hattusili loss of the western half of the empire, but domino-like, could well have led to breakaway movements of states in its central and finally eastern parts. The only reasonably coherent record of Hattusili's personal intervention in the west, the 'Tawagalawa letter', tells of the king's failed attempts to come to terms with, or capture, the renegade Piyamaradu. But that is only part of the story of Hattusili's western venture or ventures. The first two thirds of the 'letter' are lost to us, and the extremely fragmentary remains of what may have been a more comprehensive western campaign, perhaps including the Piyamaradu episode, may well have provided a more positive account of Hattusili's western ventures.

Human resources

Yet, particularly because of their costs in human resources, Hattusili kept his military operations in the west, as well as elsewhere, to a minimum. In Chapter

10, I've argued that the number of able-bodied male subjects of the empire, from which a military force could be mustered, had become increasingly limited in the empire's last decades. This must have played heavily in Hattusili's overall policy of seeking to resolve conflicts by diplomatic rather than military means – even when a campaign was already underway, as we've seen in TL.

In Chapter 10, I discussed estimates of the Hittite world's total population ranging from 140,000 to 200,000 or more. This is a small number from which to build a fighting force able to maintain a widely spread empire, especially when you consider the proportion of females (non-combatants by virtue of their sex), underage males, the aged and the infirm which this number includes. Further, a likely population decline in the years leading up to Hattusili's reign and during it placed all the greater strain on the king's ability to maintain the security and stability of his subject states, as well as protecting the peoples of his homeland and ensuring an adequate supply of able-bodied persons to produce food for them. This is why I believe that population size was an important determinant in Hattusili's policies to make peace instead of war, wherever possible, in his own territories as well as with foreign powers. The 'Eternal Peace' is the outstanding example of this.

In the aftermath of Qadesh

One of the two parties contracting the treaty had to set the ball rolling, and I have no doubt this was Hattusili. Seeking a peace agreement might well be construed as an act of submission and, given the ambiguity of the Qadesh engagement's immediate outcome, Ramesses would hardly have conceded the contest tacitly to the Hittites by initiating the peace process himself. On the contrary, he would have welcomed the opportunity provided by his royal brother's initiative to claim Hittite confirmation of the Egyptian 'victory' he had emblazoned on the walls of five Egyptian temples. But, for Hattusili, pharaonic propaganda mattered little if it was the only price to pay for settlement of a permanent peace agreement.

According to Professor Edel's restored passage in one of the letters from the Hittite-Egyptian correspondence, Ramesses invited his royal brother to meet him in Canaan, whence he would escort him to Egypt for a royal visit.[6] Whether or not this restoration is correct, Hattusili would never have accepted such an invitation. Great Kings sent their representatives on diplomatic visits to their royal brothers. To go themselves would make them no better than subjects paying homage to their royal masters.

But this visit that never was prompts me to ask a question. If the two Great Kings had met, how, physically, would they have compared? What would they have looked like? Let me begin with a negative. Almost all Bronze and Iron Age Near Eastern sculptural representations of kings and other human beings are conventional, impersonal images which give us no sense of the actual physical attributes of their subjects. In any case, surviving Hittite sculptures of kings and queens are few in number and in some cases badly worn. The latter applies particularly to the only remaining identifiable sculptures of Hattusili and his queen Puduhepa. Weathered almost beyond recognition, the sculptures are carved into a rock-face at a place called Fraktin in southern Anatolia, as we noted in Chapter 6. They are identified by their names carved in hieroglyphs next to them.

By contrast, Egypt abounds with sculptural representations of the pharaoh, often well preserved, and often spectacularly monumental, like the four statues of Ramesses at Abu Simbel. Yet, for all the excellent state of preservation of many of them, they are still no more than impersonal, conventionalised pharaonic images. It is not until the Classical era of Greece and Rome that we have images, painted or carved in stone, that give us any indication of what their subjects really looked like. What we *do* have are Ramesses' well preserved mummified remains. The pharaoh was around ninety when he died, but in his earlier years, he must have been a handsome man, with a fine head of auburn hair and a distinguished aquiline profile. At a height of 1.7 metres, he would have towered over most of his subjects, and very likely over Hattusili had they ever met. (Incidentally, he did not die of drowning, as his biblical counterpart reputedly did.)

Though sculptural representations tell us almost nothing about what Hittite (and Egyptian) kings and queens actually looked like, we know that one of the Hittites' distinguishing features was that both males and females wore their hair long, and the males were cleanshaven. Figure 14.1 may be a reasonably good likeness of Hattusili. It is a 'still' from Tolga Örnek's documentary, *The Hittites*, which is by far the most thoroughly researched and accurate portrayal on film of the Hittites and the empire they ruled. In Tolga's film, the Hattusili depicted in Figure 14.1 is actually the first king of that name. But to my mind, his shifty, cunning look makes him an appropriate representation of *our* Hattusili. By the time of their hypothetical meeting, probably some years after the peace treaty, Hattusili must have been well into his fifties, perhaps his early sixties, some twenty years or so older than the Egyptian and maybe showing the ravaging effects of his lifelong illnesses.

Figure 14.1 Hattusili. Courtesy Tolga Örnek, from *The Hittites* (2003), [TV programme] Dir. Tolga Örnek, Turkey: Ekip Film.

Puduhepa's role in the empire in her husband's last years

That brings us to the question of how great a role Hattusili's queen played in the conduct of the empire's affairs in her husband's final years. We have noted that her seal appeared with his on the 'Eternal Treaty', that she partnered him in making important official appointments, like that of Kuruntiya to the kingship of Tarhuntassa, and that she deputized for him in secular affairs of the kingdom, like the dispensing of justice. All this alongside her primary role as Chief Priestess of the Hittite world, and her efforts to sort out the chaotic jumble of deities in the Hittite pantheon. Did she, in fact, progressively take over many of her husband's administrative responsibilities as he became increasingly less able to perform these himself? She undoubtedly made enemies if she did – even apart from Hattusili's long-standing enemies, who were never reconciled to his seizure of the throne and eagerly awaited his demise to try to seize it back and restore it to Muwattalli's family line. The queen's heartfelt appeals to the gods for her husband's health may have had as much to do with fears for her own safety when he died as with a display of genuine love for her husband, and grief at his impending death.

The men behind the masks

My biography of Hattusili has clear limitations. As with all Hittite kings, we have mainly official records from which to build our picture not only of this king's successes and failures as ruler of an empire but of what he was like as a human being – his personal qualities, his strengths and his weaknesses, his virtues and vices, his likes and dislikes. This is where we miss the services of a third-party chronicler, like a Hittite Thucydides, Herodotos, Livy or Tacitus. In a limited way, I have attempted to take on this role in my account of Hattusili's life and career, and the political and social environment which helped mould them. As I have commented in one of my earlier books, the world of the Hittite royal court was probably no less byzantine in its character and behaviour than the court at Constantinople during its thousand-year kingdom. And it would indeed be surprising if the Hittite royal dynasty in the course of its own 500-year history failed to come up with at least one or two corrupt, paranoid, depraved despots when imperial Rome managed to produce a whole crop of them within the space of a few decades. Any long-lasting monarchy which is absolute and unaccountable almost inevitably spawns a few creatures of this sort in the course of its history. Why should the Hittite royal dynasty have been any different?[7]

Of course, even 'independent' chroniclers put their own spin upon their perception of events, based on their own biases, conscious or not. But, without such observers and commentators, we can with few exceptions do no more than deduce what a king was like behind his official facade. Occasionally the tablets reveal a little more. We learn something of the first Hattusili's deep disappointment in his highly dysfunctional family, and of the heart-rending grief of our Hattusili's father Mursili at the death of his first wife, murdered by his stepmother.

We are, however, provided with a slightly more comprehensive range of material about Hattusili's reign. The king's *Apology* and extensive, though now fragmentary, correspondence with Ramesses are notable examples of this; the former is unique in Hittite documentary history. Yet our knowledge of this king as a person is still very limited, and most of what I've said about him is deduction rather than fact. Thus, he tells us that the goddess Ishtar gave him and Puduhepa 'the love of husband and wife'. From the extreme rarity of the use of the word 'love' to characterize what were almost always arranged marriages in the Hittite world, from the length of the marriage, from Puduhepa's prayers for her husband's health, and from her partnership with him in the affairs of state, I have *deduced* a lifelong relationship based on love, which underpinned a working partnership between Great King and Chief Wife throughout their marriage. Contrary to partnerships in which a Hittite king's Chief Wife exercised a disruptive, malevolent role within the royal household and sometimes within the kingdom at large, theirs was one which provided the glue that helped hold the empire together throughout Hattusili's reign.

From the king's spurious claim that he had himself selected his predecessor, his nephew Urhi-Teshub, as his brother's successor to the throne, from his overthrow of Urhi-Teshub, and from his own seizure of the throne on equally spurious grounds, I have *deduced* that Hattusili was devious, deceitful, manipulative and possessed of a ruthless, long-standing ambition to occupy the throne himself. From his own alleged claims of his military achievements (which I largely believe), particularly the reoccupation and restoration of the holy city of Nerik, and from his divisional command at Qadesh (though he says nothing of his part in the battle), I have *deduced* that Hattusili had a distinuished military career, and that his military skills were early recognized and put to use in his young adult years by his brother.

From the frequent references in the texts to his poor health and the illnesses from which he suffered, I have *deduced* that Hattusili had a chronically weak disposition that did not affect his capacity to rule, with Puduhepa's support, or cut short his unusually long life. I have *deduced* that he was in his seventies, perhaps well into them, when he died. From his treaty with Ramesses, of which I believe he was the instigator, from his persistent but fruitless attempts to reach a peace settlement with a notorious insurrectionist in the west, from the general peace and apparent stability which prevailed throughout the kingdom during much of his reign, and from his emphasis on establishing and maintaining friendly relations with his foreign peers across the Euphrates as well as in the land of the Nile, I have *deduced* that Hattusili saw his role as primarily that of a peacemaker rather than a warlord in the traditional manner of Hittite kings. From archaeological evidence provided by Hattusa and from various other factors, including a serious reduction in the supply of transplantees to the homeland during his reign, residual effects of the plague which allegedly decimated the homeland during Hattusili's father's reign, and heavy battle casualties at Qadesh, I have *deduced* that the empire was becoming increasingly short of manpower, both for the purposes of food production and army recruitment, and that this may well have been an important consideration in Hattusili's attempts to maintain his empire by diplomacy rather than by force.

In the end, I believe that Hattusili left his empire pretty much as he found it, neither smaller nor significantly larger, neither significantly stronger nor weaker. Despite the manner of his accession to Great Kingship, his difficulties in gaining recognition from his royal peers, the hostile elements within his own extended family that were a constant threat to his rule, and his limited resources for keeping his enemies at bay and his vassal states subservient, he maintained a relatively firm grip on the reins of empire, preventing it from fragmenting and descending into anarchy.

Even so, the empire in this period might be compared to an old manorial building that is reasonably well maintained within the limited resources available, undergoes some minor renovations from time to time and to outward appearances changes very little for many decades. All this time, its foundations are crumbling and will eventually give way, causing the entire edifice to collapse. Hattusili could not prevent the ultimate decline and collapse of the Hittite empire. He may, however, have helped delay it a few years.

APPENDIX 1

Chronicle of Events

From Suppiluliuma I to Suppiluliuma II
with particular emphasis on the life and career of Hattusili III
(Bracketed numbers = approx. regnal dates)

Suppiluliuma I (1350–1322 BC). Grandfather of Hattusili I; completes conquest of Mittanian empire (mid 1320s); establishes viceregal kingdoms at Carchemish and Aleppo; attacks Egyptian subject territory in Syria and carries back plague with prisoners of war; dies of plague, briefly succeeded by son Arnuwanda II, who also dies of plague.

Mursili II (1322–1295 BC). Grandson and second successor of Suppiluliuma, father of Hattusili; establishes firm control over Hatti's rebellious states and drives enemies out of Hittite territory; wife murdered by his stepmother, the Babylonian Tawannana, who is banished from the capital for this and various other offences.

Muwattalli II (1295–1272 BC). Son of Mursili and brother of Hattusili; shifts Hittite capital to Tarhuntassa; Ramesses II's adversary in battle of Qadesh (1274 BC).

Urhi-Teshub (1272–1267 BC). Son (by concubine) and first successor of Muwattalli; shifts capital back to Hattusa; unseated by Hattusili and sent into exile in Syria; escapes place of exile and seeks refuge in Egypt; continues to seek reinstatement to throne.

Hattusili III (1267–1237 BC). Youngest child of Mursili and brother of Muwattalli; appointed ruler of northern part of kingdom by Muwattalli, who also assigns his younger son Kuruntiya to Hattusili as his ward; participates in battle of Qadesh; appointed by Muwattalli post-Qadesh as temporary administrator of the Damascus region; during return to his northern kingdom, he meets and marries the Hurrian priestess Puduhepa, who becomes his lifelong Chief Wife; seizes throne from Urhi-Teshub in a brief civil war; concludes an 'Eternal Peace' treaty with Ramesses (1259 BC); undertakes an ultimately unsuccessful expedition against a western activist Piyamaradu, in the context of volatile relations with the king of Ahhiyawa, a Greek kingdom; appoints Kuruntiya ruler of Tarhuntassa, in effect a third viceregal kingdom.

Tudhaliya IV (1237–1209 BC). Son and successor of Hattusili; faced with growing unrest among the vassal states and the beginnings of the disintegration of the empire; Urhi-Teshub and Kuruntiya possibly seek reinstatement of their family line as the kingdom of Hatti's ruling dynasty.

Arnuwanda III (1209–1207 BC?) and Suppiluliuma II (*c.* 1207–1178 BC?). Sons of Tudhaliya and last rulers in succession of the collapsing Hittite empire.

APPENDIX 2

The Economy[1]

As you've been reading this book, especially the chapter on 'Managing the Empire', you may think of a number of questions I haven't answered, such as 'How was everything actually paid for: the building and maintenance of the palaces and temples; the lavish festival programmes; the military campaigns; royal weddings and bridal dowries; the maintenance of the state bureaucracies; and the sustenance of the kingdom's population?' And so we could go on. Demands on the kingdom's resources were substantial and seemingly endless. What were its sources of revenue and how successfully did they meet the demands upon them? Of course, these questions belong to a broader study of the Hittites, not just a biography of one of their kings. And the answers will vary from one period to another. But I thought it worth devoting a small part of this book to addressing some of them, particularly as they apply to Hattusili's career before and during his kingship, and to the reigns of his successors – the last three Hittite kings.

Oikonomia

Let me begin with the key word in the famous, if rather fatuous, statement by US President Bill Clinton's political adviser James Carville: 'It's the economy, stupid!' 'Economy' is a simple word in origin. It's derived from Classical Greek *oikonomia*, which means 'the management of a household or family'. In many cultures the household, Greek *oikos*, was not just limited to a parental couple and their children or even to a more broadly based family organization. It might also include a household of servants and slaves, and maybe extend to a motley collection of hangers-on.

Not unusually, the *de facto* head of the extended family was the wife or chief wife of the patriarchal head. Examples of this abound in Classical legend and history. It typically happened during a husband's prolonged absences on military campaigns. Thus, Penelope ruled over her household of servants and slaves, both loyal and treacherous, all the while fending off the unwanted advances of her many suitors, during her husband Odysseus' absence fighting the Trojan War and on his long journey home.[2] The 'household' *largely* managed by Livia, the feared, all-powerful wife of Rome's first emperor, Augustus, consisted virtually of the entire imperial court, with a substantial retinue of clients and toadies ready to do her every bidding.

In the Hittite world, we have examples of at least two, and perhaps three or more, Chief Wives who managed and exercised a powerful and sometimes malign influence over the royal 'household'. Hattusili's stepgrandmother, the Babylonian Tawannana, was the most notorious of these; his wife Puduhepa the one upon whom history looks most kindly. And at lower levels of society too, in both the Hittite and other worlds, the widows or wives of men absent on long military campaigns must often have assumed a *de facto* role as head of the household. Perhaps the practice of levirate marriage, enshrined in Hittite law, was partly intended to ease the household burdens of a woman suddenly deprived of her husband by war or some other misfortune.[3]

My *Oxford Engish Dictionary* defines 'economy' as 'the management or administration of the resources (esp. the financial resources) of a community or establishment'. In its broadest sense, this covers the administration of the financial affairs of a whole country, which is what Clinton's political adviser had in mind. But in its narrowest, traditional sense, the term 'economy' or *oikonomia* might be applied to multiple household units throughout the Hittite world. Here, I use 'household' loosely to cover any family-based organizations ranging from large estates owned or operated by high-ranking Hittite officials, to the households of commoners, with nuclear families at their core; the householders might have a small number of labourers at their disposal, hired or slave, and a modest landholding, enough for growing crops or orchards or running a few livestock.

At all levels of Hittite society, it's not unlikely that women often played a major role in the management of their family's and household's affairs, just like our legendary heroines and their historical counterparts. This may in part have been due to the exigencies of military campaigns, requiring frequent call-ups of the patriarchal heads of households, and other able-bodied males within it, with lengthy periods away from home, and the risk that they might never return. In the absence of adult males, many women must have developed the experience and skills necessary to ensure that a household, whether large or small, continued to function productively until its master returned, and permanently if he did not.

And many such women may have been property-owners in their own right, particularly those whose dowries included a portion of food-producing land, and thus a source of revenue. On marriage, the husband became custodian of this land, but it remained his wife's property, and presumably reverted to her in full, if she outlived him.

An agro-pastoral economy

At macro-level, the economy of the Hittite state is best described as agro-pastoral.[4] Grain cultivation[5] was the basis of agriculture, though a wide variety of fruit and vegetables seems to have been a regular part of the Hittite diet. Grain was stored in silos in the Hittite capital, at other distribution centres throughout the homeland, and on campaign routes regularly trodden by Hittite troops. Most of the grain was probably cultivated on large estates owned or leased out by the palace, and on land granted by the palace to those who had served it with distinction – or were expected to. Fruit and vegetables were likely to have been the produce of smaller households on their allotments, sold in small local markets or requisitioned by the palace.

In what I believe was the peak period of Hittite history, from the last decades of the fourteenth century BC through the middle decades of the thirteenth, the Hittites' pastoral lands were well stocked with herds of cattle and flocks of sheep, many the result of plundering campaigns against rebellious states. As Klinger observes, the abundance of livestock is indicated by 'the astonishingly large proportion of animal sacrifices in the context of rituals, but also in the archaeological record'.[6] The livestock, including goats, served not only to provide meat for the evening meal or a banquet for the gods, but were also important in the production of wool (in the case of sheep and goats), as beasts of burden for both transport and ploughing (in the case of cattle) or as sources of milk (cattle, sheep, and goats).

The question of who actually owned the land of the state has been much debated. In theory, one might argue that all land was the property of the gods and thus belonged to the king as their chief earthly representative. In practice, to cut a very long debate short, the king probably claimed large areas of choice arable and pastoral land as his own personal property, with revenue from its produce filling his own personal respositories. This land could be leased out by the king or bestowed as land grants upon those favoured by the king, as a reward for services they had rendered the king on the battlefield or in other fields of endeavour – or in anticipation of services they were expected to supply.

Maintaining the food supply

From king to lowliest peasant, the Hittites generally fed themselves well, in accordance with their station in life, from a variety of food sources, produced by animals harvested for their flesh, or from plant foods harvested from the soil, on the estates of large landowners or land grantees, or on allotments leased and sometimes owned by small farmers.[7] Of course, nature, or in Hittite terms disgruntled gods, sometimes intervened with violent crop-destroying storms or prolonged periods of drought. In some periods, silos constructed in the Hittite capital and other centres of distribution could help tide the population over short intervals of crop failure. Such failures were only to be expected in the semi-arid region of the central Anatolian plateau with its hot, often dry summers and harsh snow-laden winters. However, Jörg Klinger comments that the second half of the second millennium (which includes the period when Hattusili was king) saw rather favourable climatic conditions, even if this period was interspersed with short regional droughts.[8]

But almost certainly the Hittites in maintaining their food supplies were subject to another danger – a human one. From a series of brief letters, more appropriately called daily bulletins, exchanged between Hattusili's great-grandfather Tudhaliya III and his chief officials stationed in various administrative centres of the homeland, we learn of constant incursions by Kaska bands, deep into Hittite territory where some of the most important of Hatti's grain fields were apparently located. The dangers these Kaskans posed to stealing or burning the crops are evident in many of these bulletins, with the king demanding urgent action to take all means possible to capture the raiders and protect the crops.[9] No doubt, too, cattle-rustling was another threat posed by the invaders. Though we have no evidence of such threats to Hatti's food supplies in later periods, no doubt the constant conflicts in which Hattusili claims to have engaged against enemy forces in regions north of the capital were as much intended to protect the kingdom's food-producing areas in the region, as to reassert control over them for their own sake.

Moreover, we should not underestimate the human resources required not only to maximize food production within the kingdom, but also to ensure adequate defence of the food-producing lands and the livestock which were essential to the kingdom's existence. This is of particular relevance to the issues I have raised in earlier chapters about how limited these resources probably were, particularly in terms of able-bodied men, on which Hattusili could call in defending his homeland. Military enterprises beyond it were costly, when the soldiers required for them might well have meant significant reductions in the number of persons available for more productive activities within their own region. Hattusili was all too aware of this. It must have underpinned what I see as his policy of using diplomacy rather than force, whenever possible, to maintain control of his kingdom, and helps explain why in a reign lasting thirty years or more, there appears to have been very few major military campaigns (perhaps only one or two) undertaken by a Hittite army far from the homeland.

The relationship between palace and temple

Then there is the vexed question of the relationship between the palace and the state's temple establishment. Did the temples function as independent entities, with lands of their own and their own economic resources? Divisions between temple and state, as later between church and palace, have been sources of friction and conflict in many periods of history, beginning with the power struggles between temple and palace in third millennium Sumer, southern Mesopotamia. In the Hittite world, the relationship between the palace and the multitudinous temple establishments – as we've noted, the remains of thirty-one temples have so far been uncovered in the capital – seems to have been a seamless, cooperative one. As the kingdom's Chief Priest, the king was *ipso facto* the head of all the kingdom's religious establishments and was the ultimate owner of any lands which were attached to them. Directly or indirectly, he oversaw all their activities, subsidized their operations when necessary, and could lay claim to any of the income they produced.

The fact that many members of the royal family also had important priestly functions, notably, the king's Chief Wife who was Chief Priestess of the Hittite world, strengthened further the interconnectedness of palace and religious establishments. A classic example of this is provided by the young Hattusili's dedication to the service of Ishtar, quite possibly serving as a novitiate in her temple in Hattusa. Klinger observes that 'numerous text finds in connection to temples in Hattuša … indicate a fluent transition in function and that both temple as well as palace were part of one and the same organisation'.[10]

Revenue from the land and the temples

All beneficiaries of the king's largesse were expected to provide revenue for the palace and the state. Thus, temples were not merely places of worship and cultic rites. They also served as locations for craftsmen, who produced a range of goods, including storage vessels, tools and certain luxury items. Some of these may have served cultic purposes, but others were very likely commissioned by the palace or produced for sale in the open market.[11] It's also not unlikely that at least some of the temples were allocated parcels of land for fruit, vegetable, or grain production, or for pastoral purposes. Revenue from them helped fund the temple's expenses, with perhaps a portion of it paid to the palace.

No doubt written records were kept of all these transactions, as well as of a host of other activities, especially those concerned with the temple's service to its deity. The likely numerous roles in which Hittite temples engaged (and they were far from being the only temples to do so in the Near Eastern temple world) call to mind the multifunctional activities of many monasteries of the medieval period. The comparison may well be appropriate, to judge from the archaeological evidence of the Temple of the Storm God in Hattusa's Lower City, and possibly some of the text finds associated with temples in the Upper City.[12]

International trade[13]

Both textual and artefactual evidence indicate that Hatti had a wide range of international trading contacts, including Babylon, Egypt, Cyprus, Mittani (before its destruction by Suppiluliuma) and the Syro-Palestinian states.[14] On the other hand, as Eric Cline observes, there is almost no evidence to indicate commercial links between the Late Bronze Age Greek (Ahhiyawan) and Hittite worlds. Cline suggests that this was due to a trade embargo on Ahhiyawan goods, but other explanations are possible.[15] The main point is that, although Hattusili and perhaps at least two of his predecessors considered it important to establish and maintain good relations with the kingdom of Ahhiyawa, they did so primarily for political and strategic reasons, rather than for any perceived commercial benefit.

It seems ironic that some of the most important contributors to the Hittite economy and to the kingdom's security and well-being are almost completely unknown to us. These people, merchants and traders, barely rate a mention in Hittite texts. Though the Hittite world was, inevitably, a part of the international

Bronze Age trading network, the Hittites themselves were beneficiaries of rather than active participants in international trading enterprises. Such enterprises seem to have been left largely in the hands of foreign intermediaries. Upon these, Hittite kings were largely, if not completely, dependent for the supply of vital raw materials, especially tin, an essential component in the manufacture of bronze weaponry for the king's armies and in the production of a multifarious array of other wares, from workmen's tools and ritual vessels to a wide range of domestic utensils.

Archaeology has yet to provide evidence that local sources of tin could be mined in sufficient quantities to sustain a bronze-making industry within the kingdom. The likelihood is that the sources of tin supplied to the Hittite world came from as far afield as Afghanistan. It was probably from the same sources that in the pre-Hittite period Assyrian traders of the so-called Assyrian colony period obtained their supplies of tin which were then transported by donkey caravans into the early, pre-Hittite, second millennium kingdoms of central and northern Anatolia.[16]

Similar means of transportation may have been used on the long treks from the sources of supply in the far east to the foundries of the Hittite world. And along the lengthy routes of travel, the risks from enemy forces or marauders to such vitally important merchandise must have required substantial military protection for the caravaneers, perhaps supplied directly by the Hittites, perhaps by the caravans' own military escorts. Even so, the merchant's life was a harsh and dangerous one, as is evident from the Babylonian king Kadashman-Enlil's complaint to Hattusili about his merchants being killed in Hittite territory. Merchant convoys were always attractive targets for roving bands of predators, because their consignments probably included a range of luxury items intended to grace the royal palaces and the mansions of Hittite society's elite classes. No doubt merchants who reached their destination with their goods intact were handsomely rewarded for their services, with a high mark-up on all they had to sell, taking into account the risks they ran and the hardships they had to endure.

Among the very rare references to merchants in the Hittite texts, there is a clause in the collection of two hundred laws that imposes a penalty of four thousand shekels of silver on anyone responsible for the murder of a merchant,[17] a sum far higher than any other penalty specified for criminal offences in the laws. A later version of this law provides further detail. The person who commits the murder will also pay three times the value of his victim's goods. But there is an appendage to this. If the merchant has no goods with him and is killed in a quarrel, or accidentally, the offender will pay only 240 and 80 shekels, respectively, for these actions. This might suggest that the merchant himself was of little account once he had disposed of his goods. But we really need more context to understand what it was that prompted this law, particularly its later version.

In any case, the Hittite term for merchant, *unnattallaš*, refers exclusively to wealthy and important men who under royal protection conducted the business of international trade with allied countries.[18] And, although the texts say almost nothing about merchants within the Hittite world, it's clear that Hittite kings attached considerable importance to their protection, at least when they were still in possession of their merchandise. The severe penalties imposed on those who stole from them is further illustrated by the substantial fine of one and a third talents of silver which the king of Ugarit, a Hittite vassal state, had to pay for seizing four hundred donkeys, worth four thousand shekels of silver, from the caravan of a merchant called Mashanda.[19] Indeed, many of the cases judged in the courts of the Hittite viceroys concerned crimes against merchants, including robbery, hijacking and murder. If the offenders were not caught, the inhabitants, or the authorities, of the districts, in which the crimes were committed, were obliged to pay substantial compensation for failing to exercise their communal responsibilities.

Currency and wages

Shekels, minas and talents were standard forms of currency in the Ancient Near East. Each was a measurement of weight, often of metal bars, whose value depended on what the metal was – copper, bronze, silver or gold, going from cheapest to most valuable. The other factor determining the worth of a metal bar was the ratio between shekel, mina and talent. This varied from one civilization to another, and from one period to another. In the Hittite world, the ratio between shekel and mina seems to have been forty shekels to the mina. (In other systems, the ratio was sixty to one.) Correspondingly, and also in accordance with the Near Eastern sexagesimal system, there were sixty minas to the talent, and thus 3,600 shekels to the talent. A mina was roughly half a kilogram in weight, and a shekel a mere 8.3 grams. But a talent weighed around thirty kilograms.

Silver was the most common form of currency used, made into bars of varying weight. So what were these bars worth, in buying and spending terms? My reply would be the old fall-back cliché: 'That's a good question!' The best we can do is to look at some prices set down in the Hittite laws, along with the hire rates the laws specify for farm labourers; the latter, we shall suppose, earned the equivalent of a basic wage. You could buy 150 litres of wheat for one shekel of silver, an uncultivated plot of land, around 3,600 square metres, for no more than two or three shekels, whereas the price of a vineyard of the same size would set you back about forty shekels of silver. And, if you were a member of the elite class, you could well afford the luxury of a chest full of fine linen garments, at thirty shekels apiece.

On the other hand, if you were a male farm labourer, you'd probably earn no more than one shekel of silver a month, if a female labourer, only half that amount. You'd be better off taking your payment in kind – that is, a share of the harvest – 1,500 litres of barley, if you were a male, which would supply you and your family's staple food needs until the next harvest season, a niggardly six hundred litres, if you were a female. The different rates of pay for males and females probably reflected the physical demands of a farm labourer's work and the male's ability to be twice as productive as the female in a role where natural physical strength played a major part. But, just as with the provisions made in the rest of the laws, all prices and wages were merely suggestive, not prescriptive. They could vary considerably from time to time as circumstances required. It's likely, for example, that female hire rates rose significantly at times when much of the state's able-bodied male population was engaged on military operations.

Merchants operating within the Hittite world

Most of the texts referring to merchants belong within the context of international trading operations. But we have a small fragment which appears to refer to merchants operating purely within Hittite world. Here is Professor Hoffner's translation of it:

We, the merchants of Ura and Zallara[20] are coming, and have plenty and abundance in our possession. We are bringing many NAM.RA-people (i.e. transplantees). We are driving cattle, sheep, horses, mules and asses in large numbers. We have barley and wine in large amounts in our possession. We have in our possession valuable items as well: silver, gold, lapis lazuli, carnelian, Babylonian stone, quartz, copper, bronze, and tin – whatever is within our prerogative, all in large amounts.[21]

This is a very large, very rich consignment, comprising not only a treasure trove of precious stones and valuable metals, but also large numbers of captured peoples and livestock. Though it's not stated in what survives of the text, the consignment is almost certainly destined for Hattusa. And almost certainly more than a mere commercial operation is involved. The consignment is most likely the plunder of a successful Hittite military operation. Part way on its journey to Hattusa it was handed over to agents of the Hittite king, who were responsible for delivering it to its final destination. Presumably a large armed escort ensured the security of the consignment throughout its journey.

Let me suggest the following scenarios. After a successful campaign against an enemy or rebel state, the Hittite king (not identified) decides that he will return home as quickly as possible with all his troops, perhaps to attend to urgent matters in his homeland territories. He has contracted out the job of escorting home the human and material spoils of conquests to 'merchants', in this case, hired mercenaries who assemble their own armed force for the purpose. We've already noted that Muwattalli allegedly supplemented his army with mercenary troops for the battle of Qadesh (according to Ramesses' account of the conflict). Mercenaries may have been used on other occasions as well; for example, as a prisoner-escort service when the king's own forces could not be spared for this task, especially in periods when Hittite manpower was in short supply. Alternatively, these 'merchant' mercenaries may have, on their own initiative, undertaken plundering expeditions with a formidable fighting force of their own, presumably in lands not subject to Hittite control, and are offering the spoils to Hattusa; no doubt at a substantial price. The piece of surviving text suggests that the document is a progress report from these 'merchants', with a list of the goods for sale.

Exports

Now we must engage in further speculation. We don't have any texts that tell us explicitly what the Hittites exported to other parts of the Near Eastern world in return for what they imported. A text from Ugarit, Hittite vassal territory, suggests that the Hittite nobility sold slaves, presumably surplus to their own requirements, to wealthy Ugaritian citizens.[22] But further afield, gold, silver and commodity metals like copper that were mined in central Anatolia and other areas under Hittite control probably found ready markets in resource-poor regions like parts of Mesopotamia, homelands of the kingdoms of Assyria and Babylon. What of exports to Egypt, which had access to abundant supplies of these metals? Horses bred from stock originally imported from Mittani may have figured amongst these exports. The rigorous training and culling programme of horses used in the Hittites' elite chariot contingents must have produced animals of the finest quality for action in battle. Their offspring could well have provided Hatti with a lucrative export item in its trade with Egypt and other Bronze Age kingdoms.

How were the state's services paid for?

Let me conclude this discussion by returning to the questions I asked at the beginning of it. How were the services both sacred and secular provided by the state, more specifically, the palace, actually paid for, and with what? No doubt part of the state's funding came from state-owned silver, gold and copper mines, which were productive enough to finance many of the state's bureaucratic and religious activities, part of the costs of its military operations, and some of its imports from eastern sources. The metals could either be moulded into bars of various weights used as a form of currency (silver, in particular), or shaped into writing tablets (bronze, in particular), or, in larger quantities, transformed into statues of kings or gods or used for plating the inner wooden cores of such statues.

Plunder from successful military campaigns provided a valuable source of revenue, all the more so when these campaigns were frequent, as they were during the reign of Hattusili's father Mursili. 'Booty-people', i.e. transplantees, from these campaigns provided a much needed boost to the homeland's population and labour and military force. And the large numbers of captured sheep and cattle helped restock the estates of the palace, the lands bestowed on the king's officials and probably, in some cases, the farmlands or grazing lands managed by temples. Treasures from looted enemy cities, like the spoils of Babylon brought back by the first King Mursili, no doubt adorned the palaces and the Great Temple of the Storm God in Hattusa and other temples. Mursili's predecessor, the first King Hattusili, had already adorned the temples of sundry gods with plunder from his Syrian campaigns.

We've already noted the precious metals and jewellery included in the loot collected by the 'merchants' of Ura and Zallara, probably destined for Hattusa for His Majesty's personal pleasure, and/or also for disposal by him to a range of palace and temple functionaries. Transplantees, gold, silver and copper provided a new source of income from the reported conquest of Alasiya by Hattusili's son Tudhaliya. The text recording this also stipulates what tribute is to be paid by

Alasiya in the future, in this case, primarily to a number of Hatti's gods, beginning with the Sun Goddess of Arinna.[23] Presumably a vassal treaty was drawn up by Tudhaliya with the Alasiyan king, in which the annual tribute to be paid by the new vassal to Hattusa was specified – *if* Tudhaliya did succeed for a time in maintaining control over the island, or at least its capital. (But see my account of the Alasiyan enterprise in Chapter 13.)

Almost certainly all Hatti's vassal states were obliged to pay an annual tribute to their overlord, thus providing him with one of his regular sources of income, though the treaties seldom refer to such payments. Two exceptions are treaties signed by Suppiluliuma with the king of Nuhashshi, a Syrian vassal state, and Mursili with the king of Amurru, another Syrian vassal. In both cases, the amount stipulated is 300 shekels of silver.[24] For a wealthy vassal, this seems little more than a token payment and, if typical of the payments imposed on other vassal states, would not have done much to swell the royal coffers of Hattusa. But assessments may have varied markedly from state to state and for each state from time to time, depending on a range of factors of which we have no knowledge.

That brings me to a series of questions. How were public works like the construction and maintenance of the kingdom's defensive structures, such as the walls of Hattusa, funded? How were the king's defence forces paid for? Who funded the festivals that filled the kingdom's religious calendar, and how? We have no statement of accounts, no financial records to help us answer these questions. Such information must have been written down somewhere; it's possible that wooden tablets which no longer exist were used partly to store financial records, erased from wax-coated tablets and replaced by new data once the old data had become obsolete.

Let me speculate further on these questions. Silver was probably a common form of payment, though payment in kind, offered on highly favourable terms, would likely be preferred by an employer, like food supplies for a season, and basic materials for making clothes or furnishing workmen's dwellings. Perhaps a mixture of the two forms of payment was on offer to some employees, mainly the army of bureaucrats who played an important role in the kingdom's administration, in both the capital and its regional centres.

The paymaster in many of the above situations was likely to be the king, from income accrued from his personal estates where livestock was tended and crops grown, and from taxes imposed on the income earned by estates allocated to temples and by the lands bestowed by the king on his officials.

Let's return to the religious festivals.[25] These, especially the most important annual ones honouring the deities of spring, autumn etc., and often repeated in various cult centres throughout the homeland and further afield, must have involved substantial costs of one kind or another. I suggest that, while the king's treasury may have covered some of the expenses, the bulk of these were the responsibility of the temples of the relevant deities, and/or wealthy *protégés* of the deities, those who claimed these deities as their patrons. Poorer folk, too, may have made what contributions they could afford, to ensure their god's protection in the year ahead.

The vast quantities of food that must have been prepared for these occasions – the roasted meats, the great variety of breads, the fancy pastries, the sweetmeats, the wine and beer, and all the other trimmings – were provided, I suggest, from the estates of wealthy devotees of the deities to whom the festival was dedicated. These were banquets fit for the gods, and it was *for* the gods, or a particular god, that they were, quite literally, intended. Indeed, the god took the honoured seat at the banquet and participated in it. After the appropriate rituals were performed, all those privileged to share the god's table fell to relieving it of its contents. When the god had finished eating, whatever he or she left behind was available to the priests who presided over the festival, to the festival's sponsors, and perhaps also to other participants once the privileged ones had eaten their fill.

Of course, all this food had to be prepared by an army of cooks and their assistants, complemented by those who served the food and attended in other ways upon the guests. Then there were the entertainers – acrobats, jugglers, minstrels, hired for the occasion (Figure A2.1). Actors may also have been hired to perform sacred dramas designed to ensure that the crops grew once more in the spring, and that evil forces were once more confined to their underground pits. Special ritualists may have been called upon to ensure that the appropriate incantations were uttered at various points during the proceedings. All these needed to be paid in one way or another, perhaps with an all-you-can-eat banquet of their own, from the leavings of the main banqueters. But no doubt many of them would have preferred a 'cash' payment, and a fund of shekels was probably reserved for this purpose.

What of the king's troops? My guess is that the pay of the common soldier in the king's standing army was little more than his uniform and weapons, and his food and lodgings in military barracks. So, too, was the basic 'pay' of reservists called up for military service. And, when on campaign, the soldier had little to sustain him beyond the daily ration of 'soldier's bread' and no doubt a flagon or two of wine or beer, supplemented by extra supplies when the army's campaign route took them through a subject state. Here, on what I imagine was a brief stopover, the troops received extra rations in their host's territory, requisitioned

Figure A2.1 Sword swallower and acrobats, Alaca Höyük. Author photo.

and paid for by the king. But, once they reached enemy territory, they were expected to find their own supplies through foraging and looting expeditions to small farmsteads and the like. Plundered livestock, fruit and vegetables provided a welcome supplement to a ration of 'soldier's bread'.

But perhaps the greatest incentive for military service for the common soldier was a likely share, even if just a small one, in the plunder extracted from conquered cities. The larger the city, the greater the risks, but the richer rewards split up amongst all. I think it likely, too, that, when not on campaign, or even during a campaign, a soldier received some discretionary income in the form of shekels of silver. He must have been granted leisure time when the opportunity arose, which meant that there were tavern-keepers to pay, as well as brothel madams for those who rounded off their evenings with various horizontal forms of entertainment.

Notes

Introduction

1 Exodus Chapter 5. The pharaoh is not actually named and, though he is commonly equated with Ramesses, the tradition has also been attributed to other pharaohs. More on this in Chapter 9.
2 The only exception is the comprehensive record of the life and career of Hattusili's father Mursili II.
3 Thus speaks Alfred Lord Tennyson's Ulysses.
4 Theo van den Hout, *A History of Hittite Literacy: Writing and Reading in Late Bronze Age Anatolia (1650–1200 BC)* (Cambridge: Cambridge University Press, 2020). 15. However, Professor van den Hout warns that we should refrain from 'excessive speculation without proper evidence'. I would see this more as a question of knowing where to draw the line between theories that are credible though as yet lacking evidential support, and theories without evidential support that clearly exceed the limits of credibility.

Chapter 1: 'He Will Not Live Long'

1 The Hittite expression literally means 'one-of-the reins' (thus, van den Hout). My assumption is that the prince was destined to become a member of the elite Hittite chariot corps.
2 Ritualists as well as physicians were regularly employed to help cure the sick, and I have assumed their presence in my scenario. Some of the details of the ritual carried out come from a Hittite ritual healing text, though its purpose is quite different.
3 She is equated with the Hurrian goddess Shaushka.
4 The appearance of the goddess Ishtar in the king's dream, and the king's consequent action are recorded in the so-called *Apology* or *Autobiography*. This document is discussed in later chapters. It is transl. by Theo van den Hout, 'Apology of Hattusili III', in *CoS* I, 94–8.
5 For a concise account of the excavated remains of the palace and the entire capital, see Jürgen Seeher, *Hattusha Guide: A Day in the Hittite Capital*, 4th edn (Istanbul: Ege Yayınları, 2011).

6 See Richard Beal, *The Organisation of the Hittite Military* (Heidelberg: Carl Winter, 1992), 224–7.
7 Dirk Paul Mielke, 'Key Sites of the Hittite Empire', in *OHAA*, 1031–7, provides a concise account of the archaeological history of the site to the date of writing his article.
8 I use interchangeably the terms 'empire', 'kingdom' and 'Great Kingdom' in referring to the lands over which the kings of Hatti held sway, though 'empire' is perhaps too grand a term for the kingdom, at least up to the end of the first half of the fifteenth century. In Chapter 10, I discuss my concerns about the use of 'empire' to describe the Hittite world.
9 See Trevor Bryce, *The Kingdom of the Hittites*, new edn (Oxford: Oxford University Press, 2005), 38.
10 Though I believe Hattusili I was almost certainly responsible for refounding Hattusa, there has been much debate about when and by whom the city was rebuilt and became the capital; see Stefano de Martino, 'Hatti: From Regional Polity to Empire', in *HHE*, 217–19.
11 On possible reasons for the transfer of the Hittite capital to Tarhuntassa, and a suggested location of the new capital at Türkmen-Karahöyük in the Konya Plain, see most recently de Martino, 'From Regional Polity', 240–4.
12 Trevor Bryce, *Warriors of Anatolia: A Concise History of the Hittites* (London and New York, NY: I. B. Tauris, 2019), 7.
13 Covering the last part of the Middle Bronze Age and the whole of the Late Bronze Age.
14 For a more detailed account of the events which follow, with references to the relevant ancient sources, see Bryce, *Kingdom*, 61–245.
15 Transl. Theo van den Hout, 'The Proclamation of Telipinu', in *CoS* I, 194–8.
16 Hurrians provided the main elements of a political and military confederation called Mittani.
17 On this question, see Bryce, *Kingdom*, 122–3.
18 Though Tudhaliya does not provide us with any genealogy at all in his five surviving state treaties; thus, Metin Alparslan and Meltem Doğan-Alparslan, 'Hittite Kings: Self-presentation and Historiography', in *HHE*, 473.
19 See de Martino, 'From Regional Polity', 243–4.
20 His name is often transcribed in slightly different ways – as Urhi-Teshshup, Urhi-Teššub etc. I have adopted the simplest form of the name.
21 Thus, also, de Martino, 'From Regional Polity', 212. However, Richard Beal comments that the future king could just as well have borne the name Hattusili from birth: 'The Predecessors of Hattušili I', in *Fs Hoffner*, 25.

Chapter 2: Our Sources

1 These are called cuneiform signs today, after the Latin word *cuneus* for a wedge.
2 On the drafting and editing of documents, see van den Hout, *Hittite Literacy*, 246–56.

3 In general, for accounts of Hittite written records, the scribes who produced them, tablet collections and writing traditions, see van den Hout, *Hittite Literacy*, and Jörg Klinger, 'The Hittite Writing Traditions of Cuneiform Documents', in *HHE*, 93–155.
4 A selection of letters exchanged between Hattusili and his royal peers and other members of their courts are transl. by Beckman, *HDT*, nos 22A–24B, pp. 128–49.
5 Itamar Singer, *Hittite Prayers* (Atlanta, GA: Society of Biblical Literature, 2002), no. 21, pp. 97–9.
6 For an English translation, see van den Hout, 'Apology'.
7 Some of the publications I cite in the Bibliography and Endnotes are in German. These are for the benefit of those who read German and may wish to pursue in greater depth the topics I've dealt with. If you don't read German, don't worry. I've tried to cover in my discussions information relevant for the general reader which these publications contain.
8 William W. Hallo and K. Lawson Younger, Jr, eds, *The Context of Scripture: Canonical Compositions from the Biblical World*, 3 vols (Leiden and Boston: Brill, 2003) (cited as *CoS* I, II, III). A supplementary volume was added in 2018.
9 The opening words of a vassal treaty of Hattusili's brother Muwattalli; transl. Beckman, *HDT*, no. 14, p. 93.
10 Elmar Edel, ed., *Die ägyptisch-hethitische Korrespondenz aus Boghazköi*, 2 vols (Opladen: Westdeutscher Verlag, 1994) (cited as *ÄHK*).
11 Oliver Gurney, *The Hittites* (London: Penguin, 1990).
12 James Macqueen, *The Hittites and Their Contemporaries in Asia Minor*, rev. edn (London: Thames & Hudson, 1986).
13 Trevor Bryce, *Life and Society in the Hittite World* (Oxford: Oxford University Press, 2002).
14 Billie Jean Collins, *The Hittites and Their World* (Atlanta, GA: Society of Biblical Literature, 2007). For a concise, comprehensive account of Hittite political history, see Richard Beal, 'Hittite Anatolia: A Political History', in *OHAA*, 579–603.
15 Peter Neve, *Hattuša: Stadt der Götter und Tempel* (Mainz: Verlag Philipp von Zabern, 1993).
16 Jürgen Seeher, *A Mudbrick City Wall at Hattusa: Diary of a Reconstruction* (Istanbul: Ege Yayınları, 2007).
17 Sharon Steadman and Gary McMahon, eds, *The Oxford Handbook of Ancient Anatolia (10,000–323 B.C.E.)* (Oxford: Oxford University Press, 2011) (cited as *OHAA*).
18 Stefano de Martino, ed., *Handbook Hittite Empire: Power Structures* (Berlin and Boston: de Gruyter Oldenbourg, 2022) (cited as *HHE*).
19 Trevor Bryce, *Warriors of Anatolia: A Concise History of the Hittites* (London, New York: I.B. Tauris, 2019 [Hardback], London: Bloomsbury, 2023 [Paperback]).

20 Horst Klengel, *Hattuschili und Ramses: Hethiter und Ägypter – ihr langer Weg zum Frieden* (Mainz: Philipp von Zabern, 2022).
21 I've also published a review of the book, in English, summarizing much of its contents (Trevor Bryce, 'Review', *OLZ* 100 [2005]: 53–8).
22 Theo P. J. van den Hout, ed., *The Life and Times of Hattušili III and Tuthaliya IV: Proceedings of a Symposium held in Honour of J. de Roos, 12–13 December 2003, Leiden* (Leiden: Nederlands Instituut voor het Nabije Oosten, 2006).
23 *CANE* II, 1107–20.
24 Full publication details of this and the following documentaries are listed under their titles at the end of the Bibliography.
25 Michael Wood, *In Search of the Trojan War*, latest rev. edn (London: British Broadcasting Corporation, 2005) (original publication date: 1985).

Chapter 3: Benefactors of a Young Prince

1 She died in the ninth year of her husband Mursili's reign, c. 1212 BC. I believe that Hattusili was no more than five or six at the time, possibly younger.
2 For the relevant prayer, see Singer, *Prayers*, nos 17–18, pp. 73–9.
3 The king's wife, traditionally called the Tawananna, generally held and retained the rank of the kingdom's Chief Wife if she outlived her husband, until her own death. The king's stepmother, a Babylonian princess, adopted the title 'Tawananna' as her personal name.
4 Bryce, *Kingdom*, 209–10.
5 Attested in Hattusili's prayer (when king) to the Sun Goddess of Arinna (Singer, *Prayers*, no. 21, p. 98). The sons were presumably Danuhepa's offspring from a previous marriage. For the identification of Danuhepa as Mursili's second wife, see most recently J. D. Hawkins, 'The Seals and the Dynasty', in *Die Siegel der Grosskönige und Grossköniginnen auf Tonbullen aus dem Nişantepe-Archiv in Hattusa*, edited by Suzanne Herbordt, Daliah Bawanypeck, and J. David Hawkins, 92–3. Mainz: Philipp von Zabern, 2011.
6 See e.g. Richard H. Beal, 'The Ten Year Annals of Great King Muršili II of Hatti', in *CoS* II, 85, col. 1, Year 3.
7 For a detailed discussion of Hittite land management, see Jörg Klinger, 'Hittite Economics', in *HHE*, 625–30.
8 See e.g. Trevor Bryce, *Babylonia: A Very Short Introduction* (Oxford: Oxford University Press, 2016), 53–4.
9 Van den Hout notes that there is no evidence that any Hittite kings were literate, though he implicitly leaves open this possibility, particularly for Hattusili's father Mursili (*Hittite Literacy*, 234–5). A similar case could be made for Hattusili.
10 Adapted from translation by van den Hout, *Hittite Literacy*, 322–3.

11 Ibid., 323.
12 Bryce, *Kingdom*, 90–1.
13 See Bryce, *Kingdom*, 296, with nn. 6 and 7.
14 He may well have learnt Akkadian while mastering his literary skills (if indeed he acquired such skills). Akkadian was the international *lingua franca* of the age, used especially for diplomatic communications. The ability to speak and read Akkadian would, for example, have enabled Hattusili as king to read and hear *directly* the many letters he received from the pharaoh Ramesses II. Of course, any such documents would still have been translated into Hittite. But there were obvious advantages for Hattusili (and no doubt other kings as well) in not having to rely on an intermediary to tell him what his foreign peers had written to him.
15 Hans G. Güterbock, 'The Deeds of Šuppiluliuma as Told by His Son, Muršili II', *JCS* 10 (1956): 41–68, 75–98, 101–30.
16 The Ten Year Annals are transl. by Beal, 'The Ten Year Annals of Great King Muršili II of Hatti'.
17 This term, used by Gary Beckman, is a translation of the logogram NAM.RA^{MEŠ}, which in Hittite texts refers to prisoners taken from their own countries and resettled in the Hittite homeland. The more common translation 'deportees' is a little misleading, since it is generally used of persons being forcibly returned to their own countries from places where they themselves have sought to resettle.
18 See Bryce, *Kingdom*, 224–6.
19 Transl. Beckman, *HDT*, no. 13, pp. 87–93.

Chapter 4: The Prince Goes to Court

1 See Bryce, *Kingdom*, 145–8.
2 The relevant information, provided by a decree issued by Hattusili when king, is transl. by Boaz Stavi, *The Reign of Tudhaliya II and Šuppiluliuma I* (Heidelberg: Carl Winter, 2015), 38–9. ('Tudhaliya II' equates with 'Tudhaliya III' in our book.)
3 See e.g. Jörg Klinger, 'Der Kult der Ištar von Šamuha', in *Investigationes Anatolicae: Gedenkschrift für Erich Neu*, Studien zu den Boğazköy-Texten 52, ed. Jörg Klinger, Elisabeth Rieken and Christel Rüster (Wiesbaden: Harrassowitz, 2010), 153–67.
4 See Beal, *Organisation of the Hittite Military*, 327–42.
5 Extract from *The Apology*, §4, transl. van den Hout, 'Apology', 199–200. I'll have more to say about this document – its nature, purpose and validity – in the next chapter.
6 Extract from *Apol.* §4; transl. (slightly adapted) van den Hout, 'Apology', 200.
7 For a discussion of these laws, see Bryce, *Life and Society*, 32–55, and for a translation, see Harry Hoffner, 'Hittite Laws', in *Law Collections from Mesopotamia and Asia Minor*, ed. Martha T. Roth, 2nd edn (Atlanta, GA: Society of Biblical Literature, 1997), 213–47.

8   *Apol.* §§6–8.
9   Extract from *Apol.* §9, transl. van den Hout, 'Apology', 202.
10 Translation of extract from *The Proclamation*, §50, by van den Hout, 'The Proclamation of Telipinu', 198.
11 Based on Hoffner's transl. of §44b of the laws, 'Hittite Laws', 223.
12 Clause 111 of the laws.
13 Clause 170 of the laws.
14 The case, its prelude and its outcome are recorded and transl. by van den Hout, 'Apology', §10a, 202.

Chapter 5: Unseating the Rightful King

1   Extract from the *Apol.* §12b.
2   Extract from the *Apol.* §10b, based on transl. by van den Hout, 'Apology', 202. The precise meaning of the epithet, here translated as 'legitimate', remains unclear; see most recently Hawkins, 'The Seals and the Dynasty', 93. However, here, as elsewhere in this book, the Hittite word has legal rather than moral connotations; in this case, the matter of the legal right of royal succession.
3   David Hawkins gives no indication of such seals in the relevant section of 'The Seals and the Dynasty', *Die Siegel der Grosskönige und Grossköniginnen auf Tonbullen aus dem Nişantepe-Archiv in Hattusa*, ed. Suzanne Herbordt, Daliah Bawanypeck, and J. David Hawkins (Mainz: Philipp von Zabern, 2011), 94-8.
4   Extract from *The Proclamation*, §28.
5   The name previously read as Kurunta.
6   Just one passing reference to it occurs in an oracle text probably dating to Puduhepa's time; see Theo P. J. van den Hout, 'Khattushilish III, King of the Hittites', in *CANE* II, 1112.
7   Kaskans are listed by Ramesses amongst the troops who fought on the Hittite side at Qadesh: Sir Alan Gardiner, *The Kadesh Inscriptions of Ramesses II* (Oxford, Griffith Institute, Ashmolean Museum, 1975), P. 44, p. 8, B. 44, p. 29.
8   Bryce, *Kingdom*, 253, with n. 26.
9   Further on this, see ibid., 252–3, with 457, nn. 23, 25, 26.
10 For reference information, see ibid., 253.
11 Even if climatic conditions saw some improvement in the second half of the millennium; thus, Klinger, 'Hittite Economics', 610.
12 Singer, *Prayers*, no. 21, p. 98.
13 For references to differing opinions on the authorship, see Bryce, *Kingdom*, 459, n. 53.
14 Based on transl. by Beckman, *HDT*, no. 24A, p. 147.
15 For a discussion of this expression, see Trevor Bryce, *Letters of the Great Kings of the Ancient Near East* (London and New York, NY: Routledge, 2003), 76–94.

16 I'll have more to say about the 'Benteshina affair' in Chapter 10. Hattusili's later claim that he himself, during his own reign, restored Benteshina to his throne is almost certainly false. See Bryce, *Kingdom*, 254, with refs.
17 Singer, *Prayers*, no. 21, pp. 97–9.
18 Extract from §2 of the Bronze Tablet treaty (discussed in Chapter 13), transl. Beckman, *HDT*, no. 18C, p. 114.
19 Nerik was captured by the Kaska people in the reign of the fifteenth-century Hittite king Hantili II and, though Hattusili's father Mursili made a pilgrimage there to celebrate the festival of the Storm God, Hattusili claimed to have fully restored it to Hittite control, apparently early in Urhi-Teshub's reign.
20 *AhT* 2 §7, pp. 56–7. See also Bryce, *Kingdom*, 252.
21 This was after enemies had invaded the homeland from many directions; and the king was forced to abandon Hattusa and set up his base of operations in a more secure location.
22 Thus, Gurney, *The Hittites*, 28; *Apol.* §11, lines 32–3.
23 We can be highly sceptical of Hattusili's claim that he had the backing of 'all Hattusa' (at the instigation of Ishtar) in his coup (*Apol.* §11).
24 For a translation of the relevant part of the oath, see van den Hout, 'Khattushilish III', 1114.

Chapter 6: 'And She Gave Us the Love of Husband and Wife'

1 Hattusili's appointment in the Damascus region (Aba) immediately after Qadesh is recorded in a fragment from a text which he authored; see Bryce, *Kingdom*, 240. Perhaps it's part of a genuine autobiography. The surviving text is referred to again briefly and transl. in Chapter 9.
2 Figure 6.1 is an artist's impression (courtesy Hannah Bryce) of these unfinished sculptures.
3 See Jan de Roos, 'Materials for a Biography: The Correspondence of Puduhepa with Egypt and Ugarit', in *Life and Times*, ed. van den Hout, 19. Further on the Fraktin monument, see Chapter 14, and Figure 14.1.
4 *Apol.* §9 tells us that the couple 'made (themselves) sons and daughters', no doubt their own children, in addition to those Hattusili sired from his concubines, both before and after his marriage to Puduhepa.
5 *Apol.* §9.
6 Attested in the preamble to a document which contains the so-called 'case against Arma-Tarhunda'; ref. in Bryce, *Kingdom*, 469, n. 91. Cf. Fiorella Imparati, 'Apology of Hattusili III or Designation of his Successor', in *Studio Historiae Ardens (Ancient Near Eastern Studies Presented to Philo H. J. Houwink ten Cate on the Occasion of His*

65th Birthday), ed. Theo van den Hout and Johan de Roos (Leiden: Nederlands Instituut voor het Nabije Oosten, 1995), 146, n. 21.

7 See Bryce, *Kingdom*, 286–7. The text is transl. by Beckman, *HDT*, no. 34, p. 179.
8 Indeed, she seems to have become increasingly active in judicial affairs in the first years of her widowhood. For her involvement in other matters which were judicial in nature, see Muhibbe Darga, 'Puduhepa: An Anatolian Queen of the 13th Century BC', in *Mélanges Mansel*, no stated editor (Ankara: TTK Ankara, 1974), 944–5.
9 E.g. in Puduhepa's (draft) letter to Ramesses, transl. Beckman, *HDT*, no. 22E, §10, p. 134. The letter provides the basis for an imagined scenario at the end of this chapter.
10 Transl. Beckman, *HDT*, no. 18A, pp.108–9, and no. 18B, pp. 109–13 (esp. §6, p. 111). Kuruntiya is identified by his Luwian name Ulmi-Teshub in the second of these texts; for the identification, see Beckman, *HDT*, no. 18, pp. 107–8; Bryce, *Kingdom*, 270–1.
11 The reason for the inverted commas will be explained in Chapter 8. Information about the Hittite royal seals and the silver tablet on which they were stamped is provided by Ramesses in his version of the Hittite treaty carved on the walls of two Egyptian temples. See J. A. Wilson in Pritchard, *ANET*, p. 201.
12 Beckman, *HDT* no. 22E, §11, p. 134. I think we can discount the possibility that the 'wives', or concubines, were those of Muwattalli, since the Great King was now firmly settled in Tarhuntassa, as was no doubt his matrimonial establishment. Of course, it's possible that some of his older children were still based in Hattusa; cf. Theo van den Hout, 'Khattushilish III', 1110.
13 See Bryce, *Life and Society*, 128–9.
14 As implied, e.g. in Puduhepa's (draft) letter to Ramesses, transl. Beckman, *HDT*, no. 22E, §9, p. 134.
15 See van den Hout, 'Khattushilish III', 1112.
16 For Puduhepa's prayers to the gods for Hattusili's health and well-being, see Singer, *Prayers*, 103–5.
17 Transl. Singer, *Prayers*, 104.
18 See Bryce, *Kingdom*, 288, with refs.
19 Ibid.
20 Darga, *Puduhepa*, 953–4.
21 Transl. Beckman, *HDT*, no. 22E, pp. 132–5.
22 As Beckman, *HDT*, 132, notes: 'The fact that (Puduhepa's response) is written in Hittite rather than Akkadian indicates that it is a preliminary draft.'
23 See Bryce, *Letters of the Great Kings*, 118, with refs.
24 Klengel, *Hattuschili und Ramses*, 99; de Roos, 'Materials for a Biography', 24.
25 See Kenneth A. Kitchen, *Pharaoh Triumphant: The Life and Times of Ramesses II* (Warminster: Aris & Phillips, 1982), 88–9, 110.

Chapter 7: 'Uneasy Lies the Head …'

1. In full, the line reads: 'Uneasy lies the head that wears a crown', from Shakespeare (*Arden Complete Works*, 1998), *Henry IV Part II*, 3.1.31, Henry.
2. Thus, Alfonso Archi, 'Trono regale e trono divinizzato nell'Antolici ittita', *SMEA* 1 (1966), 76–120.
3. *Apol.* §11.
4. On the communication with the Assyrian king, see Bryce, *Kingdom*, 264, with 461, n. 72. Shalmaneser was Adad-nirari I's successor.
5. Favoured by Itamar Singer, 'The Urhi-Teššub Affair in the Hittite-Egyptian Correspondence', in *Life and Times*, ed. van den Hout, 33.
6. *Apol.* §11.
7. For other proposals, see refs in Bryce, *Kingdom*, 461, n. 74.
8. De Martino, 'From Regional Polity', 247–9.
9. Extract from letter of Hattusili to Adad-nirari, §4, transl. Beckman, *HDT*, no. 24B, p. 149. The heading of the letter which would have identified its author and recipient is missing, but it is virtually certain that the persons in question are Hattusili and Adad-nirari; see Beckman, *HDT*, 147–8.
10. But this had not deterred him from writing to Hattusili with a request for some blades of iron, a rare and precious metal in that era, in exchange for Assyrian-made suits of armour he'd sent him (§3 of the same letter). Hattusili had agreed to meet his request as soon as the items became available – and perhaps in the expectation of backing by Adad-nirari for admission to the 'club'.
11. *ÄHK*, no. 5, obv. 10', pp. 24–5.
12. *Apol.* §12b.
13. The Babylonian king Kadashman-Turgu seems to have been an exception.
14. According to the Babylonian chronology I have adopted, one of several that have been proposed.
15. This and the information on which the following paragraphs are based are contained in a letter Hattusili wrote to Kadashman-Turgu's son and successor Kadashman-Enlil. Translations of what survives of the whole letter are provided by Beckman, *HDT*, no. 23, pp. 138–43; Harry Hoffner, 'Letter from Hattušili III of Hatti to Kadašman-Enlil of Babylon', in *CoS* III, 52–3; Kathleen Mineck, 'A Letter from the Hittite King Hattušili to Kadashman-Enlil II, King of Babylonia', in *ANE*, 275–9.
16. Cf. de Martino, 'From Regional Polity', 250–1.
17. Transl. Beckman, *HDT*, no. 23, §4, p. 140.
18. For further comments and perspectives on this document, see Alparslan and Doğan-Alparslan, 'Hittite Kings', in *HHE*, 482–3.
19. Though explicit evidence for this, e.g. on seals bearing both Muwattallis and Urhi-Teshub's names as Great Kings, has yet to be found, as noted on p. 48, with n. 3.

20 van den Hout, 'Apology', 199.
21 One of the reasons for dating the *Apology* after the treaty is that, in reviewing his reign, Hattusili speaks of concluding peace with those who had been enemies 'in the days of my fathers and grandfathers'; see van den Hout, 'Apology', 199. If the dating is correct, it is surprising that Hattusili does not extend references to enemies in his own days and to his conclusion of peace with Ramesses, which he must surely have regarded as one of the highlights of his regnal career.
22 The tablet is inscribed with the text of a treaty between Tudhaliya, Hattusili's son, after his accession to the throne, and Kuruntiya, while king of Tarhuntassa and a viceroy of the empire. Henceforth, the text will simply be referred to as the Bronze Tablet. For translations of it, see Beckman, *HDT*, no. 18C, pp. 114–24, and Hoffner, 'The Treaty of Tudhaliya IV with Kurunta of Tarhuntašša on the Bronze Tablet found in Hattuša', *CoS* II, 100–6.
23 Further on Nerikkaili's parentage, see Bryce, *Kingdom*, 464, n. 31.
24 The possibility raised by van den Hout ('Khattushilish III', 1111) that Tudhaliya was the son of an earlier marriage of Hattusili cannot be entirely ruled out, but I think is extremely unlikely.
25 Though not identified by name, Nerikkaili is, I believe, the brother referred to in the Bronze Tablet, §14 ii 43 (*HDT*, no. 18C, p. 118), whom Tudhaliya, in my opinion, replaced as Crown Prince. For further discussion of this replacement, see Bryce, *Kingdom*, 272–3.
26 Though all surviving fragments of it were discovered in the storerooms of Hattusa's Great Temple.
27 Extracts from *Apol.* §12b and §14, adapted from transl. by van den Hout.
28 Cf. Imparati, 'Apology of Hattusili III', 153–4; de Martino, 'From Regional Polity', 248.

Chapter 8: The Eternal Treaty

1 Extract from the *Apol.* §9, adapted from transl. by van den Hout, 'Apology', 201–2.
2 After Edel, *ÄHK*, no. 24, obv. 16', p. 59.
3 After Edel, *ÄHK*, no. 24, obv. 17'–19', 26'–29', pp. 58–61; see Bryce, *Letters*, 89–90.
4 See most recently the brief discussion of the treaty in de Martino, 'From Regional Polity', 251.
5 Transl. Beckman, *HDT*, no. 15, §1, p. 96.
6 Transl. Beckman, *HDT*, no. 15, pp. 96–100; Yoram Cohen, 'The Hittite-Egyptian treaty', in *ANE*, 244–8.
7 Transl. John A. Wilson, 'Treaty between the Hittites and Egypt', in *ANET*, 199–201.
8 'Second Plague Prayer', §§4–5, transl. Singer, *Hittite Prayers*, 58. The plague and its consequences are further discussed in Chapter 10.

9   For a discussion of these, see Sam Jackson, 'Contrasting Representations and the Egypto-Hittite Treaty', in *Registers and Modes of Communication in the Ancient Near East*, ed. Kyle H. Keimer and Gillan Davis (Abingdon and New York, NY: Routledge, 2018), 48–56.
10 Further on this, see Nicholas Blackwell, 'Ahhiyawa, Hatti, and Diplomacy: Implications of Hittite Misperceptions of the Mycenaean World', *Hesperia* 90, no. 2 (2021): 204. Jackson, 'Contrasting Representations', 43, describes the pharaoh's introduction as 'heavily biased' and 'bombastic'.
11 Thus, Wilson's translation, 'Treaty between the Hittites and Egypt'.
12 See Jackson, 'Contrasting Representations', 46.
13 Cf. Blackwell, 'Ahhiyawa, Hatti, and Diplomacy', 204.
14 Beckman, *HDT*, no. 15, §14, p. 99.
15 Kitchen, *Pharaoh Triumphant*, 61. Cf. Anthony Spalinger, *War in Ancient Egypt* (Oxford: Blackwell, 2005), 226. For the original source, see Gardiner, *The Kadesh Inscriptions*, 39–41.

Chapter 9: The Royal Mail

1   A city located at the confluence of the Euphrates and Balih rivers in northwestern Mesopotamia.
2   This passage paraphrases Beckman's translation of an extract from Hattusili's letter to Kadashman-Enlil, *HDT*, no. 23, §6, p. 140.
3   See Bryce, *Letters*, espec. 232–6. For translations of a number of letters in the international correspondence, see William Moran, *The Amarna Letters* (Baltimore and London: Johns Hopkins University Press, 1992), 11–117.
4   Like the notorious robber-bands of Amurru during the pharaoh Akhenaten's reign. See Bryce, *Ancient Syria: A Three Thousand Year History* (Oxford: Oxford University Press, 2014), 46–61.
5   Some scholars have concluded that the dead pharaoh was Akhenaten; others, including myself, that it was Tutankhamun.
6   The plague referred to briefly in Chapters 1 and 14. For more details of the aborted marriage alliance, see Bryce, *Letters*, 187–98.
7   *AhT* 4, extract from §15, p. 119.
8   For estimations of travel times and distances travelled each day, see Gary Oller, 'Messengers and Ambassadors in Ancient Western Asia Minor', in *CANE* III, 1466–8.
9   Found at Ramesses' capital Pi-Ramesse; see Singer, 'Urhi-Teššub Affair', 28.
10 On communications with these regional centres during Tudhaliya III's reign, see Bryce, *Letters*, 170–81.

11 Specialized terms for types of letter-carriers/couriers found in Hittite texts include words for 'horseback- rider' and 'runner/courier' (see Harry Hoffner, *Letters from the Hittite Kingdom* [Atlanta, GA: Society of Biblical Literature, 2009], 53–4). But, although these two terms are not rare in Hittite texts, they seldom occur in letters.
12 *ÄHK*, no. 29, esp. obv. 17'–21', pp. 78–9; see Singer, 'Urhi-Teššub Affair', 32.
13 *ÄHK*, no. 26, rev. 15'–19', pp. 70–3.
14 Transl. Beckman, *HDT*, no. 22D, pp. 130–1. See also Singer, 'Urhi-Tesššub Affair', 30–1.
15 Transl. Beckman, *HDT*, no. 22D, extract from §5, p. 131.
16 Compiled and adapted from passages in Edel, *ÄHK*, no. 20, pp. 50–1, and no. 22, pp. 54–5.
17 Transl. Beal, with refs, *Organisation of the Hittite Military*, 307.
18 Transl. Kitchen, *Pharaoh Triumphant*, 92.
19 And so it was published; Trevor Bryce, 'How Old Was Matanzi?', *JEA* 84 (1998): 212–15.
20 *ÄHK*, no. 12, pp. 20–1.
21 E.g. *ÄHK*, nos 10 and 11, pp. 36–9.
22 Hoffner, *Letters*, 17.

Chapter 10: Managing an Empire

1 If we can so conclude from the stream of messages that passed between Tudhaliya III and his regional officials; see Bryce, *Letters*, 170–86. Archives of later periods have yet to be discovered.
2 For the role played by the first two viceroys in the administration of the empire's Syrian vassals, see Bryce, *Kingdom*, 187–8.
3 For the tribute imposed on some of the Syrian states (e.g. 300 shekels of refined, first-class gold imposed by Suppiluliuma I on the Syrian vassal state Amurru), see Elena Devecchi, 'The Governance of the Subordinated Countries', in *HHE*, 287–8.
4 Extract from *Apol.* §6, after transl. by van den Hout.
5 Extract from *Apol.* §7, transl. van den Hout.
6 Jürgen Seeher, 'Rethinking the Role and Size of Hattuša', in *Ḫattannaš: A Festschrift on the Occasion of Theo van den Hout's 65th Birthday*, ed. Petra Goedegebuure and Joost Hazenbos (Chicago: Oriental Institute of the University of Chicago, 2023), 369–85. Also, I have cited below further comments by Dr Seeher in my email communications with him, with his permission.
7 There is evidence of settlements some distance from the city – three kilometres or so – but Seeher does not believe that these would have considered themselves part of the capital.
8 Cf. Neve, *Hattuša*, 17, with reference particularly to the Upper City.
9 Zsolt Simon, *Vorarbeiten zu einer hethitischen Demographie 1: Der Einerwohnzahl des hethitischen Reichen anhand der schriftlichen Quellen* (Budapest: Eötvös Loránd

University, 2011). Combining archaeological with textual evidence, Simon classifies settlements into a three-tiered structure, which provides him with a basis for attempting to correlate the size of a settlement with the size of its population. This is extended to a calculation of the empire's overall population size.

10 See Bryce, *Ancient Syria.*, 124.
11 Simon, *Der Einerwohnzahl des hethitischen Reichen*, 12–13.
12 Beal, *Organisation of the Hittite Military*, 41.
13 Suggested by Jürgen Seeher, most recently in email correspondence.
14 Beal, *Organisation of the Hittite Military*, 296.
15 Singer, *Hittite Prayers*, 47–69.
16 The first with Ramesses' father Seti I, referred to briefly in Chapter 1.
17 Cf. the comments of de Martino, 'From Regional Polity', 256.
18 On the combined fragments, see Oliver Gurrney, 'The Annals of Hattusili III', *AS* 47 (1997): 127–39.
19 Transl. Beckman, *HDT*, no. 24B, extract from §5, p. 149.
20 Albertine Hagenbuchner, *Die Korrespondenz der Hethiter* (Heidelberg: Carl Winter, 1989), no. 188, pp. 242–5.
21 Bryce, *Kingdom*, 275.
22 Kirk A. Grayson, *Assyrian Rulers of the Third and Second Millennia BC (to 1115 BC)* (Toronto: University of Toronto Press, 1987), 136.
23 Ibid., 182–5.
24 Beckman, *HDT*, no. 14, pp. 93–5.
25 Ibid., no. 16, pp. 100–3.
26 It was, however, extremely rare for a Hittite king's *son* to be wed to the daughter of a foreign king, let alone of a vassal ruler.
27 Transl. Beckman, *HDT*, no. 22E, extract from §10, p. 134.
28 For the most recent discussion of the kingdom of Tarhuntassa and the appointment of Kuruntiya to its throne, see de Martino, 'From Regional Polity', 252–5.
29 Transl. Beckman, *HDT*, no. 18C, extract from §3, p. 114.
30 One of a series; see ibid., no. 18, pp. 107–24.
31 Further on the boundaries of Tarhuntassa, see Massimo Forlanini, 'South Central: The Lower Land and Tarhuntašša', in *Hittite Landscape and Geography: Handbook of Oriental Studies, Vol. 121, Section 1*, ed. Mark Weeden and Lee Z. Ullman (Leiden and Boston: Brill, 2017), 239–52; de Martino, 'From Regional Polity', 253–4.
32 For more detail, see Bryce, 'The Late Bronze Age in the West and the Aegean', in *OHAA*, 363–75.
33 See Stavi, *The Reign of Tudhaliya II and Šuppiluluma I*, 38–43, for translation and discussion. Stavi identifies the king I've called Tudhaliya III as just the second king so designated.
34 The letter is translated by Moran, *Amarna Letters*, no. 31, pp. 101–3.

35 This figure is based partly on the number of days recorded in his *Anabasis* by the Greek commander Xenophon for the various stages of his march through Anatolia on his way to Persia to support Cyrus the Younger's abortive expedition to seize the Persian throne (401 BC). The first part of Xenophon's route very likely passed through much the same region traversed by many westward-bound Hittite armies.
36 For the circumstances, see Bryce, *Kingdom*, 195–6.
37 See Bryce, *Kingdom*, 452, n. 18.
38 For brief accounts of each, see Bryce, *The Routledge Handbook of the Peoples and Places of Ancient Western Asia* (London and New York, NY: Routledge, 2009), 616–17, 622–3, 689–90, respectively. Further on Sarissa and Tapikka, see Mielke, 'Key Sites of the Hittite Empire', 1042–7.
39 For a general account of the texts found at Sapinuwa and other homeland regional centres, see Bryce, *Letters*, 170–86.
40 However, no tablet archives have yet been found in any of the above three centres that can be dated later than the reign of Tudhaliya, Hattusili's great-grandfather.
41 For Hittite festivals and the king's and queen's participation in the most important of them, see Daniel Schwemer, 'Religion and Power', in *HHE*, 387–91.

Chapter 11: 'Beware of Greeks Bearing Gifts'

1 Note to reader: This chapter provides an important background to one of the most significant episodes in Hattusili's career. That will be the subject of our next chapter.
2 *Aeneid* II.29. The ancient Greeks are sometimes called Danaans, especially in epic literature.
3 See Bryce, *The Trojans and Their Neighbours* (London: Routledge, 2006), 127–50.
4 The older shorter form 'Ahhiya' is twice attested (*AhT* §§1, 12) and recently equated with the island of Chios by Markus Egetmeyer, 'Woher kam der Mann von Ahhiya?', *Kadmos* 61, nos 1/2 (2022).
5 Transliterated and translated, with commentaries, by Beckman, Bryce and Cline, eds, in *The Ahhiyawa Texts*.
6 For the most recent, comprehensive account of Ahhiyawa, see Bryce, 'Ahhiyawa', in *Brill's Companion to Warfare in the Bronze Age Aegean*, ed. Lynne A. Kvapil and Kim Shelton (Leiden and Boston: Brill, 2023), 418–46.
7 Jorrit Kelder, 'The Kingdom of Ahhiyawa: Facts, Factoids and Probabilities', *SMEA* NS 4 (2018): 204–5, has argued that *all* references to Ahhiyawa are to a specific Mycenaean kingdom so called in Hittite texts, *contra* my view that in some cases Ahhiyawa might be a generic term for the Mycenaean world as a whole. See

also Jeremy Rutter, 'An Aegean Archaeologist's Response', *SMEA* NS 4 (2018): 208–16.
8   Rutter, 'Archaeologist's Response', 205–10. He believes that my view that 'the political order of the Mycenaean palatial era consisted of a "number of principalities contemporary with the Late Bronze Age Near Eastern kingdoms"' is unwarranted.
9   Blackwell, 'Ahhiyawa, Hatti, and Diplomacy', 197.
10 See Bryce, 'The Kingdom of Ahhiyawa: A Hittite Perspective', *SMEA* NS 4 (2018): 191–7.
11 See Hericlia Brecoulaki, Sharon R. Stocker, Jack L. Davis, Emily C. Egan, 'An Unprecedented Naval Scene from Pylos: First Considerations', in *Mycenaean Wall Painting in Context: New Discoveries, Old Finds Reconsidered*, Meletemata Series, no. 72, ed. Hericlia Brecoulaki, Jack L. Davis, Sharon R. Stocker (Athens: National Hellenic Research Foundation, 2015), 261–91.
12 Robert Schon, 'Response to Trevor Bryce's Article', *SMEA* NS 4 (2018): 214–15.
13 *AhT* 6, pp. 134–9.
14 Joachim Latacz, *Troy and Homer: Towards a Solution of an Old Mystery* (Oxford: Oxford University Press, 2004), 243–4.
15 Mark Weeden, 'Hittite-Ahhiyawan Politics as Seen from the Tablets: A Reaction to Trevor Bryce's Article from a Hittitological Perspective', *SMEA* NS 4 (2018): 223–5.
16 Kelder, 'Facts, Factoids', 204–5.
17 Ibid., 202.
18 The last of these replaced the Mittanian empire, destroyed by Hattusili's grandfather Suppiluliuma.
19 See e.g. *AhT* 8 §5', p. 147, with commentary, p. 149; Kelder, 'Facts, Factoids', 205, 206; Blackwell, 'Ahhiyawa, Hatti, and Diplomacy', 213.

Chapter 12: 'Bleating in Cuneiform Across the Wine-Dark Sea'

1   Denys L. Page, *History and the Homeric Iliad* (Berkeley and Los Angeles: University of California Press, 1959).
2   *AhT* 4 §1, 1–2, p. 103.
3   For a full translation, in English and with commentaries, of what survives of the document, see in addition to *AhT* 4, pp. 102–19, Hoffner, *Letters*, no. 101, pp. 296–321.
4   Susanne Heinhold-Krahmer and Elisabeth Rieken, *Der >Tawagalawa Brief<. Beschwerden über Piyamaradu* (Berlin: de Gruyter, 2020) (cited as *Taw.*). This book provides, in German (with a chapter in English by David Hawkins on the

topography), the most authoritative, up-to-date translation of and commentary on the text.

5 His fraternal relationship with the 'letter's' addressee is indicated in §8 of the document.
6 We're told this in §5 of the document.
7 See Jared Miller, 'Some Disputed Passages in the Tawagalawa Letter', in *Ipamati kistamati pari tumatimis: Luwian and Hittite Studies Presented to J. David Hawkins on the Occasion of His 70th Birthday*, ed. Itamar Singer (Tel Aviv: Sonia and Marco Nadler Institute of Archaeology Monograph Series 28, 2010), 159; and Blackwell, 'Ahhiyawa, Hatti, and Diplomacy', 206–7. For a thorough analysis of the passage, see *Taw.*, 130–43.
8 Two terms in this 'letter' are commonly translated as 'Crown Prince' and regarded as equivalents: Hittite *tuḫkanti* and Akkadian *TARTENU* (thus, Oliver Gurney, 'The Hittite Title *Tuḫkanti-*', *AS* 33 [1983]: 97–101). I have adopted this equivalence here, though it is still open to debate; see Suzanne Heinhold-Krahmer, 'Der Textkommentar aus philologischer und historisher Perspective', *Taw.*, 72–5. The identity of the crown prince attested in this 'letter' is also open to question. Three possibilities are Hattusili's older son Nerikkaili, perhaps initially designated as the king's successor, his younger son and actual successor Tudhaliya, and Kuruntiya, son of Muwattalli and entrusted by him to the safekeeping of Hattusili who, after his accession, appointed Kuruntiya king of Tarhuntassa. Kuruntiya is the only one of the three named in the letter (§5, line 73) but it is not clear how the passage in which he is named should be interpreted (see e.g. Hoffner, *Letters*, 391–2, n. 296) or what the context of the reference to Kuruntiya is. For the most recent discussion, see Heinhold-Krahmer, 'Der Textkommentar', 146–8.
9 See most recently Blackwell, 'Ahhiyawa, Hatti, and Diplomacy', 200–1.
10 The account that follows is based on information provided by the 'letter', *AhT* 4, §§2–5, pp. 102–5.
11 Iyalanda is probably the site of later Classical Alinda. On the topography, see J. David Hawkins, 'TAWAGALAWA: The Topography (with Addenda)', in *Taw.*, 348.
12 Along with a number of scholars, I have accepted the reading 'Wilusa' in *AhT* 4, §12, p. 115, of the text, though a number of other scholars regard it as highly conjectural or reject it outright. See Heinhold-Krahmer's discussion, 'Der Textkommentar', 271. However, all *Taw.*'s contributing authors regard the reading as secure (Hawkins, 'TAWAGALAWA', 352).
13 Latacz's translation of the verb as '(*over which*) *we quarrelled*' settles for a heated disagreement (*Troy and Homer*, 279). Hoffner's translation '(*over which*) *we were at enmity*' leaves open the possibility of actual conflict (*Letters*, no. 101, p. 311).
14 See Bryce, *Kingdom*, 225.
15 Cited by Hoffner, *Letters*, 297.
16 Blackwell, 'Ahhiyawa, Hatti, and Diplomacy', 206, with refs.
17 *AhT* 4, extract from §15, p. 119.
18 See Bryce, *Kingdom*, 193.

19 See Wolf-Dietrich Niemeier, 'Hattusa und Ahhijawa im Konflikt um Millawanda/ Milet', in *Die Hethiter und ihr Reich: Das Volk der 1000 Götter*, ed. Helga Willinghöfer (Stuttgart: Theiss, 2002), 294–9; Barbara Niemeier and Wolf-Dietrich Niemeier, 'Projekt "Minoisch-Mykenisches bis Protogeometrisches Milet": Zielsetzung und Grabungen auf dem Stadionhügel und am Athenatempel', *AA* 2 (1997): 189–248.
20 *AhT* 13, pp. 87–93.
21 Kelder, 'Facts, Factoids', 202.
22 Blackwell, 'Ahhiyawa, Hatti, and Diplomacy', 194.
23 The website GKTODAY is one of the rare sources I've found that differentiates them when it states: 'A pact may or may not be a written document A treaty is an official, express written agreement which is legally binding in most cases.' My assumption in using the term 'treaty' is that the agreement was recorded in writing and regarded as legally binding. Blackwell may well attribute the same meaning to the term 'pact', while perhaps leaving open the possibility that a pact may sometimes have been a purely verbal agreement.
24 See Eric H. Cline, *Sailing the Wine Dark Sea: International Trade and the Late Bronze Age Aegean* (Oxford: BAR International Series 591, 1994).

Chapter 13: A Poisoned Chalice

1 We learn this from an oracle enquiry text. For details, see Bryce, *Kingdom*, 302.
2 This was, I believe, far more than a mere dedication to the priesthood 'like those other prior Hittite princes excluded from the succession', as Franca Pecchioli Daddi suggests, 'The System of Government at the Time of Tuthaliya IV', in *Life and Times*, ed. van den Hout, 118.
3 See van den Hout, 'Khattushilish III', 1118.
4 See Bryce, *Kingdom*, 302. We cannot be sure of the date of the decree.
5 Ahmet Ünal, *Ein Orakeltext über die Intrigen am hethitischen Hof (KUB XXII 70 = Bo 2011)* (Heidelberg: Carl Winter, 1978). The queen referred to in the document is not actually named. But it can hardly be anyone other than Puduhepa.
6 I agree with Itamar Singer's conclusion that the Babylonian princess who married into Hittite royal circles, either before or after Hattusili's death, was Tudhaliya's Chief Wife; see Singer, 'The Title "Great Princess" in the Hittite Empire', *Ugarit-Forschungen* 23 (1991): 330–3, reprinted in *The Calm Before the Storm*, ed. Billie Jean Collins (Atlanta, GA: Society of Biblical Literature, 2011), 264–7.
7 Thus, Singer, 'The Title "Great Princess"', 332 = Collins, *Calm Before the Storm*, 265–6.
8 This is a suggestion by Singer, ibid.
9 See van den Hout, 'Khattushilish III', 1112. This is commonly accepted as the age at which she died, though the chronology is uncertain, and it's possible that she may

not have lived beyond the age of seventy-five or eighty; see de Roos, 'Materials for a Biography', 18.
10 For details with refs, see Bryce, *Kingdom*, 300.
11 Daddi, 'The System of Government', 128, concludes that 'the sense of precariousness of royal power drove Tudhaliya to exercise vast control of the state bureaucracy and powerful groups through the use of traditional legal means for imposing an oath, and a vast control of the territory by means of administrative tools, also traditional, of the inventories of temple goods and cults'.
12 Theo van den Hout, 'Elites and the Social Stratification of the Ruling Class in the Hittite Kingdom', in *HHE*, 315.
13 Transl. Bryce. For the full text of this document (in German), see Einar von Schuler, *Hethitische Dienstanweisungen für höhere Hof- und Staatsbeamte*, *AfO* Beiheft 10 (Graz, 1957).
14 Van den Hout, 'Elites and the Social Stratification', 351.
15 If we can so judge from a brief reference in §15 of the Bronze Tablet, which speaks of a secession of subject states on Hattusili's death.
16 For further detail, see Bryce, *Kingdom*, 304–5.
17 See ibid., 308–9.
18 See Hans Güterbock, 'The Hittite Conquest of Cyprus Reconsidered', *JNES* 26 (1967): 81; Harry A. Hoffner, 'The Last Days of Khattusha', in *The Crisis Years: The 12th Century B.C. from Beyond the Danube to the Tigris*, ed. William A. Ward and Martha S. Joukowsky (Dubuque, IA: Kendall/Hunt Publishing Company, 1992), 48.
19 Adapted from translation by Güterbock, 'The Hittite Conquest of Cyprus Reconsidered', 77.
20 See Bryce, *Kingdom*, 333–4.
21 For the possibility that these 'enemies' were not actually Alasiyans, see ibid., 332.
22 Transl. Güterbock, 'The Hittite Conquest of Cyprus Reconsidered', 78.
23 For the most recent discussion of Kuruntiya's activities and his relations with the Hattusa dynasty, see de Martino, 'From Regional Polity', 252–5.
24 On the risks of a king appointing close members of his family to positions of high power, see van den Hout, 'Elites and the Social Stratification', 348–9.
25 Bryce, *Warriors of Anatolia*, 256–7.
26 Petra Goedegebuure *et al.*, 'TÜRKMEN-KARAHÖYÜK 1: A New Hieroglyphic Luwian Inscription from Great King Hartapu, Son of Mursili, Conqueror of Phrygia', *AS* 70 (2020): 29–43. I've indicated the amendment in the front of the paperback edition of my book, published in 2022.
27 Neve, *Hattuša*, 401–8.
28 Ali Dinçol, 'Die Entdeckung des Felsmonuments in Hatip und ihre Auswirkungen über die historischen und geographischen Fragen des Hethiterreichs', *Türkiye Bilimler Akademisi Arkeoloji Dergisi* 1 (1988): 27–35.

29 For details, see Bryce, *Kingdom*, 316–17; Masamichi Yamada, 'The Second Military Conflict between "Assyria" and "Hatti" in the Reign of Tukulti-Ninurta I', *Revue d'Assyriologie et d'Archéologie Orientale* 105 (2011): 199–220.
30 Transliterated and translated, with commentary, by J. David Hawkins, *The Hieroglyphic Inscription of the Sacred Pool Complex at Hattusa (Südburg)* (Wiesbaden: Harrassowitz, 1995), 21–65.
31 See ibid., 23, §§14–17, and 43.
32 See van den Hout, *Hittite Literacy*, 128.
33 The catastrophe scenario is comprehensively dealt with by Professor Eric Cline, *1177 B.C.: The Year Civilization Collapsed*, rev. and updated edn (Princeton, NJ: Princeton University Press, 2021). For a collection of earlier accounts, see Ward and Joukowsky, *The Crisis Years*.
34 Like those claimed in the pharaoh Ramesses III's account of the so-called 'Sea Peoples'. See, for example, the passage translated by John A. Wilson, 'The War Against the Peoples of the Sea', in *ANET*, 262–3.
35 See Trevor Bryce, *The World of the Neo-Hittite Kingdoms: A Political and Military History* (Oxford: Oxford University Press, 2012).
36 See Jürgen Seeher, 'Die Zerstörung der Stadt Hattuša', in *Akten IV. Internationalen Kongresses für Hethitologie, Würzburg, 4–8 Oktober 1999*, ed. Gernott Wilhelm (Wiesbaden: Harrassowitz, 2001), 623–34.
37 For a detailed, authoritative and well-illustrated account of the sanctuary, see Jürgen Seeher, *Gods Carved in Stone: The Hittite Rock Sanctuary at Yazılıkaya* (Istanbul: Ege Yayınları, 2011).

Chapter 14: Hattusili's Reign in Review

1 See Bryce, *Letters*, 223–31.
2 Though we cannot rule out the accident of the non-survival of texts which do refer to it.
3 It's possible that the reason for Urhi-Teshub's withdrawal of his uncle's powers in the north was rather more benign. He may simply have believed that, once the royal capital was shifted back to Hattusa, the appointments his father had conferred upon Hattusili in the north were no longer relevant. There is no hint of this in the *Apology*. But that shouldn't surprise us.
4 *Apol.* extract from §10c.
5 If there were once evidence for this, it's precisely what Hattusili would have destroyed, for it would have nullified his claim that *he alone* had appointed his nephew as Great King.
6 *ÄHK*, no. 4, pp. 22–5.
7 Bryce, *Life and Society*, 14–15.

Appendix 2: The Economy

1. For a detailed treatment of this topic, see Klinger, 'Hittite Economics', 605–47.
2. While, strictly speaking, her son Telemachos is the head of the household during his father's absence, he, too, is often absent from home – for example, when he goes on a long journey in search of his father. During the absence of both husband and son, Penelope must have become by default head of the household.
3. See Bryce, *Life and Society*, 131–2.
4. Thus, Klinger, 'Hittite Economics', 611.
5. Mainly barley and emmer.
6. Klinger, 'Hittite Economics', 613.
7. In general, on this topic, see Bryce, *Life and Society*, 72–86.
8. Klinger, 'Hittite Economics', 610.
9. See Bryce, *Letters*, 180.
10. Klinger, 'Hittite Economics', 626.
11. As indicated by archaeological evidence noted by ibid.
12. Klinger, ibid., notes what seems to be an administrative archive located at or near Temple 8 in the Upper City. It may have been one of many such archives associated with Hattusa's temples.
13. Further on Hittite trading contacts, see Devechi, 'The Governance of the Subordinated Countries', 298–301.
14. See Cline, *Sailing the Wine-Dark Sea*, 70.
15. Cline, 'A Possible Hittite Embargo against the Mycenaeans', *Historia* 40 (1991), 1–9. For a discussion of Cline's suggestion, see Bryce, 'Relations between Hatti and Ahhiyawa in the Last Decades of the Bronze Age', in *Fs Hoffner*, 59–72.
16. See Bryce, *Kingdom*, 21–32.
17. Transl. Hoffner, 'Hittite Laws', §5, p. 217.
18. Thus, Hoffner, 'Some Thoughts on Merchants and Trade in the Hittite Kingdom', in *Kulturgeschichten: Altorientalistische Studien Fur Volkert Haas Zum 65. Geburtstag*, ed. Thomas Richter, Doris Prechel and Jörg Klinger (Wiesbaden: Harrassowitz, 2001), 181.
19. Singer, A Political History of Ugarit', in *Handbook of Ugaritic Studies*, ed. Wilfred Watson and Nicolas Wyatt (Leiden, Boston and Cologne: Brill, 1999), 645–6.
20. Both Ura and Zallara were located in southern Anatolia.
21. Transl. Hoffner, 'Some Thoughts on Merchants', 184–5.
22. See Singer, 'A Political History of Ugarit', 657.
23. See Klinger, 'Hittite Economics', 632.
24. Ibid.
25. For a brief account of these, see Bryce, *Life and Society*, 187–99.

Bibliography

*The full titles of abbreviated items appear in the
List of Abbreviations at the front of this book.
Asterisked items contain translations of the original sources.*

Alparslan, Metin, Meltem Doğan-Alparslan and Hasan Peker, eds. *VITA: Festschrift in Honor of Belkıs Dinçol and Ali Dinçol*. Istanbul: Ege Yayınları, 2007.

Alparslan, Metin, and Meltem Doğan-Alparslan. 'Hittite Kings: Self-presentation and Historiography', in *HHE*, 469–95.

Archi, Alfonso. 'Trono regale e trono divinizzato nell'Antolici ittita', *SMEA* 1 (1966): 76–120.

Archi, Alfonso. 'The Propaganda of Hattušiliš III', *SMEA* 14 (1971): 185–215.

Beal, Richard. 'Hittite Anatolia: A Political History', in *OHAA*, 579–603.

Beal, Richard. *The Organisation of the Hittite Military*. Heidelberg: Carl Winter, 1992.

Beal, Richard. 'The Predecessors of Hattušili I', in *Fs Hoffner*, 13–35.

*Beal, Richard. 'The Ten Year Annals of Great King Muršili II of Hatti', in *CoS* II, 82–90.

*Beckman, Gary. *Hittite Diplomatic Texts*. 2nd edn. Atlanta, GA: Society of Biblical Literature, 1999 (cited as *HDT*).

Beckman, Gary M., Richard H. Beal and Gregory McMahon, eds. *Hittite Studies in Honor of Harry A. Hoffner Jr on the Occasion of His 65th Birthday*. Winona Lake, IN: Eisenbrauns, 2003 (cited as *Fs Hoffner*).

*Beckman, Gary M., Trevor R. Bryce and Eric H. Cline. *The Ahhiyawa Texts*. Atlanta, GA: Society of Biblical Literature, 2011 (cited as *AhT*).

Blackwell, Nicholas G. 'Ahhiyawa, Hatti and Diplomacy: Implications of Hittite Misperceptions of the Mycenaean World', *Hesperia* 90, no. 2 (2021): 191–231.

Brecoulaki, Hericlia, Sharon R. Stocker, Jack L. Davis and Emily C. Egan. 'An Unprecedented Naval Scene from Pylos: First Considerations', in *Mycenaean Wall Painting in Context: New Discoveries, Old Finds Reconsidered*, Meletemata Series, no. 72, ed. Hericlia Brecoulaki, Jack L. Davis and Sharon R. Stocker, 261–91. Athens: National Hellenic Research Foundation, 2015.

Bryce, Trevor R. 'Ahhiyawa', in *Brill's Companion to Warfare in the Bronze Age Aegean*, ed. Lynne A. Kvapil and Kim Shelton, 418–46. Leiden and Boston: Brill, 2023.

Bryce, Trevor R. *Ancient Syria: A Three Thousand Year History*. Oxford: Oxford University Press, 2014.

Bryce, Trevor R. *Babylonia: A Very Short Introduction*. Oxford: Oxford University Press, 2016.

Bryce, Trevor R. 'How Old Was Matanazi?' *JEA* 84 (1998): 212–15.

Bryce, Trevor R. 'The Kingdom of Ahhiyawa: A Hittite Perspective', *SMEA* NS 4 (2018): 191–7.

Bryce, Trevor R. *The Kingdom of the Hittites*. New edn. Oxford: Oxford University Press, 2005.

Bryce, Trevor R. 'The Late Bronze Age in the West and the Aegean', in *OHAA*, 363–75.

Bryce, Trevor R. *Letters of the Great Kings of the Ancient Near East*. London and New York, NY: Routledge, 2003.

Bryce, Trevor R. *Life and Society in the Hittite World*. Oxford: Oxford University Press, 2002.

Bryce, Trevor R. 'Relations between Hatti and Ahhiyawa in the Last Decades of the Bronze Age', in *Fs Hoffner*, 59–72.

Bryce, Trevor R. 'Review of H. Klengel, *Hattuschili und Ramses: Hethiter und Ägypter – ihr langer Weg zum Frieden*', *OLZ* 100 (2005): 53–8.

Bryce, Trevor R. *The Routledge Handbook of the Peoples and Places of Ancient Western Asia*. London and New York, NY: Routledge, 2009.

Bryce, Trevor R. *The Trojans and Their Neighbours*. London: Routledge, 2006.

Bryce, Trevor R. *Warriors of Anatolia: A Concise History of the Hittites*. London and New York, NY: I. B. Tauris, 2019.

Bryce, Trevor R. *The World of the Neo-Hittite Kingdoms: A Political and Military History*. Oxford: Oxford University Press, 2012.

*Chavalas, Mark W., ed. *The Ancient Near East*. Oxford: Blackwell, 2006 (cited as *ANE*).

Cline, Eric H. *1177 B.C.: The Year Civilization Collapsed*. Rev. and updated edn. Princeton, NJ: Princeton University Press, 2021.

Cline, Eric H. 'A Possible Hittite Embargo against the Mycenaeans', *Historia* 40 (1991): 1–9.

Cline, Eric H. *Sailing the Wine-Dark Sea: International Trade and the Late Bronze Age Aegean*. Oxford: BAR International Series 591, 1994.

*Cohen, Yoram. 'The Hittite-Egyptian Treaty', in *ANE* (2006), 244–8.

Collins, Billie Jean, ed. *The Calm Before the Storm: Selected Writings of Itamar Singer on the Late Bronze Age in Anatolia and the Levant*. Atlanta, GA: Society of Biblical Literature, 2011.

Collins, Billie Jean. *The Hittites and Their World*. Atlanta, GA: Society of Biblical Literature, 2007.

Daddi, Franca Pecchiolo. 'The System of Government at the Time of Tuthaliya IV', in *The Life and Times of Hattušili III and Tuthaliya IV: Proceedings of a Symposium held in Honour of J. de Roos, 12–13 December 2003, Leiden*, ed. Theo van den Hout, 117–30. Leiden: Nederlands Instituut voor het Nabije Oosten, 2006.

Darga, Muhibbe. 'Puduhepa: An Anatolian Queen of the 13th Century BC', in *Mélanges Mansel* (no editor), 939–61. Ankara: TTK Ankara, 1974.

Dinçol, Ali. 'Die Entdeckung des Felsmonuments in Hatip und ihre Auswirkungen über die historischen und geographischen Fragen des Hethiterreichs', *Türkiye Bilimler Akademisi Arkeoloji Dergisi* 1 (1988): 27–35.

Devecchi, Elena. 'The Governance of the Subordinated Countries', in *HHE*, 271–312.

*Edel, Elmar, ed. *Die ägyptisch-hethitische Korrespondenz aus Boghazköi*. 2 vols. Opladen: Westdeutscher Verlag, 1994 (cited as *ÄHK*).

Egetmeyer, Markus. 'Woher kam der Mann von Ahhiya?' *Kadmos* 61, nos 1/2 (2022).

Forlanini, Massimo. 'South Central: The Lower Land and Tarhuntašša', in *Hittite Landscape and Geography. Handbook of Oriental Studies, Vol. 121, Section 1*, ed. Mark Weeden and Lee Z. Ullman, 239–52. Leiden and Boston: Brill, 2017.

*Gardiner, Alan. *The Kadesh Inscriptions of Ramesses II*. Oxford: Griffith Institute, Ashmolean Museum, 1975.

Goedegebuure, Petra, and Joost Hazenbos, eds. *Ḫattannaš: A Festschrift on the Occasion of Theo van den Hout's 65th Birthday*. Chicago: Oriental Institute of the University of Chicago, 2023.

*Goedegebuure, Petra, Theo van den Hout, James Osborne, Michele Massa, Christoph Bachhuber and Fatma Şahin. 'TÜRKMEN-KARAHÖYÜK 1: A New Hieroglyphic Luwian Inscription from Great King Hartapu, Son of Mursili, Conqueror of Phrygia', *AS* 70 (2020): 29–43.

*Grayson, A. Kirk. *Assyrian Rulers of the Third and Second Millennia BC (to 1115 BC)*. Toronto: University of Toronto Press, 1987.

*Gurney, Oliver R. 'The Annals of Ḫattušili III', *AS* 47 (1997): 127–39.

Gurney, Oliver R. *The Hittites*. London: Penguin, 1990.

Gurney, Oliver R. 'The Hittite Title *Tuḫkanti-*', *AS* 33 (1983): 97–101.

*Güterbock, Hans G. 'The Deeds of Šuppiluliuma as Told by His Son, Muršili II', *JCS* 10 (1956): 41–68, 75–98, 101–30.

Güterbock, Hans G. 'The Hittite Conquest of Cyprus Reconsidered', *JNES* 26 (1967): 73–81.

*Hagenbuchner, Albertine. *Die Korrespondenz der Hethiter*. Heidelberg: Carl Winter, 1989.

*Hallo, William W., and K. Lawson Younger, Jr, eds. *The Context of Scripture: Canonical Compositions from the Biblical World*. 4 vols. Leiden and Boston: Brill, 2003 and 2018 supplement (cited as *CoS*).

*Hawkins, J. David. *The Hieroglyphic Inscription of the Sacred Pool Complex at Hattusa (Südburg)*. Wiesbaden: Harrassowitz, 1995.

Hawkins, J. David. 'The Seals and the Dynasty', in *Die Siegel der Grosskönige und Grossköniginnen auf Tonbullen aus dem Nişantepe-Archiv in Hattusa*, ed. Suzanne Herbordt, Daliah Bawanypeck and J. David Hawkins, 85–102. Mainz: Philipp von Zabern, 2011.

Hawkins, J. David. 'TAWAGALAWA: The Topography (with Addenda)', in *Taw.* 338–65.

Heinhold-Krahmer, Susanne. 'Der Textkommentar aus philologischer und historischer Perspective', in *Taw.*, 63–305.

*Heinhold-Krahmer, Susanne, and Elisabeth Rieken, eds. *Der >Tawagalawa Brief<. Beschwerden über Piyamaradu*. New edn. Berlin: de Gruyter, 2020 (cited as *Taw.*).

*Herbordt, Suzanne, Daliah Bawanypeck and J. David Hawkins, eds. *Die Siegel der Grosskönige und Grossköniginnen auf Tonbullen aus dem Nişantepe-Archiv in Hattuša*. Mainz: Philipp von Zabern, 2011.

*Hoffner, Harry A. 'Hittite Laws', in *Law Collections from Mesopotamia and Asia Minor*, ed. Martha T. Roth, 213–47. 2nd edn. Atlanta, GA: Society of Biblical Literature, 1997.

Hoffner, Harry A. 'The Last Days of Khattusha', in *The Crisis Years: The 12th Century B.C. from Beyond the Danube to the Tigris*, ed. William A. Ward and Martha S. Joukowsky, 46–51. Dubuque, IA: Kendall/Hunt Publishing Company, 1992.

*Hoffner, Harry A. 'Letter from Hattušili III of Hatti to Kadašman-Enlil of Babylon', in *CoS* III, 52–3.

*Hoffner, Harry A. *Letters from the Hittite Kingdom*. Atlanta, GA: Society of Biblical Literature, 2009.

Hoffner, Harry A. 'Some Thoughts on Merchants and Trade in the Hittite Kingdom', in *Kulturgeschichten: Altorientalistische Studien für Volkert Haas zum 65. Geburtstag*, ed. Thomas Richter, Doris Prechel and Jörg Klinger, 179–89. Wiesbaden: Harrassowitz, 2001.

*Hoffner, Harry A. 'The Treaty of Tudhaliya IV with Kurunta of Tarhuntašša on the Bronze Tablet found in Hattuša', in *CoS* II, 100–6.

*Hout, Theo P. J. van den. 'Apology of Hattušili III', in *CoS* I, 199–204.

Hout, Theo P. J. van den. 'Elites and the Social Stratification of the Ruling Class in the Hittite Kingdom', in *HHE*, 313–54.

Hout, Theo P. J. van den. *A History of Hittite Literacy: Writing and Reading in Late Bronze Age Anatolia (1650–1200 BC)*. Cambridge: Cambridge University Press, 2020.

Hout, Theo P. J. van den. 'Khattushilish III, King of the Hittites', in *CANE* II, 1107–20.

Hout, Theo P. J. van den, ed. *The Life and Times of Hattušili III and Tuthaliya IV: Proceedings of a Symposium held in Honour of J. de Roos, 12–13 December 2003, Leiden*. Leiden: Nederlands Instituut voor het Nabije Oosten, 2006.

*Hout, Theo P. J. van den. 'The Proclamation of Telipinu', in *CoS* I, 194–8.

Imparati, Fiorella. 'Apology of Hattusili III or Designation of his Successor', in *Studio Historiae Ardens (Ancient Near Eastern Studies Presented to Philo H. J. Houwink ten Cate on the Occasion of His 65th Birthday)*, ed. Theo van den Hout and Johan de Roos, 143–57. Leiden: Nederlands Instituut voor het Nabije Oosten, 1995.

Jackson, Sam. 'Contrasting Representations and the Egypto-Hittite Treaty', in *Registers and Modes of Communication in the Ancient Near East*, ed. Kyle H. Keimer and Gillan Davis, 43–58. Abingdon and New York, NY: Routledge, 2018.

Kelder, Jorrit M. 'The Kingdom of Ahhiyawa: Facts, Factoids and Probabilities', *SMEA* NS 4 (2018): 200–8.

Keimer, Kyle, and Gillan Davis, eds. *Registers and Modes of Communication in the Ancient Near East*. Abingdon and New York, NY: Routledge, 2018.

Kitchen, Kenneth, A. *Pharaoh Triumphant: The Life and Times of Ramesses II*. Warminster: Aris & Phillips, 1982.

Klengel, Horst. *Hattuschili und Ramses: Hethiter und Ägypter – ihr langer Weg zum Frieden*. Mainz: Philipp von Zabern, 2002.

Klinger, Jörg. 'Der Kult der Ištar von Šamuha', in *Investigationes Anatolicae: Gedenkschrift für Erich Neu*, Studien zu den Boğazköy-Texten 52, ed. Jörg Klinger, Elisabeth Rieken and Christel Rüster, 153–67. Wiesbaden: Harrassowitz, 2010.

Klinger, Jörg. 'The Hittite Writing Traditions of Cuneiform Documents', in *HHE*, 93–155.

Klinger, Jörg. 'Hittite Economics', in *HHE*, 605–47.

Latacz, Joachim. *Troy and Homer: Towards a Solution of an Old Mystery*. Oxford: Oxford University Press, 2004.

Macqueen, James G. *The Hittites and Their Contemporaries in Asia Minor*. Rev. edn. London: Thames & Hudson, 1986.

Martino, Stefano de, ed. *Handbook Hittite Empire: Power Structures*. Berlin and Boston: de Gruyter Oldenbourg, 2022 (cited as *HHE*).

Martino, Stefano de. 'Hatti: From Regional Polity to Empire', in *HHE*, 205–70.

Martino, Stefano de and Franca Daddi Pecchioli (eds). *Anatolia Antica: Studi in Memoria Fiorella Imparati*. Eothen 11, Florence, LoGisma. 2002.

Mielke, Dirk Paul. 'Key Sites of the Hittite Empire', in *OHAA*, 1031–7.

Miller, Jared. 'Some Disputed Passages in the Tawagalawa Letter', in *Ipamati kistamati pari tumatimis: Luwian and Hittite Studies Presented to J. David Hawkins on the Occasion of His 70th Birthday*, ed. Itamar Singer, 159–69. Tel Aviv: Sonia and Marco Nadler Institute of Archaeology Monograph Series 28, 2010.

*Mineck, Kathleen. 'A Letter from the Hittite King Hattušili to Kadashman-Enlil II, King of Babylonia, in Akkadian', in *ANE*, 275–9.

*Moran, William L. *The Amarna Letters*. Baltimore and London: Johns Hopkins University Press, 1992.

Neve, Peter. *Hattuša: Stadt der Götter und Tempel*. Mainz: Philipp von Zabern, 1993.

Niemeier, Barbara, and Wolf-Dietrich Niemeier. 'Projekt "Minoisch-Mykenisches bis Protogeometrisches Milet": Zielsetzung und Grabungen auf dem Stadionhügel und am Athenatempel', *AA* 2 (1997): 189–248.

Niemeier, Wolf-Dietrich. 'Hattusa und Ahhijawa im Konflikt um Millawanda/Milet', in *Die Hethiter und ihr Reich: Das Volk der 1000 Götter*, ed. Helga Willinghöfer, 294–9. Stuttgart: Theiss, 2002.

Oller, Gary H. 'Messengers and Ambassadors in Ancient Western Asia Minor', in *CANE* III, 1465–73.

Page, Denys L. *History and the Homeric Iliad*. Berkeley and Los Angeles: University of California Press, 1959.

*Pritchard, James B., ed. *Ancient Near Eastern Texts Relating to the Old Testament*. 3rd edn. Princeton, NJ: Princeton University Press, 1969 (cited as *ANET*).

Richter, Thomas, Doris Prechel and Jörg Klinger, eds. *Kulturgeschichten: Altorientalistische Studien für Volkert Haas zum 65. Geburtstag*. Wiesbaden: Harrassowitz, 2001.

Roos, Jan de. 'Materials for a Biography: The Correspondence of Puduhepa with Egypt and Ugarit', in *The Life and Times of Hattušili III and Tudhaliya IV: Proceedings of a Symposium held in Honour of J. de Roos, 12–13 December 2003, Leiden*, ed. Theo van den Hout, 18–26. Leiden: Nederlands Instituut voor het Nabije Oosten, 2006.

Rutter, Jeremy. 'An Aegean Archaeologist's Response', *SMEA* NS 4 (2018): 208–16.

Sasson, Jack M., ed. *Civilizations of the Ancient Near East*. 4 vols. New York, NY: Charles Scribner's Sons, 1995 (cited as *CANE*).

Schon, Robert. 'Response to Trevor Bryce's Article', *SMEA* NS 4 (2018): 214–17.

Schuler, E. von. *Hethitische Dienstanweisungen für höhere Hof- und Staatsbeamte, AfO* Beiheft 10. Graz, 1957.

Schwemer, Daniel. 'Religion and Power', in *HHE*, 355–418.

Seeher, Jürgen. 'Die Zerstörung der Stadt Hattuša', in *Akten IV. Internationalen Kongresses für Hethitologie, Würzburg, 4–8 Oktober 1999*, ed. Gernot Wilhelm, 623–34. Wiesbaden: Harrassowitz, 2001.

Seeher, Jürgen. *Gods Carved in Stone: The Hittite Rock Sanctuary at Yazılıkaya*. Istanbul: Ege Yayınları, 2011.

Seeher, Jürgen. *Hattusha Guide: A Day in the Hittite Capital*. 4th edn. Istanbul: Ege Yayınları, 2011.

Seeher, Jürgen. *A Mudbrick City Wall at Hattusa: Diary of a Reconstruction*. Istanbul: Ege Yayınları, 2007.

Seeher, Jürgen. 'Rethinking the Role and Size of Hattuša', in *Ḫattannaš: A Festschrift on the Occasion of Theo van den Hout's 65th Birthday*, ed. Petra Goedegebuure and Joost Hazenbos, 369–85. Chicago: Oriental Institute of the University of Chicago, 2023.

*Singer, Itamar. *Hittite Prayers*. Atlanta, GA: Society of Biblical Literature, 2002.

Singer, Itamar, ed. *Ipamati kistamati pari tumatimis: Luwian and Hittite Studies Presented to J. David Hawkins on the Occasion of His 70th Birthday*. Tel Aviv: Sonia and Marco Nadler Institute of Archaeology Monograph Series 28, 2010.

Singer, Itamar. 'A Political History of Ugarit', in *Handbook of Ugaritic Studies*, ed. Wilfred Watson and Nicolas Wyatt, 603–733. Leiden, Boston and Cologne: Brill, 1999.

Singer, Itamar. 'The Title "Great Princess" in the Hittite Empire', *Ugarit-Forschungen* 23 (1991): 327–38. Reprinted in *The Calm Before the Storm*, ed. Billie Jean Collins, 259–72. Atlanta, GA: Society of Biblical Literature, 2011.

Singer, Itamar. 'The Urhi-Teššub Affair in the Hittite-Egyptian Correspondence', in *The Life and Times of Hattušili III and Tuthaliya IV: Proceedings of a Symposium held in Honour of J. de Roos, 12–13 December 2003, Leiden*, ed. Theo van den Hout, 27–38. Leiden: Nederlands Instituut voor het Nabije Oosten, 2006.

Simon, Zsolt. *Vorarbeiten zu einer hethitischen Demographie 1: Der Einerwohnzahl des hethitischen Reichen anhand der schriftlichen Quellen*. Budapest: Eötvös Loránd University, 2011.

Spalinger, Anthony J. *War in Ancient Egypt*. Oxford: Blackwell, 2005.

Stavi, Boaz. *The Reign of Tudhaliya II and Šuppiluliuma I*. Heidelberg: Carl Winter, 2015.

Steadman, Sharon, and Gary McMahon, eds. *The Oxford Handbook of Ancient Anatolia (10,000–323 B.C.E.)*. Oxford: Oxford University Press, 2011 (cited as *OHAA*).

Stone, Damien. *The Hittites: Lost Civilizations*. London: Reaktion Books, 2023.

Ünal, Ahmet. *Ein Orakeltext über die Intrigen am hethitischen Hof (KUB XXII 70 = Bo 2011)*. Heidelberg: Carl Winter, 1978.

Waal, Willemijn. 'They Wrote on Wood: The Case for a Hieroglyphic Scribal Tradition on Wooden Writing Boards in Hittite Anatolia', *AS* 61 (2011): 21–34.

Ward, William A., and Martha S. Joukowsky, eds. *The Crisis Years: The 12th Century B.C. from Beyond the Danube to the Tigris*. Dubuque, IA: Kendall/Hunt Publishing Company, 1989.

Watson, Wilfred, and Nicolas Wyatt, eds. *Handbook of Ugaritic Studies*. Leiden, Boston and Cologne: Brill, 1999.

Weeden, Mark. 'Hittite-Ahhiyawan Politics as Seen from the Tablets: A Reaction to Trevor Bryce's Article from a Hittitological Perspective', *SMEA* NS 4 (2018): 217–27.

Weeden, Mark, and Lee Z. Ullmann, eds. *Hittite Landscapes and Geography: Handbook of Oriental Studies, Vol. 121, Section 1*. Leiden and Boston: Brill, 2017.

Wiener, Malcolm H. 'Oh No – Not Another Chronology!', *The Art and Culture of Ancient Egypt: Studies in Honor of Dorothea Arnold, Bulletin of the Egyptological Seminar* 19 (2015): 649–63.

*Wilson, John A. 'Treaty between the Hittites and Egypt', in *ANET*, 199–201.

*Wilson, John A. 'The War Against the Peoples of the Sea', in *ANET*, 262–3.

Wood, Michael. *In Search of the Trojan War*. Latest rev. edn. London: British Broadcasting Corporation, 2005.

Yamada, Masamichi. 'The Second Military Conflict between "Assyria" and "Hatti" in the Reign of Tukulti-Ninurta I', *Revue d'Assyriologie et d'Archéologie Orientale* 105 (2011): 199–220.

Television documentaries

In Search of the Trojan War, written and presented by Michael Wood, [TV programme] Dir. Bill Lyons. London: BBC, 1985.

The Dark Lords of Hattusha, [TV programme] Dir. Martin Wilson. London: BBC, 2006.

The Hittites, [TV programme] Dir. Tolga Örnek. Turkey: Ekip Film, 2003.

The Truth of Troy, [TV programme] Dir. Aidan Laverty. London: BBC, 2004.

Index

Personal names are briefly identified. Page nos in **bold** indicate main refs.

Aba, 99, 107, 120
Abu Simbel, 122–3, 205
'Achaia', 153
Adad-nirari I, Assyrian king, 54–6, 83, 108, 137, 138, 139
Adad-nirari III, Assyrian king, 72
adultery, penalties for, 42, 73
Aegean Sea, 11, 154, 174
Aeneas, legendary Trojan prince, 3
Aeneid, 161
Afghanistan, 219
Agamemnon, legendary Mycenaean king, 152–3, 157, 171
agro-pastoral economy, 13, 215–16
Ahhiyawa (Bronze Age Greek/Mycenaean world), 38, 145, **151–61**, 163, 169, 170, 172–7, 182, **183–4**
Ahlamu, 85, 111, 140
Akhenaten (Amenhotep IV), pharaoh, 112
Akhetaten, *see* Amarna
Akkadian language, 7, 76, 100, 116
Alaksandu, vassal ruler of Wilusa, 173
Alasiya (later Cyprus), 45, **184–6**
Aleppo, 14, 18, 128, 140, 193, 194
Amarna (mod. Akketaten), 112
Amenhotep III, pharaoh, 112, 145
Amenhotep IV, *see* Akhenaten
Amurru, 18–19, 56–7, 81, 85, 97, 105–6, 141, 224
Anatolia, 1, 10–11
Annals, Hattusili III, 134, 172, 175
Annals, Mursili II, 37
Apology (aka *Autobiography*), Hattusili III, 2, 23, 43, 48, 50, 60, 83, **87–90**, **92–3**, 97–9, 136, 198
Apology, Socratic, 88
Argos, 155
Arma-Tarhunda, Hittite royal litigant, 40, 41, **42–5**, 71, 82

Armenian mts, 11
Army, standing army (size), 133
Arnuwanda II, Hittite king, 17
Arnuwanda III, Hittite king, 188
Arzawa (lands), 38, 144–5
Assuwan Confederacy 16
Assyria, 7, 17, **53–6**, 86, 108, 111, 194
Assyrian colony period, 219
Atpa, father-in-law of Piyamaradu, 169
Attarimma, 163

Babylon, 7, 15, 17, 81, 83, 108, 142
Babylonian wife of Tudhaliya, 180
bandit gangs, 112–13, 115
Beal, Richard, Hittitologist, 133
Beckman, Gary, Hittitologist, 164
Benteshina, Amurrite vassal ruler, **56–7**, 106, 141–2
black magic, *see* witchcraft
Black Sea, 11
Blackwell, Nicholas, Classical archaeologist, 155
Bronze Tablet treaty, 91, 101, 183
'brother' as a diplomatic term, 54–5, 71
'Brother-Kings', 7

Carchemish, 17, 18, 128, 137, 193
chariot corps, 5, 83, 96, 97, 98, 108, 111, 130, 132, 133, 144, 145, 168, 174, 223
Chief, Royal Bodyguard, 40, 180
Chief Scribe, 5, 7, 21–2, 33–4
'Chief Wife', Hittite, 48–9, 57, 71, 72, 73, 74, 91–2, 217
Chios, 155, 175
City Gates, judicial venues, 42
civil war, **59–62**
clay tablet inscriptions, 21–2, 101, 173

Cline, Eric, Hittitologist and archaeologist, 218
'Concentric Invasions', 145
concubines, concubinage, 15, 19, 48, 49, 70, 72, 73
co-regency, 48,
coronations, 62, 83
court cases, judicial proceedings, **41–3**, 60, 71, 86
Crete, 158
Crown Prince, 35, 57. 90–3, 167–8
currency and wages, **220-1**
Cyprus (Bronze Age Alasiya), *see also* Alasiya, 82
Cyrus 'the Great', Persian emperor, 150

Damascus, 13, 65, 99, 107
Danaans, 151
Danuhepa, Hittite queen, 23, 31, 49, **57–8**
deportees, *see* transplantees
Diocletian, Roman emperor, 188
diplomacy, diplomatic missions, relations, 15, 85, 113, 136, 138, 146, 160, 170
divine patronage, 31–2
dowries, 78, 215
dreams, divine communications through, 5–6, 60

economy, Hittite, 13, **213–26**
Edel, Elmar, Egyptologist, 24, 117, 118, 204
Egypt, 7, 13, 17, 18–19, 56, 83, 84, **95–109**, 112–13, 120, 190
'elite overproduction', 182
empire (Hittite connotations), 127–8
end of Bronze Age, **189–90**
Ephesus, 171
'Eternal Treaty', 1, 71–2, **95–109**, 173, 193, 195, 201
Euphrates river, 13, 108, 111, 128, 137, 194, 195
exile, 31, 45, 51, 57, 58, 62, 82, 141, 146
exports, Hittite, 222–3

Faiyum, 79
festivals, 148, 224–5
Forrer, Emil, Swiss philologist, 153

Fraktin, 67–8, 205
fugitives, extradition of, 105–6

GAL *MESHEDI*, 40
Gassuliyawiya wife of Mursili II, 23
gift-giving (between kings), 160
Gill, Rosemary, medieval scholar, 148
Golden Spear-Men, 7, 32
Greece (Bronze Age), *see* Ahhiyawa
Guney, Oliver, Hittitologist, 164

Hakpis, 43, 58, 59, 60, 69–70, 180
Halpasulupi, Hittite prince, 5, 18
Hani, Egyptian ambassador, 112
Hanigalbat, 17, **138–40**
Hannibal, Carthaginian military commander, 62
Hartapu, Neo-Hittite king, 187
Hatti (= Hittite Kingdom), *passim*
Hattus, 13, 63
Hattusa, 6–10, **11–14**, 16, **52–3**, 69, 114, 115, **130–2**, 149–50, 190
    Audience Hall, 7
    Büyükkale, 6, 13
    'Lower City', 9
    Nişantepe, 9
    population numbers, **129–32**
    'Upper City', 9
    walls, 9
Hattusili I, Hittite king, 13, 14, 62, 193
(Hattusili II), Hittite king?, 63
Hattusili III, Hittite king, *passim*
Heinhold-Krahmer, Susanne, Hittitologist, 164
Hepat, Hurrian Chief Goddess, 67, 68, 191
Heshni, Hittite prince, 181
Hoffner, Harry A., Hittitologist, 23, 24, 125, 221
Homer, Greek epic poet, 3, 153
'Homeland', Hittite, 10, **147–9**
Hout, van den, Theo Hittitologist, 2, 24, 25, 27, 34, 181
Hurrians, 13, 15, 193
    cultural influences, **67–8**

Iliad, 151, 152
Ilios/Ilion, 152
Ini-Teshub, Hittite viceroy, 137
Isuwa, 18, 142

Ishtar, goddess, 6, **31–4**, 36, 39, 40, 41, 60, 65, 92–3, 179
Israelite army, size of, 132
Israelites (biblical tradition), 1
Itti-Marduk-balatu, Babylonian vizier, 84
Iyalanda, 168

Kadashman-Enlil, Babylonian king, **84–7**, 111–12
Kadashman-Turgu, Babylonian king, 83–4
Kadmos, legendary Theban king, 157
Karnak, temple of, 100, 103
Kashtiliash IV, Babylonian king, 108
Kaskan peoples, region, 13, 60–1, 69, 70, 179, 216
Kelder, Jorrit, Mycenaean scholar, 159, 160
Kitchen, Kenneth, Egyptologist, 108, 121, 122, 123
Kizzuwatna, 15, 67
Klengel, Horst, Ancient Near Eastern scholar, 27
Klinger, Jörg, Hittitologist, 215, 216, 217
Kupanta-Kuruntiya, vassal ruler of Mira, 118–19
Kuruntiya, Hittite prince, viceroy, 48–9, 58, 71, 90–1, 101, 105, **142–4**, 179, 183, **187–8, 201–2**

Lalanda, 182
land ownership, 216, 217
Laocoön, legendary Trojan priest, 151
Laverty, Aidan, film director, 28
Lawazantiya, **65–9**, 149
law courts, 42
laws, Hittite, 42
Lesbos, 155, 175
letters, 22–3, 24, 54, 72, 76–7, 83, 84–7, **111–25**, 138
letter-bearers, couriers, messengers, 114–15
Liliwani (Lelwani), Hittite goddess, 75
Linear B tablets, 153, 160, 173
literacy, Hittite, **32–3**, 35, 36–8, 85
Lower Land, 182
loyalty oaths, 181
Lukka lands, peoples, 135, 163, 165
Luwians, Luwian culture, language, inscriptions, 132, 144, 171, 184, 191

Manapa-Tarhunda, vassal ruler of Seha River Land, 146
Marassantiya river, 10, 59,
marriages
 double marriages, 141–2
 monogamous, 73
 polygamous, 73
 royal, 72, 74, 77–9
 with vassal offspring, 141–2
Martino, Stefano de, Hittitologist, 26, 82
Massanauzzi, Hittite princess, 121
Masturi, vassal ruler of Seha River Land, 61, 121, 146
Matanazi, *see* Massanauzzi
mausolea, royal, 37
mercenaries, 70, 132, 222
merchants, 85, 86, 218–20, 221–2
messengers, 86
Miletos/Miletus, *see* Millawanda/Milawata
military campaigns, 145–6
Millawanda/Milawata (Classical Miletos/Miletus), 28, 136, 159, 164, 168–9, 170–3, 176
Mira, 118
Mittanamuwa, Hittite Chief Scribe, **33–5**, 69, 72, 166
Mittani, 16, 17, 67, 108, 193, 194
Moses, biblical Israelite leader, 123
Mursili I, Hittite king, 14–15, 51
Mursili II, Hittite king, 5–6, 18, 23, 31, 40, 51, 128, 134, 146, 175, 176, 182, 194
Mursili III aka Urhi-Teshub, 51
Mursili, Neo-Hittite king, 187
Muwattalli I, Hittite king, 16
Muwattalli II, Hittite king, 5, 13–14, 18–19, 35, 38, 40, 41, 42, 47–50, 57, 58, 86–7, **95–7**, 98, 120, 128, 130, 141, 146, 160, 167, 173, 179, 198
Mycenae, 155, 157, 158–9, 173–4
Mycenaean kingdom, *see* Ahhiyawa

Nairi (Nihriya), 188
Naptera, *see* Nefertari
Nauplion, 159
naval battles, 186
Nefertari (Naptera), Egyptian queen, 122
Neo-Hittite states, 190
Nerik, 59, 69–70, 180

Nerikkaili, Hittite prince, 91–2, 118, 141–2
Neve, Peter, archaeologist, 26
New Year festival, 191
Nihriya, *see* Nairi
Ningal, Hittite goddess, 75
Nişantepe, *see* Hattusa
Nuhashshi (Nuhasse), 62, 63, 81, 224

oikonomia, 213–15
Örnek, Tolga, film director, 76, 205
Orontes river, 18, 97

Page, Denys, Classicist, 163
pax Hethitica, 135–7
Pentipsharri, Hurrian priest, 66, 67
Persepolis, 159
physicians
    Babylonian, 86–7
    Egyptian, 121–2
pilgrimages (royal), 131, 148
Pi-Ramesse, 115, 134
Piyamaradu, anti-Hittite activist, 38, **164–7**, 182, 183
plague, 17–18, 101, 134, 175, 194
plague prayers, 134
Plato, Greek philosopher, 88
Pontic mts, 11, 13
population numbers, management of, **134–5**, 204
prayers and hymns, 23, 75–6
Priam, legendary Trojan king, 151
Puduhepa, Hattusili III's Chief Wife, 23, 60, 64, **66–79**, 91–2, 103, 117, 124, 142, **180**, 195, 196–7, 206
Pylos, 155–6, 159, 190
Pyrrhus, Greek king, 96

Qadesh, 18–19, 96, 120, 134
    battle of, 18–19, 47, 48, 65, **95–8**, 193

Ramesses II ('The Great') pharaoh, 1, 18–19, 22, 71, 72, 76–9, **98–100**, 103–4, 117, **118–23**, 124, 132, 142, 173, 180, 193, 194–5, 205
revenue and payments, **223–6**
Rhodes, 158, 163
Rieken, Elisabeth, Hittitologist, 164
rituals (healing), 5
Rutter, Jeremy, Mycenaean scholar, 155

Sammu-ramat (Semiramis), Assyrian queen mother, 72
Samos, 155, 175
Samuha, 16, 39, 40, 44, 45, 61, 93
Sapinuwa (mod. Ortaköy), 114, 147
Sarissa (mod. Kuşaklı), 147
Schliemann, Heinrich, archaeologist, 157
Schon, Robert, Mycenaean scholar, 156
seals, seal impressions, 58, 71, 72
seaports, 13
Seeher, Jürgen, archaeologist, 130–1, 148, 149
Seha River Land, 61, 146, 183
Seti I, pharaoh, 18, 56, 123
Shalmaneser I, Assyrian king, 81, 138, 140, 195
Shalmaneser III, Assyrian king, 132
Shapili, Amurrite vassal ruler, 141
Sharrumma, Hurrian god, 191
Shattuara (no. 1), Hanigalbatean rebel leader, 138
Shattuara (no. 2), Hanigalbatean rebel leader, **138–40**
Sidon, 185
Simon, Zsolt, Hittitologist, 132
Singer, Itamar, Hittitologist and archaeologist, 23, 27
Sippaziti, son of Arma-Tarhunda, 45, 82
Socrates, Greek philosopher, 88
sorcery, *see* witchcraft
Starke, Frank, Hittitologist, 157–8
Storm (Weather) God, 9, 13, 67, 191
    of Lightning, 14
    of Nerik, 60
succession, rules of, 15, 48, 73
Südburg inscription, 189
Sun Goddess of Arinna, 23, 32, 67, 75, 185, 191
Suppiluliuma I, Hittite king, 16–17, 36–7, 101, 112, 128, 134, 145, 193, 194
Suppiluliuma II, Hittite king, 184, 186, 188
Syria, 13, 14, 15, 16, 17, 57, 99, 111, 137, 193

Talmi-Sharrumma, Hittite viceroy, 140
Tapikka (mod. Maşat), 114, 147–8
Tarhunaradu, vassal ruler of Seha River Land, 183
Tarhundaradu, Arzawan ruler, 145

Tarhuntassa, 14, 18, 49, 50, 52–3, 69, 71, 91, 101, **142–4**, 179, 189, 190, 202
Taurus mts, 11
Tawagalawa, brother, and regnal predecessor (?), of Mycenaean king, 164
Tawagalawa 'letter', 23, 28, **163–77**, 202, 203
Tawananna (personal name, wife of Suppiluliuma I), 18, 31, 49
Tawananna (title of several Hittite queens), 74–5
Telipinu, Hittite king, 15, 48, 73
Telipinu, Hittite viceroy, 140
Temple, Storm (Weather) God, 9
Teshub, Hurrian Chief God, 67, 191
Thebes (Greek), 155, 157, 159
Tiglath-pileser, Assyrian king I, 111
tin, 219
trade, international, **218–20**
transplantees ('booty-people'), 37, 134–5, 136, 175, 185, 221
travel
 hazards of, 85, 111
 times and distances, 114, 115
treaties, see also Bronze Tablet treaty, 'Eternal Treaty'
 international, 83
 (with Ahhiyawa?) 172–7
 with vassal rulers, 21–2, 61, 129, 141, 173, 183–4
 with viceroys, 140–1, 183
tribute payments, 223–4
Trojan horse, 151
Trojan War, 151, 160–1, 174
Troy, see also Wilusa, 3, 28, 151–2
Tudhaliya I/II, Hittite king(s), 16
Tudhaliya III, Hittite king, 16, 37, 39, 114, 145, 147, 216
Tudhaliya IV, Hittite king, **91–3**, 101, **179–88**, **190–2**, 202

Tudhaliya the Younger, Hittite king, 16
Tuya, Egyptian queen, 123
tuḫkanti, 91
Tukulti-Ninurta, Assyrian king, 108, 188
Tutankhamun, pharaoh, 17
Tuttul, 111
Tyre, 185

Ugarit, 85, 185, 186, 190
Ulmi-Teshub 143
 Ulmi-Teshub (= Kuruntiya), see 143–4
Upper Land, Hittite, 39, 41, 42, 60
Ura, 221
Urhi-Teshub (aka Mursili III), Hittite king, 19, **48–62**, 81–3, 88–9, 98, 106, 117, 118–20, 137–8, 143, 146, 175, 179, 196–8, 201

vice-regents, 52, 85, 128, 137
Virgil, Roman poet, 151

Wasashatta, Hanigalbatean rebel leader, 138
Weather God, see Storm God
Wilusa, see also Troy, 38, 152, 167, 168–170, 173
'Wise Women', 5
witchcraft, sorcery, black magic, **43–5**
Wood, Michael, documentary presenter, 28, 170

Xenophon, Greek military commander, 37

Yazılıkaya, **190–2**

Zallara, 221
Zenobia, Queen of Palmyra, 72
Zida, father of Arma-Tarhunda, 41